Muscular
Christianity

Tony Ladd (Ph.D., Ohio State University) is chair of the department of kinesiology and athletics and athletic director at Wheaton College, where he has taught since 1983. He regularly makes presentations to professional organizations, parachurch groups, and college audiences. He has served on the boards of several ministry groups, including Sports Outreach Chicago and Friendship Sport, Inc.

James A. Mathisen (Ph.D., Northwestern University) is professor of sociology at Wheaton College. He has made presentations to professional organizations, parachurch groups, and college audiences on sports ministry topics for over ten years. He is a member of a number of professional groups, including the American Sociological Association, the North American Society for the Sociology of Sport, and the North American Society for Sport History.

A
BRIDGEPOINT
BOOK

BridgePoint,
an imprint of
Baker Books,
is your connection
for the best in
serious reading
that integrates
the passion of
the heart with
the scholarship
of the mind.

Muscular
Christianity

Evangelical Protestants and the Development of American Sport

Tony Ladd
James A. Mathisen

A BridgePoint Book

Baker Books
A Division of Baker Book House Co
Grand Rapids, Michigan 49516

© 1999 by Tony Ladd and James A. Mathisen

Published 1999 by BridgePoint Books
an imprint of Baker Books
a division of Baker Book House Company
P.O. Box 6287, Grand Rapids, MI 49516-6287

Printed in the United States of America

Library of Congress Cataloging-in-Publication Data

Ladd, Tony.
    Muscular Christianity : evangelical Protestants and the development of American sport / Tony Ladd, James A. Mathisen.
        p.   cm.
    Includes bibliographical references and indexes.
    ISBN 0-8010-5847-3 (pbk.)
    1. Sports–United States–Religious aspects–History.
    2. Evangelicalism–United States–History. I. Mathisen, James A.
    II. Title
    GV706.42.L34   1999
    796'.088'2044–dc21   99-10255

For current information about all releases from Baker Book House, visit our web site:
                http://www.bakerbooks.com

Contents

Preface

As we write these comments setting the stage of our interpretation of the relationship that organized sport has had to conservative Protestant Christianity in North America, contemporary examples of our subject abound and long-standing confusion persists. Mike Singletary, formerly of the Chicago Bears, has made an impassioned acceptance speech at his induction into the Pro Football Hall of Fame, with his commitment to Jesus a rallying cry of his talk. A fellow football player, Reggie White of the Green Bay Packers, continues to fend off criticism following his provocative speech to Wisconsin's state legislature in which he expounded on his understanding of the Bible's opposition to homosexuality. Similarly, the proselytizing tactics of Champions for Christ have come under heavy fire, with two professional football teams asking the National Football League to investigate this organization.

Who are these people? Where did they come from? How did they become so visible? How might we best understand their relationships to their two contexts of organized sport and conservative Christianity? In the pages that follow, we try to provide some answers, informed not only by our familiarity with the two worlds we care passionately about—sport and religion—but also by our academic backgrounds in history and sociology. Episodically for the past 140 years, the peculiar interaction between religion and sport called "muscular Christianity" has carried many connotations. We do not write with the intention of settling once and for all any nagging questions about the origins, meaning, and significance of muscular Christianity. Indeed, as befits our postmodern world, there are probably multiple muscular Christianities. So we write to call particular attention to one version of them.

Two primary audiences have prompted this interpretation of muscular Christianity. One is our professional and academic colleagues in sport history, sport sociology, sociology of religion, and religious studies. Throughout the 1990s, we have made numerous presentations and written a variety of papers and articles attempting to inform interested peers, and thereby contribute to an ongoing conversation on the significance of the religion-and-sport relationship, past and present. In the process, we have learned much and made numerous midcourse corrections in our analysis.

Simultaneously, we have interacted with scores of acquaintances from a second audience of practitioners who are "doing sports ministry" in colleges, churches, and affiliate organizations. Since 1988 and the Olympic Games in Seoul, we have participated in conferences, workshops, and informal gatherings of groups of contemporary muscular Christians, seeking to learn from them while providing historical and sociological perspectives.

We therefore come to finalizing this project with a great sense of appreciation and indebtedness. Institutionally, our dean at Wheaton College, Ward Kriegbaum, has supported us with funding and other forms of encouragement. Katy Wasisco, Judy Kawakami, and Jill Huttar have provided valuable word processing and editing. We also have received support—individually or as a team—from the Pew Charitable Trusts, Princeton University, Texas Tech University, Whittier College, Reformed Theological Seminary (Orlando), Sports Outreach America, and the National Association of Church Recreators and Sports Ministers. Professionally, especially helpful have been conversations at meetings of the North American Society for Sport History, the North American Society for the Sociology of Sport, the American Sociological Association, the Association for the Sociology of Religion, and the Society for the Scientific Study of Religion. Librarians and archivists at the University of Chicago, Springfield College, University of Kansas, Wheaton College, and the Billy Graham Center have provided timely assistance.

Intellectually, Tony traces his lineage back to Timothy Smith and Bruce Bennett. Jim is indebted to Rockwell Smith and Richard Tholin from the early days. More recently, colleagues including Shirl Hoffman, Bill Baker, John MacAloon, Michael Oriard, Tim Weber, Tim Stafford, Chris Stevenson, Kathryn Long, Mark Elliott, and Al Mawhinney have asked good questions and provided insight, but bear no responsibility for the interpretations we have made of their comments. We have enjoyed open access at meetings of Sports Outreach America and the International Sports Coalition. In those settings, conversations with Eddie Waxer, Dave Burnham, Jim Riley, Tom Felten, Ralph Drollinger, Rodger Oswald, Max Helton, and others have been invaluable. Our brothers—Bob Mathisen and Dennis Ladd—have read most or all of the manuscript and provided gentle correctives. Donna Berg has helped reshape some of our garbled prose, and Robert Hosack has been a most enthusiastic editor.

We have reflected our individual interests and separate backgrounds in theology, history, and sociology in our shared research and writing. But as much as possible in any jointly authored work, we have worked as one in developing our interpretations. Our initial attraction to the topic of muscular Christianity came through our fascination with some of its key practitioners over the past 140 years—men like Amos Alonzo Stagg, James Naismith, Billy Sunday, Gil Dodds, and Bill Glass. Our hope is that we convey some of our fascination to you, and that together we can begin to understand better these muscular Christians on their own terms.

9

Introduction

As Orville Gardner rose to testify during a revival meeting in March 1858 at the Methodist Church on Green Street in New York City, a sense of anticipation filled the sanctuary. Before the curious and the committed stood a man who had reached the pinnacle of his profession. Yet by many in attendance, he was perceived as being as far from the church as one could possibly be. Orville Gardner was a professional prizefighter.

Not only had "Awful" Gardner, as he was nicknamed, earned a reputation as a famed pugilist, but his fighting skills earned him great notoriety outside the ring. In 1853 he bit off an opponent's ear in a barroom brawl. Two years later he was sentenced to a six-month term in Sing Sing Prison for assault and battery after starting a fight and breaking the jaw of a business traveler in New York City.[1] Yes, Awful Gardner was bad. Now with some hesitation, Gardner related his conversion story.

> I feel it my duty to tell you what God has done for me. I hope you will hear all I have to say. There are many here who have known me for ten years—have known me when I was fearfully wicked. Now I am on the Lord's side. . . . [On Saturday] after I had my dinner I resolved that I would seek the Lord that night. I made a strong resolution; I felt where I stood that perhaps it was the last time the Lord would strive with me. Saturday night the invitation was given to come for-

ward to the altar—on my shoulders my load of sins—up I
went with them, the cross of Christ upon my back. I got up
and threw my sins down by the altar. I tried as hard as a man
ever did, and I got no religion. Sunday night I attended with
a like result. That night I could not sleep, my sins looked so
bad; they came up on every hand and looked at me; all the
sins of my life crowded upon me, many I should never have
thought of, had not the devil brought them before me. I
could not sleep; I wiggled and waggled around the bed all
night; the Lord was striving with me. Monday morning I got
up and prayed; I did the best I could; I asked the Lord to
take away the weight that bore me down so. There was a
friend came to me that day and said he was going over to
White Plains, and I could go with him. Knowing I would be
in good company, I concluded to go, thinking he might do
me some good. There was little said on the way, but he told
me to keep looking for the Savior; that I was trying to get
religion, and had let everybody know it; the Lord was willing to bless me at any time or anywhere. I was riding along,
singing a hymn, and in an instant I felt as though I was
blessed. I am sure I gave up my soul and body. The first thing
I knew God spoke peace to my soul. It came like a shot—it
came like lightning, when I was not anticipating it, and the
first thing I said, "Glory! God blessed me." My friend said
he knew it; he felt the shock too. We rode against a stone
fence two or three times, and came near tumbling on the
ground. The change was surprising; the trees looked as they
had been blessed; everything appeared to have been blessed,
even the horse and wagon. I felt strong. I could almost fly.
Glory to God, this religion is good! The Lord has blessed me
ever since. My faith in Him grows stronger every day. I would
face all the people that God ever put on the earth and tell
them all I am bound for heaven. My heart says, see the
scorner: I say, I will go pray for him. Everything is pleasing.
I love those I used to hate. Now, that shows pretty good for
religion—don't it, brothers? (Yes, yes.) Men that I used to
seek to injure I love now; I pray for them. I don't hate a soul
that God ever put breath in. As I look around, you all look
good to me: I love the Christian a little better than the sin-
ner, but I love you too. I would not swap this religion for all
New York City. . . . [2]

After his Damascus road–like conversion experience, Gardner used his celebrity status as a sports hero to work in society, especially in prisons, to convert others to Christianity. He became one of the first peculiarly American, muscular Christians who used sport not only as an arena for character development but also as a means for Christian outreach to change evil to good. He helped clear a path that other practically minded muscular Christians such as Dwight L. Moody, James Naismith, Amos Alonzo Stagg, Gil Dodds, and Bill Glass would follow over the next century.

Orville Gardner is one notable example among others in the United States illustrating how the revivals in the nineteenth and twentieth centuries contributed to the engagement of a distinctively American form of religion with a unique approach to sport. As these muscular Christians emerged in the United States, they became more than popularizers of muscular Christianity in England, where the most prominent goal was to make the "good of society better." In America that strain of muscular Christianity existed as well.[3] But in the new world a succession of revivals propelled the social phenomenon of sport beyond the character-development ideology to take on the added goal of making the "bad of society good." By such means Christianity and sport reversed their relationship from being aliens to being allies. American revivalism helped form a symbiotic relationship, so that the eventual engagement of religion and sport infused a missionary zeal in those who participated in sports and stimulated the idealism of a generation of muscular Christians who felt called to win the world to Christ in their generation. Sport became an essential element in their strategy to reach the world.

Although the seeds for the muscular Christian movement had been sown earlier on British soil, by the third quarter of the nineteenth century, the movement had spread to other parts of the English-speaking world. The term "muscular Christianity" probably first appeared in a critical review of Charles Kingsley's novel *Two Years Ago* in the February 21,

1857, issue of *Saturday Review*.[4] For Kingsley the phrase carried negative overtones. His Christian socialist and literary friend, Thomas Hughes, liked the term, however, and emphasized its positive potential by attaching it to concepts of manliness, morality, and patriotism. Although Hughes did not incorporate the specific term "muscular Christian" into *Tom Brown's Schooldays,* published in 1857, he used it in the sequel, *Tom Brown at Oxford,* which appeared in 1860.[5] Hughes's use of muscular Christian ideas in both books suggests he was greatly influenced by Kingsley, with the term taking on specific significance after 1857.[6]

Nevertheless, even though Hughes and Kingsley are generally credited with the "social construction" of the term, the ideal of the muscular Christian who was pure in spirit, fair in relationships, and who actively pursued Christ's kingdom existed long before in the consciousness of Christian sportsmen.[7] What Hughes and British culture of the 1850s contributed was a direct connection to modern sport. Although this connection was made most explicit in England, by mid-century a muscular Christian movement was spreading and adapting to cultural circumstances elsewhere, including the United States.

No single voice has ever spoken with undisputed authority and clarity on the definition or meaning of muscular Christianity. This circumstance becomes problematic at the end of the twentieth century as we attempt to understand what the early proponents of muscular Christianity intended. Our lenses are clouded by developments since the mid-nineteenth century in the religion-and-sport relationship in British and North American contexts. We can make several inferences, however, as to how various groups have come to be designated muscular Christians.

In *Tom Brown at Oxford,* the sequel to *Tom Brown's Schooldays* written in 1860, Thomas Hughes sought to describe muscular Christians in contrast to another group of "musclemen." Hughes wrote in chapter 11, "The only point in common between the two being, that both hold it to be a good thing to have strong and well-exercised bodies. . . . Here all likeness ends. . . . The least of the muscular Christians has hold of the old chivalrous and Christian belief, that a man's body is given him to be trained and brought into subjection, and then used for the protection of the weak, the advancement of all righteous causes, and the subduing of the earth which God has given to the children of men."[8]

At least three characteristics seem primary here for Hughes. Muscular Christianity meant physicality and manliness—"a good thing to have strong and well-exercised bodies . . . a man's body is given him to be trained and brought into subjection." It meant using those bodies in morally uplifting ways, "for the protection of the weak, the advancement of all righteous causes." And it meant at least a tacit acknowledgment of godly or Christian motivation in any subsequent activity, "Christian belief . . . subduing of the earth which God has given."

Gerald Redmond has located these qualities among the components or "sentiments of the muscular Christian gospel—i.e., that physical activity and sports (especially team games like cricket and football) contributed significantly towards the development of moral character, fostered a desirable patriotism, and that such participation and its ensuing virtues were transferable to other situations and/or to later life."[9]

Peter McIntosh has argued that muscular Christianity constituted a "new philosophy" consisting of "two new basic theories." "The first was that competitive sport, especially team games, had an ethical basis, and the second was that training in moral behavior on the playing field was transferable to the world beyond."[10] Andrew Miracle and Roger Rees, as well as Michael Oriard, have further suggested that early notions about muscular Christianity were virtually identical in English and North American settings, although it is likely that "the pattern of health, discipline, morals, and military preparedness was replayed in discussions of sport on this side of the Atlantic, as Americans both followed the lead of British intellectuals and addressed their own similar con-

15

cerns." Historically, team sports performed similar functions on both sides of the Atlantic, specifically, "extending institutional control, teaching 'manliness,' developing school leaders, and preparing athletes for elite colleges and universities. Through participation in organized sport, the boys would learn to be 'gentlemen' by developing the 'masculine ideal of self-control and fair play.'"[11]

For the purposes of our discussion, we will extract highlights from these representative attempts at definition and emphasis. Four characteristics of muscular Christianity were, and continue to be for many, essential—manliness, morality, health, and patriotism.

These characteristics composed an initial "core ideology" within a cultural ethos that was evangelically Christian. Muscular Christians focused on the transformation of society, assuming that participation in games and sports by adolescent males had inherent value immediately and in later life. So Charles Kingsley, although reluctant initially to endorse the term muscular Christianity, by 1874 wrote in *Health and Education* that "games conduce not merely to physical but to moral health; that in the playing fields boys acquire virtues which no books can give them; not merely daring and endurance, but, better still, temper, self restraint, fairness, honour, unenvious approbation of another's success, and all that 'give and take' of life which stand a man in such good stead when he goes forth into the world, and without which, indeed, his success is always maimed and partial."[12]

It seems clear to us that although Thomas Hughes and Charles Kingsley may have had approximately the same notions in mind in their uses of the term muscular Christianity, subsequent proponents adapted the core ideology and its implications for their own purposes in a wide range of settings, which is not unusual and probably should not surprise us. Thus, muscular Christianity for the leaders of the Young Men's Christian Association (YMCA), for Charles T. Studd, for Baron de Coubertin, and for D. L. Moody meant quite different things. But we are getting ahead of ourselves; that diversion, especially in the United States, is a large part of our story. Similarly, not only do we care about understanding muscular Christianity on its own terms, but we will attempt to explain how its advocates affected the development and institutionalization of sport in America.

As will be evident in chapter 1, muscular Christianity as a concept did not develop in a vacuum. Throughout Western literature a strong historical connection was drawn between the idealized knightly soldier and the athlete as Christian. And the societal agents significant in the emergence of muscular Christianity in the United States were the same ones that effected the rise of sport in the nineteenth century—industrialization, immigration, education, and capital development. Industrialization produced a technological explosion which altered the means of production and consumption. It also created increased leisure time and led to the development of major population centers. The ability to sustain modern sport occurred not only through technological expansion but also through the growth of a critical population mass and the development of new patterns of consumption. Also, between 1865 and 1900, more than fourteen million immigrants came to the United States.[13] In that same period, the population more than doubled, increasing from thirty-one to seventy-six million, leading to the emergence of the modern city. That environment provided a means by which spectator sports could be supported. At the same time, it highlighted a perceived need for Christian evangelistic activity. In less than a generation after the Civil War, team sports with managerial structures developed in American cities. Muscular Christians living in an industrialized, urban culture capitalized on this development and served as catalysts to help make modern sport possible.[14]

As we shall see in chapter 2, the engagement of sport and muscular Christianity during the late 1800s was the result both of design and of circumstance. While much has been made of the forces affecting America in general and the development of sport in particular, less has been said of the designers, pioneer muscular Christians. Emphases on involvement in sports as a common ground for evangelism, as a means to manliness, as a method for character development, or as a basis for socialization into a competitive society assume the presence of activists who pursued innovation and change. Amid these changes, a complementary group of stabilizers was essential to secure the advances of sport in society. As the United States was developing into a world political power, as industry boomed, and as the frontier closed, muscular Christians oversaw the development of modern sport. While political power became more centralized, and, some feared, more distant and corrupt, Christian evangelists worked through educational and social agencies such as the YMCA to attempt to meet perceived problems emerging from this dynamic situation. Sport was one of the tools they employed. A receptive environment and active muscular Christian agents such as Amos Alonzo Stagg, Dwight L. Moody, and Luther Gulick coalesced to help shape a distinctively American muscular Christianity within modern sport and as an arm of the evangelical church.

As important as the engagement of sport and evangelical muscular Christianity was, of perhaps even greater significance was the interaction between the two over the next century. After an initial linkage, strong forces within the Christian community, within the growing world of competitive sport, and within American society led to a disengagement of evangelical muscular Christians from sport. Chapter 3 traces that disengagement up to the Depression era. Of major significance was the disillusionment of many evangelical Christians with sport, resulting in the abandonment of sport by some prominent evangelicals. Billy Sunday was perhaps the most renowned Christian sportsman who emerged from the sports culture and then became antagonistic to it.

In chapter 4 we will examine how muscular Christians again engaged with sport in the World War II era. This time, however, they were dependent on and shaped by sport, an opposite impetus from that leading to the initial engagement in the nineteenth century. Critical in this realignment were efforts of Billy Graham, the innovative practices of evangelical fundamentalists in specialized youth work, and a growing use of sport in an effort to overcome the cultural isolation of fundamentalists from the American mainstream.

Chapter 5 will develop the theme of the reengagement of evangelicals and sport as institutionalized in the second half of the twentieth century through major organizations such as Sports Ambassadors, the Fellowship of Christian Athletes, and Athletes in Action. Further institutionalization in the form of sports chaplains and overarching networks such as the International Sports Coalition and Sports Outreach America contribute to this story.

A more comprehensive account of the interinstitutional arrangements of muscular Christianity in the 1980s and 1990s is presented in chapter 6. Here is the story of how the institutions of sport, the evangelical church, and education came together in mutually supportive networks and programs, so that sport assumed additional purposes compatible with the ministry and educational intentions pursued by evangelicals. How sport fit into the ministry of the modern megachurch and Christian colleges complements this account.

Finally, chapter 7 explores the meaning of muscular Christianity at the close of the twentieth century. Interpreting the role of muscular Christians as moral crusaders and explaining the theology and modern myth of evangelical muscular Christianity provide understanding of the current state of the movement. The concluding question explores whether another disengagement of evangelicals from sport is likely or even possible.

In contrast to the story presented here, traditional interpretations of muscular Christianity typically emphasize its British origins and the interaction of British sport and Anglicized Christianity. From that perspective most scholars have assumed that British muscular Christianity served as the norm and then was merely transplanted to America and adopted by sports activists. While we do not deny the presence of the British understanding of muscular Christianity among some American activists, we wish to present two alternative theses that will guide our interpretation of the American evangelical presence in sport in the nineteenth and twentieth centuries.

First we suggest that another type of muscular Christianity, distinctively evangelical and premillennial in its theology and culturally American in its process and methods, developed parallel to and complementary of the existing British brand of muscular Christianity. This American evangelical form was more utilitarian and extrinsic in its attitude toward sport, more practice-oriented and less idealistic in its strategies, and more closely linked to American Protestant revivalism. By the late 1880s, then, this Americanized muscular Christianity had developed its distinctly evangelical platform and was poised to move into the American sport-and-religion mainstream (see chap. 3). Because of our concern for developing this thesis, examining the relationship of either Catholicism or Judaism to the development of American sport—important as those considerations are for the larger story of religion and sport—lies outside the scope of this study.[15]

A second thesis we will argue is the sequence of engagement, disengagement, and reengagement represented by chapters 2–4. For better or for worse, this sequence paralleled the cultural visibility of evangelical Protestantism in America and also interacted with significant developments in the institutionalizing of American sport. As it was in the 1880s, so it is in the late 1990s. One cannot understand the contemporary sport-in-religion movement without knowing something about its more recent reemergence in the 1940s and 1950s. Sport historians and sociologists have generally overlooked those cultural circumstances surrounding the reestablishment of this evangelical Protestant phenomenon. Further, American muscular Christianity of the past fifty years owes little to the British original and is clearly in the tradition of the more indigenously American version of the late nineteenth century, but without any direct connections to it. This study also not only argues for a distinctive American evangelical approach to muscular Christianity but is one of the first serious attempts to reconstruct the story of how evangelical Christianity and sport found each other again in the post–World War II era.[16]

Since American muscular Christianity owes much to its revivalist roots, the authors will emphasize revivalism in the nineteenth and twentieth centuries. These revivals were marked by significant strategic changes in the ways American Protestants pursued their evangelistic and social goals. The nineteenth-century revivals, as evident from D. L. Moody's work, revolutionized evangelism in America by targeting adult males rather than children, by approaching the rising middle class rather than the educated elite, by focusing on urban more than rural populations, and by using lay leaders rather than ministers as engineers of the movement. Then, once business and educational enterprises were linked with manly Christianity, the stage was set for sport to emerge as a cultural phenomenon. A similar framework antedated the revival movement of the 1940s and 1950s, especially as exemplified by the efforts of Billy Graham and his Youth for Christ associates.

In summary, amid the dynamic changes in the nineteenth and twentieth centuries, evangelical muscular Christians played key roles as change agents and filterers in the transformation of American sport. They engaged wholeheartedly in the development of sport, reinforcing—and often bringing legitimacy to—sport. In this context, the calls by muscular Christians to manliness, character development, and healthful living occurred within the framework of an evangelical Protestant ethos that called for personal salvation as well as development. How this process worked is a major piece in the writing of this important story.

The Rise of Evangelicals and the Development of Sport in America

Perhaps no one reflected the idealized version of the mid-nineteenth-century muscular Christian as did Henry Ward Camp. His life stood as an icon to a generation of evangelical Christians who came to see participation in sports as a training ground for living and dying. Henry Camp was one of numerous muscular Christians on college campuses whose experiences reflected those of the mythical Tom Brown.

Educated in the public schools of Hartford, Connecticut, Henry Camp was described as a thorough athlete, strong and compact. One of his teachers indicated that he attracted all who knew him.

> I never had a pupil who possessed a finer character or more completely won the respect, and even admiration, of his teachers. He despised everything mean, everything vulgar; and his generosity and manliness in his intercourse with other boys made him a general favorite among them. He was remarkably truthful also, and this never from a fear of consequences, but with a spontaneity which showed that truth was at the foundation of his character. As a scholar he was very faithful, accurate, and prompt in his recitations. . . . No

one stood above him in his class; and he took some prizes while in the school, for English composition and other exercises. But it was chiefly his uncommon nobleness of character which made him conspicuous then, as in later years. . . .

At Yale, 1856–60, Camp was a campus leader, especially in athletics. As a member of the university crew, he rowed number three. A college friend wrote, "Those who saw his heart in this respect will cherish the revelations made to them as something sacred. I know one who was brought to Christ, who, had it not been for him, for his Christian character as revealed in his conversation, and for the sincerity and wholeheartedness of his trust in Christ, would not, as far as I can see, have ever been a Christian. Others I knew who were influenced by him whom he did not know or dream of—whom he knows *now*."[1]

After graduation, Camp taught school for a few months and then went off to war. He was killed at Richmond after "gloriously leading a charge." He asked to be placed in the first line, "where he fell riddled with bullets." Shortly thereafter, a life-size portrait of Henry Ward Camp was placed in Alumni Hall at Yale. Over his grave in Hartford, a granite and bronze monument bore the inscription, "A true knight: Not yet mature, yet matchless."[2]

Muscular Christianity in Mid-Nineteenth-Century America

Although the seeds of the muscular Christian movement had been sown earlier on British soil, by the third quarter of the nineteenth century the movement had spread to other parts of the English-speaking world. And as early as the end of the Civil War, the term muscular Christianity had penetrated American society. Writing in a denominational journal in 1867, one writer concluded, "We like this phrase, though it is 'new coined,' because it expresses the idea of that robustness and vigor which ought to characterize those who are strong in the Lord and the power of His might. It is suggestive of force and that high-strung, nervous energy which by constant exercise has developed its possessor into the stature of a perfect man in Christ Jesus. We need such a Christianity now."[3]

Broadly defining the concept, the writer advocated a personal muscular Christianity and a social context for it. By building up the individual, American muscular Christianity would have positive social benefits and create a more vibrant church. The writer concluded, "[I]f we shall evince that degree of 'muscular Christianity' which we ought to possess, there will no longer be a doubt of our success as an independent branch of the church of Christ."[4] That "success" would be tested by the ability of the church "to extend the kingdom of the Redeemer upon the earth, and little by little, as a foothold may be gained here and there, to push forward the great cause of true religion towards its glorious consummation in subduing the hearts of all men to obedience to the law of Christ. . . . [T]here is a pressing need for the full development and exercise of 'muscular Christianity.'"[5]

The term muscular Christian was by no means restricted to the religious press. In describing the new YMCA building in New York in 1869, the *New York Times* identified the term and lauded the concept.

> But what the Association *certainly* will have is a splendid gymnasium—a gymnasium which in size and appointments will be unequaled in the City. This concession to the muscular Christianity of the time has been made, we are glad to hear, almost without dissent, nor can any one who appreciates the moral force of the *sana mens in sano corpore* find fault with the athletic character it is proposed to give the young Christians of New York. If the association succeeds in drawing to its gymnasium a large number of the young men of the City, and in giving them sound bodies and muscles of iron, as well as healthy religious principles and moral characters more enduring than steel, it will deserve and receive a double commen-

dation. We may then hope for a next generation of New-Yorkers fully equal to the occasions of an advancing civilization.[6]

Muscular Christianity was mentioned in a wide variety of sources. In his book *The Indian Club Exercise* in 1866, S. D. Kehoe attempted to connect the use of Indian clubs to muscular Christianity. Similarly, a book reviewer in *Godey's Lady's Book* in 1871 cited the increasing popularity of muscular Christianity as a stimulus for books on strength and skill.[7] The term appeared as the field of sport was becoming a phenomenon in society. Whether muscular Christianity helped to develop sport or merely engaged itself with it is the focus of some scholarly debate.[8]

While some Christians continued to debate the efficacy of sport itself, the focus of argumentation began to shift to the meaning of sports activity and how participation in sports fit into a theological construct. Justification criteria focused on gambling or physical harmfulness (sports such as boxing or bear baiting), cultural practice (limits on Sunday activities), or environmental concerns (such as playing in smoke-filled rooms).[9] At the Methodist General Conference in 1872, a specific list of sinful amusements was identified, including "dancing, playing at games of chance, theater-going, horse-races, circuses, dancing parties or balls, patronizing dancing schools, and taking such other amusements as are obviously of misleading or questionable moral tendency."[10] In the end, however, many agreed with the editors of the *Spirit of the Times* who at midcentury argued, "Let religion recognize and restrain them [sports] . . . but let it throw around them its gentle and holy bonds, to make them pure, cheerful, healthful—helpful to the great ends of life."[11]

Although appreciation for sports ran through various strata of American society, a group of eastern intellectuals, Henry David Thoreau, Calvin Stowe, Lyman Beecher, and Thomas Wentworth Higginson, most effectively promulgated ideas with their pens and from their pulpits.[12]

Higginson was one of the most significant of these early advocates for muscular Christianity. Writing in the *Atlantic*

Monthly in 1858, he specifically used the term.[13] His muscular Christian message that America's development rested on a balance between spiritual and physical health emphasized the Greek concept of a strong mind in a strong body (*mens sana in corpore sano*). In the nineteenth century this conceptual framework served as the foundation for a broad-based coalition to support the use of games and sports to create a new society. Muscular Christianity was a means for providing the message and lighting the pathways of human progress for the kingdom of God.[14]

The impetus for sports and fitness was also nurtured by those who campaigned for moral reform as well as health and fitness. Helping fuel these moral reform movements were the efforts of American revivalists.[15] The optimism of evangelical Protestant firebrands seemed unquenchable. Matthew Simpson, an outspoken champion of American manifest destiny, concluded that the United States held the "sympathy of the masses all over the world" and that "God could not afford to do without America."[16] As theologian Stanley Gundry indicates, this was essentially a postmillennial view of Christianity as an all-conquering faith destined to convert the world and to turn it into one vast realm under Christ's spiritual rule.[17] This view of America's place in the world and its role in bringing about the kingdom of God on earth was at the heart of Christian activity in the United States through the middle of the nineteenth century.[18]

Yet there was a gradual transition in many Christians' views about the end of the world and Christ's return and in the motivations for Christian activism in the interim.[19] While a majority of Protestant theologians continued to articulate a version of postmillennialism, the premillennial presuppositions of many evangelicals were clearly never far below the surface. And although discredited by William Miller's errant prediction of the end of the world in 1844, the premillennial position gradually reemerged with new force by building on a dispensational view of biblical history and an emphasis on literalism in Bible prophecy.[20] As we shall see, the interplay between the two viewpoints is evident in the work of Dwight L. Moody and other muscular Christians.

Muscular Christians, energized by a postmillennial view of progress, a sense of duty, and a concern for health, used the dynamic environment fostered by the technological revolution[21] to engage the gears of the sports machine in culture. The development of sport among Christians accompanied the great social movements of the nineteenth century—to free slaves, to improve sanitation, to incorporate rights for women, and to restrict alcohol. These movements, with individual and social consequences, would address society through two primary, overlapping institutions—education and religion.

Educators and religious enthusiasts were at the heart of these reform movements. And no one represented the reformers more clearly than Lyman Beecher, patriarch of one of the most significant families of the nineteenth century. The Congregational minister and his family dominated religious, education, and reform circles. Although other reformers may have had more influence on curricular development in education, Beecher, his family, and his friends made a permanent imprint on the institutional role of education and the extension of learning beyond school curricula. They were a unifying force providing a rationale for Protestant, missionary-minded individuals to support public schools based on "a new religious synthesis, one which would give members of the diverse sects a common faith."[22]

Members of the Beecher family were muscular Christians even before the term was coined. All five sons studied theology and several became prominent ministers. Henry Ward Beecher was perhaps the most dominant pulpiteer in the latter half of the nineteenth century. The four Beecher daughters were equally renowned. Catherine was a leading physical education theorist, and Harriet Beecher Stowe's *Uncle Tom's Cabin* (1852) galvanized the nation to action against slavery. For the entire family, education was the means for transforming society, and "schools and churches were allies in the quest to create the Kingdom of God in America."[23] Through education the Beechers developed a rationale and a means for merging American nationalism and Protestantism into a national ideology. They saw the public school as the primary agency for such social progress, and physical activity as a vital tool of education. From their perspective, the school would teach basic morality to all citizens, including recent immigrants, many of whom were Roman Catholic or non-Christian.[24] That philosophy of building a religious synthesis was the driving force not only for the development of the common school but also for the emergence of Sunday schools, for enhancement of Chautauqua and other educational associations, for opening colleges, and for driving myriad movements.[25]

By the Civil War era, the American education system seemed to fulfill those aims. The school was serving as a common denominator for the American democratic experience. At the same time, the public schools were broadening the scope of education in America. Recreation and athletics were established within that context. For example, the fifth grade text of *The American Educational Reader* published in 1873 asked, "Must we attend to our lessons and labors all day long, and never enjoy any pastime? . . . By no means! Idleness is forbidden, but not recreation. Indeed, recreation within due limits is as necessary to health and happiness as labor, especially in the case of the young, whom 'all work and no play' would soon enfeeble both body and mind."[26]

From the founding of the public school in America, most educational leaders had perceived its mission as extensive and inclusive.[27]

Revivalism and Sport: From Adversaries to Allies

If educational leaders provided the theoretical basis for the legitimacy of sport in American society, it was through religious institutions, and evangelicalism in particular, that sport was sanctified for the individual to become fully involved. While sport and Christianity historically may have been adversaries, by the last half of the nineteenth century they were becoming allies. And, as we shall see, within the evangelical communities the work of the Protestant revivalists was of great significance.

Religious historians have described the important role revivalism played in shaping the social and moral character of America, beginning with the efforts of Jonathan Edwards and George Whitefield. Yet histories of physical education and sport portray a generalized picture of Protestant Christianity that seldom identifies various levels of commitment and enthusiasm or clearly distinguishes evangelical Protestants from other Christians. Even among the revivalists there were distinct differences. Besides theological distinctions such as millennial interpretations, there were significant social and cultural differences. For example, the urban revivals of the 1850s were different from the frontier revivals of the early nineteenth century. So too were the people they attracted and served.[28]

Serving as a transitional figure between the rural and urban revivals was Charles Grandison Finney.[29] When he left his law office in 1821 to devote his life to saving souls, he inaugurated a new era in American Christianity. Not only did he develop innovative techniques for promoting conversions, but he also transformed the philosophy and process of evangelism. Finney's theological view was essentially post-millennial, which reinforced the idea of improving society in addition to converting individuals. His perfectionist theology gripped converts with a sense of urgency and challenged them to work with haste to bring forth the kingdom. This position would provide the theological and philosophical underpinnings for Luther Gulick, James Naismith, and other second-generation muscular Christians to develop sports as character-development activities to improve society. The perceived goodness of masculine activity and sports was implicitly part of the vision to win the world for Christ and thereby usher in the millennium. Later, Gulick acknowledged this position when he asserted that the "first object of the Young Men's Christian Association Athletic League is to increase the good and decrease the evils in connection with athletic sports."[30]

While Finney's theology drove the revival movement, it also directly affected muscular Christianity. George Williams, who developed the YMCA in England, was significantly influenced by him.[31] Also, Luther Gulick, the leading theorist of the YMCA movement in America and the head of the YMCA training school at Springfield, came from a long line of missionaries. His grandmother had committed her life to mission work under Finney's influence.[32] Moreover, the development of a nationally prominent program of physical education and athletics at Oberlin College was a direct result of Finney's leadership as president there during the formative years of the muscular Christian movement. For nearly half a century after Finney, Oberlin College served as the cradle for the fledgling physical education profession and the muscular Christian movement.

While Finney served as the prototype for evangelical revivalists, Henry Ward Beecher became muscular Christianity's first national preacher. The son of Lyman Beecher expanded his father's social and evangelical ideas when he became the minister at Plymouth Church in Brooklyn. Regarded by many as a liberal, Beecher at one time was identified with various Protestant movements. His connection to the evangelical revival of 1857–58 is one direction of his eclectic approach to ministry.[33]

Beecher laid out the extended possibilities for social innovation combining education and athletics. He loved sports, and he could be quite partisan, as when he cheered on his grandson, the quarterback of the Yale football team. In an 1887 sermon, he thundered, "I stood yesterday to see Yale and Princeton at football. I always did hate Princeton, but I took notice there was not a coward on either side, although I thank God that Yale beat."[34] As Michael Oriard indicates, one of Beecher's more consistent themes was "a muscular Christian emphasis on 'winning' life's promised rewards."[35]

Beecher was a broad centrist theologically and a post-millennialist who served as a legitimizer of athletics. He frequently described the benefits to individuals and the community. When advocating a new gymnasium for a YMCA, he claimed that "nothing can come more properly in the sphere of Christian activity than the application of the cause of physical health in the community. If general health is not religion, if it is not Christ, it is John the Baptist; it goes before him."[36] For Beecher and other evangelicals, the need for salvation or revival rested on both millennial assumptions and ideas of human progress. And progress depended on opportunities for education. The coming of God's kingdom was predicated on the accessibility of education to all people. "The way to make a man safe," Beecher said, "is to educate him."[37] The connection between Christianity and education was firmly established.

Beecher's approach to recreation and physical activity as "preceding Christ" required a diversity of activities to meet the needs of all those who would be brought to Christ's kingdom.

> It is well, therefore, that so many muscular games are coming into vogue. Baseball and cricket are comparatively inexpensive, and open to all, and one can hardly conceive of better exercise. Boat-clubs for rowing are springing up. . . . This gives an admirable development to the muscles. But all these are yet but a little for the thousands who need exercise.
>
> There ought to be gymnastic grounds and good bowling-alleys, in connection with reading-rooms . . . under judicious management, where, for a small fee, every young man might find various wholesome exercises, and with all good society, without the temptations which surround all the alleys and rooms of the city, kept for bowling and billiards. It seems surprising, while so many young men's associations are organized, whose main trouble it is to find *something to do*, that some Christian association should not undertake this important reformation, and give to the young men of our cities the means of physical vigor and health, separated from temptations to vice. It would be a very gospel.[38]

Reflecting a concept of progress and a passionate sense that right would always defeat wrong, Beecher argued that "there ought to be so many clubs under moral and Christian influences that it shall be the fault of every young man if he joins a bad one."[39] In the end, Beecher believed that self-evident truths embedded in the gospel would persuade men.

Beecher's views reflected an emerging position in society. For example, the writer of an article on "Amusements" in the 1867 *New Englander* argued that games like baseball should not be denounced, because they were not "expressly discountenanced in the Bible."[40] That writer maintained that "different persons need different forms of recreation. There are some who need excitement, while others need quiet. Some need bodily exercise, others need to have their minds diverted and soothed."[41] Indeed, in matters of sport and spirit, Beecher was an ecumenist, "a man who sought to unite Americans of all faiths in the love of God and country."[42] Beecher's views paralleled those of many in American society.

Because of Beecher's pulpit and his connection with the eastern intellectual establishment, he helped sanctify the sports arena for muscular Christians. William McLoughlin indicated that "Henry Ward Beecher's contribution to American religious development was to effect a workable marriage between the romantic, idealistic, individualistic aspects of transcendental philosophy and the conservative, well-ordered, institutional aspects of Christianity."[43] Social action and personal salvation were pragmatically linked by Beecher, and one important connection was provided through recreation and sports.

If Finney established the theoretical underpinnings for the acceptance of sport in society, and if Beecher wielded the power of the mainline Protestant church with evangelical emphases on behalf of sports and recreation, then Dwight L. Moody was the champion of an indigenous, American brand of muscular Christianity in the final decades of the century. While scholars have firmly established Moody's role in American revivalism, his association with muscular Christianity has been largely ignored. The reasons for this are complicated and may result as much from the narrow focus of scholars of both evangelicalism and sport as from any bias among or neglect by historians.[44]

Although reared in New England as a Unitarian, Moody converted to Trinitarian Christianity in his late teens. Shortly thereafter in 1856, he moved to Chicago to seek fortune. His entrepreneurial skills were evident, first as a salesman and then in "pitching" Christianity. Within a few years he had made his mark in business and then moved to full-time Christian endeavors. Working in mission churches and Sunday schools in Chicago during and after the Civil War, Moody aligned himself with two powerful forces—the emerging young business community and novel methods of evangelism, including muscular Christianity.[45]

Moody associated with John T. Farwell, a prominent Chicago merchant. Later he extended his associations to Marshall Field and John McCormick, and then to a host of other national and international businessmen. These alliances provided a sound financial base from which he worked as an evangelist. They also aided fund-raising for the YMCA and other social agencies. But more important, they established a supporting network of relationships among evangelicals, businessmen, and sports enthusiasts for the development of muscular Christianity.

Moody's muscular Christian methods grew out of a personal involvement with the YMCA in Chicago. That organization was formed in 1858, two years after he arrived in the Midwest. The association demanded the "evangelical test" for all voting members. Any male of good standing in any evangelical church that held the doctrine of justification by faith in Christ alone could join.[46] In 1865 Moody was elected president of the Chicago branch, a position he held for four years.

Moody's early work in the YMCA occurred as "his religious fervor was intensified by the urban revivals of 1857–58."[47] Not only did these immediately impact his work with the YMCA, but they firmly connected him with the larger evangelical movement. Converts from the revivals with direct ties to Finney and Moody influenced the development of the YMCA.[48]

As Orville Gardner's story and the experiences of Finney, Beecher, and Moody demonstrate, these revivals indirectly accomplished several purposes simultaneously. First, they provided continuity, linking the activities of earlier revivalists like Finney to their eventual successors, including Moody. Second, they moved revivalist activity into the domain of middle-class, urban-based males. Known alternatively as "the prayer meeting revival" and "the businessmen's revival," the religious enthusiasm of 1857–58 "found a ready audience in the business culture of large cities," especially on the East Coast and in the Midwest.[49] Third, the YMCA was the immediate beneficiary of this time of revival that transcended restrictive denominational identities. "Local units of the YMCA found it easy to begin such [noonday prayer] gatherings. Some which had been struggling for survival suddenly attracted huge crowds."[50] And fourth, revival catapulted some converts into a celebrity status hitherto unknown. For example, Orville Gardner's story was repeated for weeks in newspapers around the country.[51] In one sense, he was the first American muscular Christian celebrity, antedating by a century scores of modern Christian sports heroes.

Historians continue to debate the importance of the revivals of 1857–58.[52] For the purpose of this study, however, the revivals "showed that those who advocated revivalism, soul-saving, and rescue out of this world were the same people who wanted to devote virtually equal energies to the reform of the society."[53] By connecting evangelical Protestants to the needs of growing cities, the revivals gave further impetus to the efforts of muscular Christians, especially through the expanding activities of the YMCA. Thus the revivals served as an early linchpin connecting social action, the cities, and the YMCA. Ultimately it aided in the engagement or alliance of sport and evangelical Protestants.

By the mid-1870s Moody's fame had spread throughout the eastern United States and to England. In 1875 he moved his headquarters from Chicago to Northfield, Massachusetts. Later that year he visited Princeton and helped spark a revival among students in the Philadelphia Society, the predecessor to the college YMCA there. Influenced by that revival, Luther Wishard later played a significant role in the YMCA and the development of the Northfield conferences in the 1880s.[54] At the international convention of the association in 1879, Moody was enthusiastically elected president. He declined, arguing that he could not give himself to both evangelistic work and the national leadership of the YMCA.[55]

Still, his efforts on the local level were significant. Under his leadership the Chicago branch had become a model for those who saw the association as a means for evangelism and social assistance. Every Sunday evening Moody preached to large audiences. During the week he visited neighborhoods to speak to community groups. The Chicago association's goal was to reach all without distinction of gender or age.[56] Moody's work was directed to a large social constituency even though, in practice, his efforts focused on a more narrowly defined program of evangelism.

Moody's position was critical at this point in YMCA history. He represented one of two groups who fought for control of the associations. At the Albany convention in 1866, Moody forcefully proclaimed, "God wants us to go forth and preach the gospel to the whole world."[57] He encouraged his audience to use the YMCA as an evangelistic institution. As was evident in his work with college students when he visited many campuses or when he convened the Northfield conferences, his focus was evangelism. He utilized his practical muscular Christianity, and his "manly, genuine, whole-souled personality won the students."[58]

On the other side in the debate were those who held broader program goals, although perhaps among a narrower constituency. This group was led by Robert McBurney of the New York association, who opposed Moody's views so strongly at the Albany convention in 1869 that Moody believed McBurney was opposed to him personally.[59]

The key element in McBurney's program was the use of the gymnasium. At first the gym was perceived as a means of drawing young men into Bible studies and prayer meetings. This enticement was soon expanded by attempts to meet the needs of the whole person, including the spiritual, mental, and social as well as the physical. The New York association, under McBurney's leadership, opened the first gym in 1869. This served as a prototype throughout the nineteenth century.[60] When some criticized that the gym had turned the New York association into a social club, McBurney offered the following defense: "It is exceedingly difficult for an unconverted man to leave one of our meetings without a direct effort being made in his behalf. At all our meetings a personal invitation is given to all who desire to find Christ as a personal savior, to signify it by raising the hand. But we do not rest there. As men pass out of the meetings, if we do not know them, we ask them if they are believers, and if not, we endeavor to detain them and point them to Christ. I am not acquainted with a religious organization, mission, or church in this city or in any other place where such vigorous spiritual effort is put forth to win men to Jesus Christ."[61]

McBurney remained singular in his dedication to serve young men. Over the next fifteen years, his philosophy gradually prevailed, as the YMCA program moved to meet physical needs.[62]

In the meantime, Moody's experiences overseas affected his preaching, his fund-raising, and his theology.[63] During a trip to England for the YMCA in 1867, he met J. N. Darby, the leader of the Plymouth Brethren, a small evangelical sect operating outside the established Anglican Church. Between 1867 and 1884, when Moody traveled to England five times, Darby influenced the evangelist to accept a premillennial position on eschatology which predicted that only Christ's return could establish his kingdom in a world becoming more evil. This was in stark contrast to the optimistic, postmillennial expectations of gradually making the world better so Christ would return.[64] By the end of the 1870s the new directions in Moody's career path and theological underpinnings were firmly established. Though still aligned with the YMCA, Moody had gone far beyond its operations in establishing an outreach to the world. His visits to Britain, ironically, also broadened his views on athletics and the role of athletics in his ministry.

After McBurney emerged victorious over Moody, the evangelist moved to matters largely not involving muscular Christianity. When rejecting the presidency of the international commission in 1879, he said, "It is not the work of the YMCA to invite evangelists. Let ministers and churches do that. . . . The work of the secretary is too important for him to engage in anything but his distinctive work of reaching young men. I would recommend a gymnasium, classes, medical lectures, social receptions, music, and all unobjectionable agencies. These are for weekdays—we do not want simply evangelistic meetings. I've tried that system in Association work and failed, so I gave up the secretaryship and became an evangelist. You cannot do both and succeed."[65] Yet even at the height of his career when involved in the Boston revival, Moody was still identified with muscular Christianity. Walt Whitman inveighed against Moody in the Sunday *Times* that he was not only "a mesomeric but also a muscular Christian."[66]

Revivalists from Finney to Moody popularized an evangelical message that rode a rising tide of aggressive Protestantism, emerging nationalism, and social consciousness. In their efforts to bring about the kingdom of God in America, evangelicals embraced a muscular Christian doctrine as one means to that end. Although divisive conflicts over evolution, millennialism, and higher criticism would emerge later, by the 1880s muscular Christians in America were linked directly to Christian revivalism and evangelism. Both Moody and McBurney, though disagreeing on methods, represented this call to change lives through individuals' acceptance of the Christian message.

But the gradual ascendancy of a new American evangelicalism that accepted a dominant premillennialism forced a change in the way some muscular Christians operated. Since this emphasis was occurring at the same time sport was becoming institutionalized, it is small wonder that the society-saving imagery of muscular Christians became exaggerated and detached from social affairs. There was no longer a cohesive force such as the postmillennial ideal of making the world better. Even though "winning the world for Christ" had meaning for all who marched in the evangelical army, the meaning differed from one person to the next. The muscular Christian movement was a flexible consensus at best.

An Organizational Context for Muscular Christianity: Practitioners

During the nineteenth century, as educators and religious leaders were espousing a theoretical framework for supporting muscular Christianity, a platoon of evangelical practitioners emerged to lead the athletics and new physical education movement under its banner—Edward Hitchcock, who was the first college professor of physical education, Dio Lewis, who founded the first teacher training institute for physical educators, and Luther Gulick, who became the movement's main theorist as the head of a college dedicated to physical education.

Open about their Christian beliefs, many leaders in physical education and sport actively incorporated the practice of faith in their educational programs. For example, Edward Hitchcock emphasized his pietistic roots: "I put implicit confidence in God, by daily and sometimes hourly prayer—that he will bless and keep me and at least save me. I feel—and have for years—perfectly confident that God will save me in a better world simply because he says he will."[67] That religious commitment guided Hitchcock as the "father of physical education" and in the development of physical education in American colleges during the nineteenth century.

Like Hitchcock, Dio Lewis was an extremely devout educator. Early in life he had anticipated studying for the ministry. The teacher training pioneer, who would later introduce the Swedish system of light gymnastics to America, indicated he was molded by the prayers of his mother. "We grew up with a very large estimate of the power of prayer. The day was never so dark at our house that mother could not go upstairs and open the clouds. . . . I believe in my heart that woman's prayer is the most powerful agency on earth."[68] This same conviction enabled him to work so faithfully in other social action areas as well as muscular Christianity. Raised a Baptist, Lewis later affiliated with a Brethren sect and spent most of his adult life in the temperance and women's suffrage movements.[69]

Even Dudley Sargent, who became the head of the physical education program at Harvard in 1879 and who was perhaps the most influential physical educator of the early twentieth century, was influenced by the revivalists. Though not an evangelical, he was attracted by the preaching of Henry Ward Beecher and had planned to study for the ministry at Tufts, where he also used his gymnastics ability to support himself. What these men and others shared was a vision of muscular Christianity proclaimed not from the pulpit but from the gymnasium and the playing field.[70] But it was not the educators who would make muscular Christianity part of mainstream culture. That would be left to the Young Men's Christian Association.

Nowhere did the philosophy of teaching character and instilling values through games take on larger significance than in the YMCA. The association was one of several evangelical societies trying to reach young males in the cities. At first, the founder, George Williams, directed his efforts toward developing men through prayer groups in churches and in mutual improvement societies. His personal approach and his connection with the revivalism of Charles Finney produced an emphasis on religious experience rather than on doctrine. He believed that converted men, aware of the treasure within each unconverted soul and painfully aware of the "old Adam" within themselves, would need mentors "to turn this old Adam to good account in others."[71] Converting young men to Christianity would improve society. Therefore, revivalism was a key ingredient in the development of the YMCA.[72]

The emergence of the YMCA in Britain, though significant in its own right, is important in this context to identify the close connection of the revivalists with the organization of the association on both sides of the Atlantic. The central aim of the Young Men's Christian Association from its inception through the rest of the nineteenth century was to improve the spiritual condition of young men.[73] Until the twentieth century, the YMCA avoided theological discussions or debates over social issues that might have divided the organization. This unity gave strength to the early development of the association and aided the legitimization of sport within the organization and within culture generally.

Robert McBurney expressed the goal of the association as being "to help men in their daily life."[74] This was a concise statement of an attitude that became characteristic of the American YMCA. As the association emerged, its program was built on the general goal of character transformation.[75] The early movement was more concerned with moral development and the role sport played in that development than with theology.

Meanwhile, American life after the Civil War was enmeshed in a civil religious culture which was becoming more pluralistic and less self-assured. Within the YMCA movement, when controversies arose in conventions or meetings, it was customary to "engage in prayer or sing a hymn."[76] As described by Howard Hopkins, the YMCA chose to exhibit a movement not as a system of the law but as a "state of the heart."[77] Thus, as the YMCA emerged, it generally implemented its goals by serving clientele through character development rather than by attempting to change structures that were social or environmental.[78]

With an inclusiveness that reflected the evangelical thinking of both liberal and conservative, the movement evolved as an American institution. McBurney argued, "It is touching men's hearts and lives for Christ that is our business," adding that creeds and specific patterns of belief rarely helped in those endeavors. Moody tacitly endorsed a similar framework. When some conservative Northfield sponsors criticized him for inviting the more "liberal" Henry Drummond to the 1887 conference, Moody argued that Drummond seemed to be "so much a better Christian than I am."[79] During this formative engagement with sport, the YMCA encompassed many facets of Protestantism in America. It stood before the world "as a recognition of the fact that the Church of Christ is one." McBurney believed that the record of the organization in the nineteenth century was an eloquent testimony to the practice of unity.[80]

Although Moody and McBurney were able to subordinate their differences to the overall purposes of the YMCA, the fragile consensus among various Protestant groups was about to be tested and eventually found wanting. Following the Civil War, forces both outside and within Protestantism led to what religious historian Martin Marty has aptly depicted as the "two parties"—premillennialists and postmillennialists.[81] These two parties adopted contrasting positions on nonreligious issues as well as on Christian theology and action.

While much of nineteenth-century theology and social activism (including muscular Christianity) was based on postmillennial assumptions, by 1875 premillennialists were strong and confident enough to convene the first of twenty-five annual Niagara Bible conferences "to hear the older evangelical doctrines confirmed and preached."[82] From these conferences emerged seven periodically convened prophecy conferences beginning in 1878, as the premillennialists were both "broadening their own movement" and "accentuating the differences" between them and other Protestants.[83] Not incidentally, many of the Niagara and prophecy conference speakers also would appear on the platform at Moody's Northfield summer meetings beginning in 1886.[84]

Simultaneously, the endorsement for sport accelerated in the 1880s. Hopkins and others indicate that the YMCA quickly promoted recreational activity even to the extent of endorsing ball games. In addition, the organization encouraged other activities, such as billiards and bowling, which Christians had spurned because of associations with gambling or questionable environments. Although the YMCA was breaking new ground among its Christian constituents, it was also reflecting acceptance in the wider culture. In 1886 the editor of the *New Englander and Yale Review* lauded the role of athletics in society.[85] And even though the YMCA endorsed other social movements such as Sabbatarianism and temperance, there were counterpoints to some of that activity. The YMCA became an agency for Sunday activity and for greater social freedom within culture. McBurney himself had counseled the convention of 1873 against becoming "prosecuting attorneys in connection with this or that other work."[86]

One way revivalistic methods were used in a context supportive of sports was in young men's meetings. For example, in the 1880s at the New York City association, some of these meetings developed into a series of "Athletic Sundays" managed by Henry H. Webster. The gospel message was offered through the testimonies of prominent athletes such as A. A. Stagg, then a student at Yale; members of the Princeton football team; and Billy Sunday, a professional baseball player who had recently converted to Christianity. The meetings were developed to attract men who did not go to church. That "these speakers faced capacity audiences" and that "the young men's meetings came to be regarded as an index of the effectiveness of the Association's program" are clear indications of the developing engagement of evangelical Christians with sports.[87]

Thus, until their deaths in 1899, Moody and McBurney served as an important tandem in the development of mus-

cular Christianity generally and in the YMCA organizationally. Moody's greatest influence was an ecumenically oriented emphasis on the spiritual, though he continued as the
association's best fund-raiser. McBurney's gift was organizational with an emphasis on the physical. At a joint memorial service in 1900, a YMCA secretary pointed to remarkable
parallels in their careers. "These two men undoubtedly stand
as the greatest figures in the history of the YMCA [for] each
was an evangelist, a preacher of the gospel, a messenger of
good tidings and a worker for the extension of the Kingdom
of the Lord Jesus Christ." Described as having "minds of
poets and hearts of women," Moody and McBurney were
identified as brothers who shared the same vision and who
followed a pattern of prayer, Bible study, and evangelism.[88]

The development of the YMCA in the United States relied
on a muscular Christian agenda to reach a white, middle-
class culture. In Great Britain that cause was similar. Nevertheless, in the United States, the flood of immigrants added
another factor. In his important analysis of the YMCA's development in the two countries, L. L. Doggett reported that "the
percentage of foreign born inhabitants in the fifty leading
American cities was in 1880 eighteen times as great as the
percentage of foreign born persons in London." Half of the
young men in American cities were foreign by birth or parent-
age, reflecting an essential naturism, Doggett believed. These
young men were especially at risk. For the social managers
of the YMCA, this class of young men was open to a "special
temptation"[89] and posed a particular challenge for early muscular Christians.

Although there were exceptions, which could be expected
in a movement as diverse and expansive as the YMCA, by the
mid-1880s the work of the organization was narrowing. Most
agencies began to concentrate on males as opposed to females,
on boys as opposed to men, and then on boys from better
homes as opposed to street children. This reflected changes
in social dynamics and signaled the emergence of the middle class.[90] The YMCA in its formative years had been a "sort

of a cooperating agency for the advancement of any good work." During this new phase, the emphasis changed to developing manliness and moral character to win men to Jesus Christ.[91] That position would be enhanced by the work of muscular Christians.

Setting the Stage for Engagement: The Studds

J. E. K., C. T., and G. B. Studd were all captains of Cambridge University's cricket teams in the early 1880s.

Perhaps no single family affected the muscular Christian movement among evangelicals in America more than the Studds of Great Britain. Members of the family personified the English-American linkage of muscular Christianity. They did it via Moody's revivalism. Edward Studd, a wealthy tea planter, converted to Christianity in 1877 during one of D. L. Moody's revival campaigns in England.[92] In the next few years his son Charles (C. T.) was converted through his father's influence. Two other sons, George (G. B.) and Kyneston (J. E. K.), were converted shortly thereafter. The young Studds were international cricketers, and their athletic renown gave them a platform for communicating the gospel of Jesus Christ. Each served as captain of the Cambridge University cricket team in succession—G. B. in 1882, C. T. in 1883, and J. E. K. in 1884. C. T. was the best player of the three, rising to become a member of the All-England Eleven.[93]

The Studds played athletics at a significant time in the history of Cambridge University and when cricket was the preeminent international game for gentlemen of the British Empire. Games between Oxford and Cambridge drew more than thirty thousand fans in the 1880s. And the English test team, of which C. T. was a member, toured throughout the world.

When C. T. returned from touring Australia, he found his brother G. B. deathly sick. While watching his brother hover between life and death, he thought to himself,

> Now what is all the popularity of the world worth to George? What is all the fame and flattery worth? What is it worth to possess all the riches in the world, when a man comes to face Eternity? . . . All those things [he said] had become as nothing to my brother. He only cared about the Bible and the Lord Jesus Christ, and that taught me the same lesson. In His love and goodness He restored my brother to health, and as soon as I could get away I went to hear Mr. Moody. There the Lord met me again and restored to me the joy of His salvation. Still further, and what was better than all, He set me to work for Him and I began to try to persuade my friends to read the Gospel, and to speak to them individually about their souls.[94]

Such a testimony illustrates the personal piety of many evangelical athletes. In 1885 C. T. forfeited his international standing in cricket to become a missionary pioneer. He became the first muscular Christian to gain international standing both as a sportsman and as an evangelical. As a leader of the Cambridge Seven, a band of missionary volunteers, he caught the attention of Queen Victoria and the imagination of the Western world when they sailed for China in 1885. For C. T. the obsession to serve God was little different from his obsession with cricket. After his conversion the focus of his playing changed, but he did not reject the benefits of playing cricket. C. T. wrote his brother, "By all means play and enjoy them [cricket or games], giving thanks to Jesus for them. Only take care that games do not become an idol to you as they did to me."[95] This practical approach, "to play for the glory of God," paid evangelistic dividends when Studd entered the mission field in India in 1904 and "joined a cricket tour in order to get opportunities of holding meetings with soldiers."[96]

The Cambridge Seven received a hero's send-off when they departed Britain's shores for missionary service in China in 1885. C. T. Studd is on the far left in the back row.

The connection between the Studd family and other evangelical Christians interested in sports is vital to understanding muscular Christianity as it developed in the United States. As indicated earlier, the most direct tie was the elder Studd's conversion through the Moody campaigns. There were tangible results as well. C. T. gave away part of his personal fortune and contributed money to D. L. Moody for evangelistic purposes. And at Moody's invitation, J. E. K. spoke at a series of American colleges, which led to the conversion of John R. Mott and the founding of the Student Volunteer Movement (SVM) as an outgrowth of the YMCA movement. As we shall see in chapter 2, the SVM and Mott played significant roles in the next generation by affecting the career choices of many muscular Christians.[97] The relationship between the Studds and Moody was nurtured in England in the decade prior to J. E. K.'s appearance in the United States. Members of the English test team heard Moody and "one by one . . . they had accepted Christ." They were often invited to the spacious grounds of wealthy patrons on London's outskirts, where Moody "would throw himself into games with as much zest as he took up all his other work." Since he did not like to lose, he generally secured "one of the brothers Studd or Mr. Steel to play on his side!"[98] It was no accident that most of the Cambridge Seven were converts of or helpers to Moody in his mission in Great Britain.

For American muscular Christians, the Studd connection marked two important contributions. First, a financial dividend was felt immediately. Not only had C. T. given part of his inheritance to Moody, but Edward Studd had previously given Moody money to buy a home in Northfield, Massachusetts, a center for student activity. Moody's interaction with the Studds had given him a substantial financial base from which to continue his evangelistic work and develop a new means of reaching the world for Christ. Second, this new strategy combined Moody's early work of evangelism in the YMCA with the emphasis on sport which was emerging so prominently in the 1880s. Norman Grubb's analysis captures the essence of what muscular Christians came to appreciate most in sport: "C. T. never regretted that he played cricket (although he regretted that he had allowed it to become an idol), for by applying himself to the game he learned lessons of courage, self-denial and endurance, which, after his life had been fully consecrated to Christ, were used in His service. The man who went all out to be an expert cricket player, later went all out to glorify his Savior and extend His Kingdom."[99]

By the mid-1880s Moody was staunchly premillennial, and that theological shift affected the direction and outcome of the rapidly expanding muscular Christian program. The ironic result is that while Moody had fewer ties to the YMCA, his experiences with the Studds in England moved him closer to McBurney's social position on evangelism yet laid the foundation for evangelical muscular Christian activity at the Northfield conferences. Thus the stage was set, not only to make the "good of society better" and thereby usher in the kingdom (a postmillennial emphasis) but also to make the "bad of society good" before Jesus would return to earth (a premillennial emphasis). As we shall see, evangelical Christianity was moving rapidly toward an engagement with sport.

The Engagement of Religion and Sport

When J. E. K. Studd, a younger brother of missionary C. T. Studd, visited the United States and Canada in 1885, he was welcomed by college students as an incarnation of the fictional muscular Christian prototype, Tom Brown. The association of Studd with Brown was direct and purposeful. Reflecting on his tour after he had returned to England, Studd told of a student he met who had "ever since reading *Tom Brown's School Days* longed to see some specimen of an English schoolboy." When it was announced that the Cambridge graduate would hold meetings at Cornell, where the young man attended, curiosity drew the student to hear Studd speak. At the meeting, the inquisitive student "decided for Christ."[1] He was John R. Mott, who would later lead the Student Volunteer Movement.

Tom Brown in America: Muscular Christian Revivalist

Evaluating the presence of J. E. K. Studd in America, Luther Wishard, the head of the college YMCA program, explicitly linked Studd's athletic reputation with Christian revivalism and evangelism. "Mr. Studd's prominence in athletics in Cambridge, where he was captain of the University Cricket

Eleven, contributed to secure for him a hardy welcome from many students in the leading institutions of the United States and Canada. His experience in Christian work, in which he was also a leader in his own university, enabled him to accomplish results which can scarcely be over-estimated. He is intimately acquainted with the missionary movement which proceeded from Cambridge and led several of its prominent men, including his brother Charles T. Studd, and his friend Stanley Smith, two of England's most prominent athletes to go as missionaries to China."[2]

J. E. K. Studd's tour of twenty colleges began in November 1885 and extended over the next four months. At each institution, Studd stayed three to six days, holding group meetings for prayer and Bible study. It was in his individual meetings with students, however, that he had the most influence. He effectively used the stimulating narrative of the Cambridge Seven's exploits, but it was his "earnest Christian manliness" that won the hearts of many students. As the YMCA *Collegiate Bulletin* reported, "his own personal experience in college life, as leader of athletic and Christian work of the university, has appealed strongly to our students and has led many to consecrate their lives to Christ."[3]

J. E. K. Studd's college tour had been encouraged by D. L. Moody. Studd confirmed Moody's influence and connected it to an emphasis on the Keswick-style consecrated life for the emerging muscular Christian movement. "D. L. Moody last summer, at Northfield, was much stirred by hearing the way God had led and used those men who recently left our University of Cambridge for the mission fields of China. He felt strongly that such testimony of blessing on consecrated lives was greatly needed and urged my giving account of it among students in your colleges. To this I agreed, and God certainly did bless it to convince men of the reality of unseen things, and many a Christian man was led not only to a life of more devotion to God and College, but to make his life a subject of prayer to God as to what He would have him do."[4]

Combining evangelism, perfectionistic theology, and manly sport was a gradual process. Finney's evangelistic efforts earlier in the century had included a strong emphasis on a second work of grace. Then, the British Keswick movement, of which the Studds were a part, had reinvigorated holiness efforts through "victorious living" strategies. By the time Moody convened the YMCA leaders in the 1880s, the holiness movement had garnered national attention. Moody's selection of "holiness" as the theme for the 1891 Northfield conference followed naturally. This was especially evident in the emphasis on sport at the YMCA training school during this time.[5]

A number of muscular Christians responded to this call and became advocates of a "second work of grace." Of the group committed to a "deeper life experience," Robert Speer and John Mott carried the banner most prominently into the twentieth century.[6] A significant example of how the consecrated life influenced social behavior was the advocacy of the White Cross movement, whose members pledged to keep themselves sexually pure. For a short period in the mid-1880s the movement was a central theme for YMCA leaders.[7]

The Northfield meetings challenged young men to consider "manly" opportunities for service to win their world for Christ. Energized by the urgency of millennial appeals, consecrated young men marched into the world for Christ and his kingdom.

Studd's influence on North American college students was both greater than and something other than the leaders of the YMCA movement had expected. In future decades, members of the SVM and the YMCA would provide much of the energy for evangelism and Christian outreach.[8] Few organizations have had a greater influence on world evangelism and relief. The attention of a generation of Christians was focused on the possibilities of changing the world order based on a religio-political idealism tied to concepts of service.[9]

Not only were Americans influenced by Studd's personal qualities and intrigued by his account of the Cambridge Seven, they also were interested in the attention Studd gave to Bible study. Based on these reactions, YMCA leaders decided to make intensive Bible study an integral part of association meetings.[10]

While Studd's tour had an immediate influence on the Northfield conferences and a long-range effect on the emerging student missionary movement, it did not expand the intercollegiate YMCA in England as some American leaders had hoped. J. E. K. Studd demonstrated no zeal to organize the YMCA in Britain as it was in the United States.[11] Wishard's hope that Studd would carry back to England "a knowledge of our intercollegiate work, which we trust will result in the formation of an intercollegiate organization among the colleges and universities of Great Britain" was never realized.[12]

Nevertheless, J. E. K. Studd's legacy for North American college students and for muscular Christianity was impressive: he brought emphases on Keswick holiness, personal Bible study, and missionary outreach. Although these were not the same messages portrayed by the Tom Brown of Thomas Hughes's writing, Studd's efforts provided exactly the necessary ingredients for a practical American muscular Christianity at the end of the nineteenth century. The *Collegiate Bulletin* reaffirmed his imprint by indicating that his "earnest Christian manliness [had] won the hearts of all students with whom he [had] come in contact."[13] In this way J. E. K. Studd was an important bridge between the idealized muscular Christianity in England at midcentury and the practical muscular Christianity as it engaged with sport in America during the closing decades of the nineteenth century.

Northfield Conferences and Dwight L. Moody

One of the most important results of Studd's visit to the United States was the development of a series of annual conferences near D. L. Moody's home in Northfield, Massachusetts. Within a few years, in the context of premillennial Bible and prophecy conferences in the United States, the Northfield meetings helped fan the flames of religious fervor among college students throughout America. Northfield set a muscular Christian agenda far different from that envisioned at midcentury.

The initial conference in 1885 was limited to a few select leaders and reflected the structure of other informal gatherings held at Northfield earlier in the decade. But the 1886 conference offered dramatic changes. By following a pattern established in the Cambridge Seven's university meetings in England, the conference fostered significant interaction among students involved in sport and religion.[14] The ingredient that emerged from these two forces was the shared vision for revival and world evangelism.

According to Kenneth Scott Latourette, the foremost historian of the missionary movement, the Northfield conference of 1886 created a sense of renewal in the Protestant foreign missionary enterprise.[15] The conference was held on the grounds of the Boys School at Mount Hermon, an institution that Moody was creating on the Connecticut River a few miles below Northfield. For twenty-six days, two hundred-fifty YMCA men from ninety-six colleges met for instruction, fellowship, and renewal.

By 1887, when the meetings became known as the College of Colleges, the muscular Christian union of sport and religion was formalized. For ten days that summer, four hundred men from eighty-two colleges gathered. Every afternoon they engaged in sports, including baseball, football, lawn tennis, boating, and swimming.[16] Those long hours devoted to athletic activities reflected Moody's personal enjoyment of competition. Sometimes he would challenge the "college boys to race him carrying enough ballast to equal his weight— and beat them over twenty-five or thirty yards."[17] This practical engagement of religion and sport emerged as muscular Christians proclaimed that "ebullient animal spirits of youth were consistent with the most intense Christian zeal."[18]

The Northfield conferences were largely informal gatherings with considerable emphasis on biblical instruction and developing a consecrated life. "I hate programs," Moody said, "and I don't have any. Then I can't break over 'em. If you want to know what is ahead, we don't know, except that we will have a good time. We want to stir you up and get you in love with the Bible, and those of you with a voice in love with music. If I find you getting drowsy in hot weather, I'll just ask the speaker to stop and we will sing. . . . Our talks are going to be conversational. If you want to ask a question, speak out: that's what we're here for, to get all the cobwebs swept away, and to go back to our college mates inspired with the truth."[19] Indeed, the Northfield meetings provided a training ground for muscular Christians. One of the best-known examples was Amos Alonzo Stagg, the All-American football player who served as chair of athletic activities for the conferences before embarking on a long career in coaching.

The conferences provided an informal means for Moody to develop personal relationships with college students and leaders. His closeness to Stagg, William Rainey Harper, and others of the Yale delegation was reinforced by the matriculation of his two sons at Yale during this period. Will graduated in 1891 and Paul in 1901. During the last decade of the century, each conference attracted more than one hundred Yale students.[20]

Speakers ranged from a popular Bible teacher like Harper to a narrower dogmatist like A. J. Gordon. Some were unknowns while others were internationally recognized speakers such as Henry Drummond.[21] Harper was so ecumenical in his approach that some evangelicals close to Moody questioned his orthodoxy. Nevertheless, Harper was one of the most popular Bible teachers at these conferences and others throughout the nation. His heartfelt enthusiasm for the values of muscular Christianity was exhibited at the University of Chicago, where as president he hired Stagg as the first football coach and professor of physical education in order to produce the most outstanding athletics teams in the nation.[22]

In contrast to Harper, Moody invited Arthur T. Pierson, perhaps the most notable of several "principal speakers [who] were confirmed premillennialists,"[23] to address the 1886 conference on "The Bible and Prophecy." A popular Presbyterian churchman among many Northfield attendees, Pierson had influenced Robert Speer to convert to Christianity during the Princeton revival earlier that year.[24] At Robert Wilder's request he changed his topic to address the Northfield conference on "God's Providence in Modern Missions." Of that July 16 talk, John Mott asserted, "Dr. A. T. Pierson gave a thrilling address on missions. He supported, by the most convincing arguments, the proposition that 'all should go and go to all.' This was the key-note which set many men to thinking and praying."[25] In retrospect Mott also credited Pierson with supplying the "watchword" of "the evangelization of the world in this generation," which was subsequently appropriated by Mott and the SVM.[26]

Of both immediate and long-term significance, Pierson's talk that summer resulted in the Mount Hermon 100, the core of the 1886 Northfield muscular Christians, who "returned to their separate colleges in the fall and began to gather bands of students . . . from around the country [who] volunteered to become foreign missionaries, and the Student Volunteer Movement for Foreign Missions came into being to conserve and to organize these students."[27]

Of all the leaders, Henry Drummond was perhaps a key figure, and another Anglo-American link, in the engagement of evangelical Christianity and sport. At Moody's encouragement this philosopher and educator from Scotland had spent two years in evangelistic work in Scotland, England, and Ireland.[28] He was an extraordinary speaker and articulated the muscular Christian principles upon which the Northfield group was acting. Speaking from his British frame of reference, Drummond argued that "the key to a boy's heart [was] athletics." Drummond indicated athletes were picked to lead meetings because they were heroes in the eyes of students. Drummond mentioned that some of the headmasters in Scotland had involved athletes as leaders at special Sunday meetings. The experiment was so successful that the meetings became an institution and had "influenced those boys in the direction of muscular Christianity."[29]

By using Drummond to supplement the earlier British influence of the Studds, D. L. Moody helped legitimize the use of sport for evangelism and discipleship in America. Although built on ideas borrowed from England, and linked to the character education values of muscular Christianity, this form was built on the traditions of revivalism and reform. After viewing the athletic activities at Northfield, Moody observed, "To see them play (tennis) you would think their lives depended on it. . . . I liked that. Whatsoever thy hand findeth to do, do it with thy might."[30] The editor of the conference record concluded, "Even the fondness for manly sports may have a determined value in the counsels of providence."[31] This emphasis fit well with Moody's, and evangelical Christianity's, newly found theological position of premillennialism.

This generation of muscular Christians felt that the work of those active in sports or supervising gymnasiums was significant. These evangelicals reasoned that, like the physician who healed the sick, the muscular Christian who served as a physical director ministered to physical and spiritual needs to "bring young men to Jesus Christ." This philosophy required YMCA staffers to persuade "the souls of men as well as their bodies."[32] The essential goal, as indicated in the *Intercollegian,* was to permeate the association with a missionary spirit.[33]

Outreach activities had a significant emphasis on reaching males and sent an obvious "masculine" message. Writing in the *Intercollegian,* Robert Lendram indicated that "if Northfield Christianity was warm and fervid, it was nonetheless robust and manly. No effeminacy, no sickly pietism flourished there. Every manly sport had its votaries. . . . Northfield Christianity was preeminently hopeful and aggressive. The tide of Christian fervor in the American and Canadian colleges is evidently gaining in strength and volume."[34]

In reality the Northfield conference inadvertently perpetuated multiple visions of the evangelical appropriation of sport, which in the end would never completely cohere. On the one hand, those with closer ties to the college YMCA movement sought to extend essentially postmillennial, arguably more middle- and upper-class, and more British-like emphases on "making the good of society better." Clearly, Moody accepted such emphases. He had benefited personally from them, both in Britain and the U.S., and the Tom Brown–like image embodied in J. E. K. Studd lingered in the minds of many.

On the other hand, Northfield also served the parallel—and sometimes competing—interests of another growing group of evangelical muscular Christians. The exploits of C. T. Studd and the Cambridge Seven were fresh in the minds of Northfield men who were bent on using sport for worldwide evangelization and to "make the bad of society good."[35] Their vision was more directly shaped by premillennialism and the sense of urgency it gave to their task. Thus, many SVM volunteers adopted the watchword of "the evangelization of the world in this generation" and fused it with a modicum of the manly Keswick emphasis on power and victory through God's Spirit. After embracing premillennialism, Moody likewise preached, "I have felt like working three times as hard ever since I came to understand that my Lord was coming back again. I look on this world as a wrecked vessel. God has given me a life-boat, and said to me, 'Moody, save all you can.' God will come in judgment and burn up this world, but the children of God don't belong to this world; they are in it, but not of it, like a ship in the water."[36]

For historian Timothy Weber, "Premillennialism not only gave its advocates a new incentive for converting sinners; it gave them a new, powerful way to shake them from their spiritual lethargy."[37] Thus those attending Northfield likely heard multiple evangelical appeals that they filtered through their own experiences, convinced that manly participation in sports related to more than one kind of service to the kingdom.

Of course, not all analysts lauded the work of muscular Christians. One commentator indicated that since "it was the period of 'the manly Christian,' some students deliberately espoused religious work as their extra curriculum activity for the sake of social rewards." Not only were some muscular Christians' motives challenged, but their intellectual character became an issue as well. As the medical profession moved away from sport and physical education at places like Yale, the social and religious work of the YMCA began to be interpreted as anti-intellectual. [38]

Sport and Christianity were fused at Northfield in the mid-1880s. So important was this connection that within a decade Luther Gulick, as head of the YMCA training school at Springfield, Massachusetts, recommended that all juniors spend their summers at the conference.[39] Full engagement of a distinctively evangelical and American muscular Christianity had occurred.

Integration of Sport, Education, and Christian Ideals

Evangelism through athletic-minded students paid significant dividends for evangelical Christians in the short run. By the 1880s American colleges had opened their doors to a broad range of students, especially at land grant institutions. The proliferation of new colleges was changing the landscape of American higher education. In this competitive marketplace, a social phenomenon also was emerging which soon would capture the soul of the campuses. Like a Trojan horse, intercollegiate sport gained a place in American higher education as educational administrators began a century-long process of explaining and sometimes deploring sports but always using sports for personal and institutional purposes.

As sports were legitimized on college campuses, they became acceptable activities for evangelical Christians. Reflecting the idealism of muscular Christians, one YMCA worker spoke enthusiastically, "These associations have wrested the gymnasium from the hands of prizefighters and professional athletes and put it into the hands of Christian gymnasts who are after the souls of men as well as their bodies."[40]

57

By the close of the nineteenth century, the efforts of inter-denominational groups like the SVM and the YMCA created high, and probably unrealistic, hopes for the emerging muscular Christian movement and for worldwide evangelism. John Mott indicated that there never was "a time when simultaneously in so many sections of the world the opportunities for the extension of the Christian religion were so numerous and so extensive."[41] Frances E. Clark, a leading Congregationalist and a participant in the Northfield meetings, commented early in the twentieth century, "The harvest seemed never so white as young reapers trooped into the fields in great numbers." He had observed "the eager faces of earnest youth, with the high resolves and splendid optimism . . . looking forward with eager vision to Christ's conquest of the world."[42]

Much of the attractiveness of these movements lay in their dynamic idealism. The "responsibility resting upon each generation of Christians to make the Gospel fully known to non-Christians of their own generation," John Mott had proclaimed, "was not only a universal challenge, but a personal one as well."[43] Mott asserted that people who think of "the world as the field of Christ as Lord" and hold that his reign will someday become coextensive with the inhabited earth "find that they cannot rest with a divided ownership in their own lives." According to Mott, God was calling "missionary statesmen as prophets to widen the realm of human understanding."[44]

The Northfield men attracted special attention on their campuses, significantly affected the development of muscular Christianity, and ultimately helped legitimize sport. By their consecrated lives and integrated lifestyles, they lifted sport to a new status; the combination of playing sports and serving humanity, while not necessarily new or exclusively American, was nevertheless carried out more visibly and with greater institutional endorsement than ever before. Building God's kingdom appeared to be a bit easier if the king's messengers were also the heroes of society. And few heroes were larger than those in sport.

In 1886 at the opening of Dwight Hall, the Yale College YMCA building, the *New Englander and Yale Review* lauded the emergence of sport, indicating that "college athletics bear part of the praise of this growing manliness. The healthy play of young life in honorable tests of ability, condemns and banishes rudeness and lawlessness of behavior, from common life."[45] By the early 1890s six of the starting eleven of Yale's football team were evangelical Christians.[46]

The YMCA on college campuses was booming. According to the 1885 annual report, there were 181 college associations, with more than ten thousand members. That membership reflected nearly one-third of the college population in the United States. One indication of their commitment was that nearly two hundred students intended to become foreign missionaries.[47]

At the local level, such figures are even more astounding. At Hamilton College in New York, for example, 110 out of 180 students belonged to the YMCA.[48] Indeed, the YMCA had become a major campus social club. It was the college fraternity of the late nineteenth century.

A building campaign to provide YMCA gymnasiums on college campuses was launched during this era. Concerns regarding secular institutions spending money for sectarian purposes were usually assuaged by the argument that the YMCA was making a significant contribution to society. Besides, most felt that sports, especially in educational settings, were "among the most important moralizing influences in America."[49]

The Protestant Christian consensus had reached new heights. Civil religious enthusiasm, with muscular Christianity at its core, reigned supreme. The primary concern, though never exactly verbalized, was whether an adequate structure was in place for the institutionalization and perpetuation of this early engagement of religion and sport. The development of YMCA colleges in Chicago and in Springfield, Massachusetts, would provide that structure. The school at Springfield would serve as the headquarters for a missionary movement that would reach the four corners of the world.

The YMCA Training School at Springfield: Training Muscular Christian Engagers

The expansion of the evangelical outreach of muscular Christianity was accompanied by institutional development to sustain its momentum. It began at the same time as the Northfield conferences and was meant to provide organizational continuity to those summer sessions within the established YMCA structure. In 1885 an institute to develop Christian workers was formed in Springfield, Massachusetts. The institute quickly forged an identity and mission within the larger framework of the association. Robert Roberts was its first physical director, but in 1887 Luther Gulick was hired to lead the program. He provided the leadership for the institutionalization of muscular Christianity within the YMCA.

As mentioned earlier, Gulick's missionary roots and his grandmother's conversion under Charles Finney connected Gulick with early nineteenth-century revivalism.[50] In explaining the special training for the gymnasium director at Springfield, Gulick indicated that "the aim of this department of the school will be twofold. First, to put into the field men of tested Christian character, men who have had thorough drill and Bible truth and association work. Second, to see that these men shall be intelligent teachers, men who shall know what to do, how to do it and why it is to be done. . . . In brief, the aim is to place Christian gymnasium superintendents in the field; men who were first Christian, then intelligent teachers; men whose object in going into the world is to serve Christ."[51] These men would work under "the idea that Christ's kingdom should include the athletic world."[52]

Howard Hopkins, the eminent historian of the YMCA, credits Gulick with being the primary catalyst for developing Springfield and integrating the gymnasium into its educational program. Gulick captured the holistic philosophy of the association with a meaningful symbol. He created a triangle to represent the integration of body, mind, and spirit, arguing that this essential unity in each person reflected God.

Paraphrasing the apostle Paul, he summarized the position: "I pray to God your whole spirit and soul and body be preserved blameless unto the coming of our Lord Jesus Christ." This served as a reference point for Gulick's early work at the Springfield institution. The model of a resurrected Christ who was perfect in body, mind, and spirit served as a foundation for subsequent muscular Christians.[53]

Gulick's work at Springfield, then, was much broader than is usually understood. Along with other early YMCA workers, he certainly was interested in manhood and in fitness. But Gulick was an organizational genius and served as a transformer of culture. His early writings indicate that he, like Harper, held a kinship with the evangelical Protestant movement of the nineteenth century.[54] With his roots embedded and nurtured in a family of missionaries, such a concern would have been normative. Nowhere was his philosophy better articulated than in one of his lectures from the early 1890s at Springfield. Titled "Oh to Be Nothing," the speech encouraged students to become involved in association work to reach young men spiritually.[55]

Students who sat under Gulick's teaching recognized the Christian commitment he brought to the classroom. Lecture notes by Edward Von DeSteiner indicate Gulick's emphasis that "body and soul are both so closely related that one affects the other." Gulick went on to identify the need for students to help the sick and the poor following Jesus' example that "you have done it unto the least of these. . . ."[56] Ethel Dorgan, in a somewhat romantic view of Gulick, indicates that his interest in physical education started with his desire to benefit humanity. To him, physical education offered a way to do this. "No religious missionary has been more sincere in his aim to gather to Christ than Luther Gulick in his twofold object of educating for character and bringing to Jesus."[57]

Gulick was adamant in advocating use of the gymnasium to build Christ's kingdom. "The gymnasium is not simply a trap to catch young men. It is equally false the gymnasium exists only for bodies of its members. Yet we do hope to reach young men through the gymnasium and do expect we are going to benefit their bodies and each of these aims is of primary importance. The gymnasium exists in the association as a fundamental and intrinsic part in the salvation of man."[58] The YMCA gradually changed and became more reflective of the culture surrounding it. Yet during this period of engagement between sport and evangelical Christianity, Gulick emphasized the positive connections, echoing Moody and McBurney. Gradually the YMCA moved to a position where the purpose of conversion was character development rather than character transformation.

As religion and sport linked, it is instructive to note how the two were affected by the culture supporting them. Typically the YMCA reflected the norms of society. For example, as the organization emerged in the Midwest, numerous mixed-gender associations were organized. But the eastern leadership rejected this idea. By the mid-1880s women were moved to a separate organization. For the next century the emphasis on manliness had a special connotation within the YMCA for muscular Christianity and for sport.[59]

Also, there was increasing tension within the YMCA about the institutionalization of sport and the role of sports managers. Before 1890, associations had encouraged competition in games of low organization and development. But as institutionalization occurred, the YMCA was caught between a policy of sports for all and sports for heroes. The idealization of sports heroes was moving sport from the status of folk tradition to one of elite performance. Various approaches were tried throughout the life of the YMCA to counteract this trend. In the early 1890s Gulick developed the pentathlon to allay the criticism that athletics within the YMCA was leading to specialization, an evident evil that athletics was meant to overcome. According to Gulick, "The object of the Association is the production of all-round Christian manhood."[60]

The tension between men playing games and games-playing men was always just below the surface. In founding the Athletic League section of the YMCA early in the 1890s, Gulick openly addressed this issue.

The first object of the Young Men's Christian Association Athletic League is to increase the good and decrease the evils in connection with athletic sports.

We recognize the elements of manliness and vigor that are cultivated by manly sports. These good elements have, however, been so often associated with the evils of betting, swearing, physical excesses, dishonesty, and a trivial view of the serious things of life that the whole influence of such sport has been doubtful in the minds of many Christian men.

The leaders in the athletic world . . . have not usually in the past been men who have taken the earnest view of life. This may have been in part a result of the nature of sport itself, but it is also a fact that resolute, earnest young men are generally connected with sport for a short time only. They soon out-grow this period, the larger things of life engage their attention, and what time is given to sport is merely for recreation.

There is always a strong temptation to place victory above honesty or courtesy. The yielding to such temptations makes success in athletic sports to depend as much upon a knowledge of technical points, ways of evading rules or penalties, or violation of the spirit of rules without being detected, as it does upon athletic skill itself. To be trained that cheating is right if it is only done skillfully, and that courtesy and Christian character are to be put off when he puts on an athletic suit, does more harm to a man than any good that can come from the sport itself.[61]

Gulick's clarion call "that Christ's Kingdom should include the athletic world" provided a philosophical rationale for operating sports in society. He hoped that Christian coaches and teachers, by virtue of higher and stronger motives and character, would change sport to increase the good and decrease the evils. Such was Gulick's emphasis on "Christian character in sport. . . ."[62] To a great degree, the legitimation of sport in society rested on the assumption that educational and moral values would be derived from participation in sports. As indicated by Gulick, one significant element in this legitimizing process was the role of the sports supervisor.

Two schools of thought quickly emerged regarding supervision. One held an activist position that promoted adult supervisors to direct the play of young men. Another held a more passive viewpoint, emphasizing that participation on the game field would inherently foster character-forming values. Although it is too simplistic to indicate that this division was between coaches and physical educators or between American and British muscular Christians, it is evident that these groups generally aligned with one or the other of these positions. In the history of educational sport in America, the two traditions emerged and conflicted. That conflict would be fully developed during the period of disengagement, as we shall see in chapter 3. According to the activists, if character was to be developed through sport, it had to be taught. Gulick would later refer to the use of the child development doctrine of "hands off" in sport as advocating a pernicious doctrine.[63] These positions can best be illustrated by the careers of Gulick's two prized pupils—Amos Alonzo Stagg and James Naismith.

A. A. Stagg: A New Manager Model

As muscular Christians developed strategies for moral education through athletic participation, many endorsed the position of coach. Previous to the 1880s most teams operated with team-directed leadership, and few external forces were exerted on the teams. Though coaches from outside the teams began to be hired in the 1880s, their jobs were restricted, with most acting as general managers. However, the emphasis quickly moved to field-managing the game. Soon these managers began to utilize time-outs, huddles, substitutions, and other aspects of management commonly accepted today. These innovations interfered with the flow of the games, but they brought a new level of cohesion, stability, and efficiency to athletic contests. Like their counterparts in business, good coaches were organizational wizards who could manipulate teams into winning combinations. And like their business counterparts, they were responsible to boards who replaced them if they did not win. As Donald Mrozek has indicated, character education for muscular Christians was moving from qualitative measures of personal growth to quantitative ones marked by performance.[64] Gradually, coaching performers to win became the priority for some muscular Christians.

Amos Alonzo Stagg was an outstanding baseball pitcher at Yale University (1884–89) before pursuing his football coaching career.

Perhaps no one exemplified this business-based model for coaching more completely than Amos Alonzo Stagg. Stagg was responsible for many of the innovations in modern coaching. Some still consider him the father of coaching. Although he was an excellent baseball player and was selected to the first all-American football team in 1889, Stagg's journey to a coaching deanship followed a circuitous route. First he studied theology at Yale under William Rainey Harper; then he applied muscular Christian principles to young men at the new YMCA training school in Springfield before Harper wooed him to Chicago. There, Harper instructed Stagg "to develop teams which we can send around the country and knock out all the colleges." His commitment was epitomized by his statement that "we will give them a palace, car and a vacation too."[65]

From Stagg's perspective in 1892, coaching football at Chicago was a call to Christian service in which he could best be used "for my Master's service." Stagg was given a position on the faculty, the first such athletic position in the United States. He idealized his role, thinking of coaching as one of the "noblest and farthest reaching" opportunities he could have imagined for developing manhood. And football was more than a mere game. It was a laboratory where his players could develop in an honest and clean environment.[66] How clean that

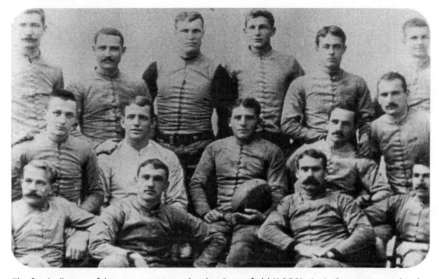

The football team of the YMCA training school at Springfield (1890). A. A. Stagg is seated in the middle, holding the football, and James Naismith is seated in the front row, second from right.

environment was would be disputed over the next century. What is certain is that winning was very important. And it required a strong coach who could scientifically and perhaps arbitrarily manage young men. What better way to build and legitimize a management team than through the discipline offered by muscular Christians? Serious effort, consecration to one's task, and laying down one's life for the team were critical ingredients for the successful muscular Christian coach.

Even as Stagg was settling into institutionalized higher education, his sports system was becoming an economic enterprise at odds with existing educational philosophy. As a model for other coaches, Stagg became a manager of a business operation under the full protection of an educational institution. Stagg informed his president soon after taking the job, "I understand that I am not to be hampered in my work in any way. . . . I am not compelled to explain for what purpose certain money is to be used."[67]

For some coaches like Stagg, intercollegiate athletics was a profitable setting which allowed their free enterprise activities to work within a subsidized system provided by schools and colleges. Endowed with free capital (gymnasiums and stadiums subsidized by state or private funds), free marketing (sports pages), and low personnel costs (salaries attached to scales in education), these coaches, especially those who were muscular Christians, followed a self-fulfilling moral imperative to conform men to their closed values system. Over the next generations Christian coaches would be among the most vociferous defenders of the sports enterprise. Few would question, as had Gulick, whether the supposed values really were being developed. In the athletic arena where testimonials carried the day, those who had the most vested interest in sport spoke the loudest and with the most heartfelt enthusiasm.

As a participant in sports, Stagg's first love was baseball. He starred on the Yale nine from 1884 to 1889, during the years of his participation at the Northfield conferences, and was offered a professional contract. He rejected six offers from National League teams, the largest from New York at forty-two hundred dollars, in part because of his concerns about professionalism in sport. Also, he wanted to return to the divinity school at Yale.[68] As a graduate student he joined the football team after consulting with Richard Morse, the general secretary of the YMCA, who, according to Stagg, "urged me to accept on the ground that it would increase my influence as a worker."[69]

Stagg's decision to become a physical educator and a coach may have rested to some degree on his discomfort with speaking publicly before religious and church groups. Stagg's decision was clinched when he overheard John Mott tell a colleague at a student conference at Lake Geneva, Wisconsin, that he couldn't understand "why Stagg simply can't make a talk."[70] Although Stagg could not easily articulate his faith, he had an exceptional ability to act it out. This was exemplified even during his college days by his starting the Yale Mission, an early attempt to apply social action to his muscular Christian views.[71]

Ultimately, even though Stagg had studied for the ministry, he decided that he could accomplish more on the athletic field than from the pulpit. The opportunity at Chicago confirmed his calling to muscular Christian work, and he wrote President Harper, "after much thought and prayer, I decided that my life can best be used for my Master's service in the position you have offered."[72]

Stagg remained at Springfield until the new university opened in October 1892. The additional year on the staff gave him a chance to hone his coaching skills and to develop his philosophy of coaching based on muscular Christian principles. He was filled with anticipation, since he felt that the opportunity to coach would give him "such a fine chance to do Christian work among the boys who are sure to have the most influence. Win the athletes of any college for Christ, and you will have the strongest working element attainable in college life."[73] He later indicated that coaching was "one of the noblest and farthest reaching (vocations) in building manhood."[74] And football was a primary means for reaching that goal.

For Stagg, football was more than a game. It provided an arena in which to test one's faith, to purify one's soul, and to develop one's character. Frank Merriwell, the fictional ideal athlete, would have felt at home on Stagg's team, where right and wrong were self-evident truths and where one would do battle to disinfect society and clear it of all wrongs.[75] But Stagg was certainly not alone. In 1891, shortly after his graduation from Yale and while he was still working at Springfield, the *Young Men's Era* indicated that football had become an established outlet for Christians on college campuses. "To those who have congratulated themselves that all outdoor sports have been of late years elevated by the participation in them of Christian men, there will come an additional cause for encouragement in the statement that more than half of the Yale team are Christians—as interested in the Lord's work as in the contest of the football field."[76]

The triumph of muscular Christianity seemed at hand. Evangelical Christianity had directly engaged with sport. Young muscular Christians flocked to the new profession of coaching. And as the gears of society turned, it was hoped that a new world would be created. Muscular Christians hoped to win the world for Christ in their generation.

The Disengagement of Evangelical Muscular Christians from Sport

Changes within the emerging institution of sport affected evangelical muscular Christians at the turn of the century in ways they never could have anticipated a mere two decades earlier. Amos Alonzo Stagg illustrated the response taken by those who endorsed the professionalization of coaching along lines compatible with American emphases on competition and winning. Another of Luther Gulick's Springfield pupils, James Naismith, exemplified a quite different attempt to adapt evangelical muscular Christianity to the demands of American sport in the twentieth century.

James Naismith: An American Tom Brown

Appearing before the Eighth Annual Convention of the National Collegiate Athletic Association in 1914, Naismith proclaimed the principles of Tom Brown—duty, honor, and manliness.

Therefore, while the immediate responsibility of this organization is primarily with intercollegiate contests, yet it should use every means to put basketball, as well as every other sport, on such a basis that it will be a factor in the molding of character, as well as to encourage it as a recreative and competitive sport. This organization should take such measures as will result in a rigid enforcement of the rules as formulated, and encourage a manly respect for the rights of others. So much stress is laid to-day on the winning of games that practically all else is lost sight of, and the fine elements of manliness and true sportsmanship are accorded a secondary place. One great problem for this organization is the formulating of the system of scoring that will take cognizance of these traits of manhood or the development of traditions which will make it impossible for a college man to take advantage of an opponent, save in those qualities which the sport is supposed to require. The bane of basket ball to-day is the attempt to evade the laws of the game and even the rulings of the officials. . . . Few college men would take money or valuables from another yet they are taught in the practices of our sports that it is not dishonorable to take an illegal advantage of another, if there is little prospect of being caught. To-day, a player hardly dares do the manly thing if it will mean a loss of points, lest he incur the ridicule of the bleachers and the sneers of his college mates. The man who does what he knows to be right, when he thereby fails to score points, too often incurs the wrath of the coach and the scorn of his team mates.[1]

During the twenty-three years between the invention of basketball and Naismith's appearance before the NCAA convention, much had changed.[2]

In 1891, while a graduate student at the YMCA training school in Springfield, Massachusetts, Naismith was given the assignment to develop a game that could be played indoors between the football and baseball seasons. To create this new activity, Naismith used elements of games he had played as a child. After experimenting with several formats, Naismith was encouraged by his advisor, Luther Gulick, to include something distinctive from other sports. Naismith finally decided upon a game based on the concept of tossing a ball on a soft arc to an elevated goal. Although most of the other elements of the new activity reflected aspects of other games, basketball was well received by the men of the YMCA. Given the missionary zeal of the students involved in the YMCA, the game was soon being played throughout the world.

For Naismith, basketball was more than a new game. It was a means to evangelize people about morality and Christian values, the essence of American muscular Christianity. Later, Naismith would remember that he had invented basketball from a thesis that "the trouble is not with men but with

James Naismith, center, rowed competitively while at Springfield.

the system."[3] Cities were overflowing and many immigrants appeared to hold few of the sociocultural values of Tom Brown. Moreover, health and sanitation conditions were limited; educational opportunities were minimal. Perhaps greatest of all, at least for muscular Christians, was the perceived need for a Christian witness. As an evangelical Christian, Naismith felt a new game would provide a means to meet both social and spiritual needs. That approach—inventing basketball as an act of social engineering—has reinforced the interpretation of Naismith's act as a reflection of the Social Gospel movement. At least as Naismith remembered it forty years later, his intent was to meet the "needs" and to change the "systems" in which he was involved during the 1890s.

Reflecting both Enlightenment and Christian philosophies, Naismith was convinced that placing an individual into a game would yield a positive educational experience. Basketball would become a self-instructional, character-development activity. To a degree, this philosophy also reflected Naismith's acceptance of a prevailing theory of physical education based on a modified Rousseauian view of child devel-

71

opment that children should be given freedom to develop on their own. Naismith believed that he had gained a great educational advantage as a youngster by playing games in rural Canada. Unfettered by institutional chains, Naismith and his friends were free to play the games as they saw fit.

Naismith's original intentions for the game (and for muscular Christianity) may be less clear than his reflection forty years after its invention. Freedom of play was probably not as open as Phog Allen, the coach who replaced Naismith at the University of Kansas, asserts. Nevertheless, Allen's indication that Naismith's original concept of basketball instruction had been "to throw the ball in and let them fight over it" identifies a position that the players would control the game from within, not abdicating control to forces outside the game. For Naismith basketball was a game to be played, not to be coached.[4]

As basketball developed in the twentieth century, it became less self-directed and more coaching-directed. In response to this trend, Naismith became rigid. He rejected most attempts to adapt the rules to the changing athletic culture. He believed that the game would nurture and develop players on its own without intervention. With that theory, Naismith represented a solid constituency within physical education and athletics who believed in "throwing out the ball" and letting the students learn by playing within an agreed-upon set of rules and cultural expectations.

A Theology of Sport in the Early Twentieth Century

James Naismith, as a muscular Christian, was confident that a personal God oversaw the universe and predestined the actions of those who were part of God's system. Within those Presbyterian theological constraints, personal responsibility for individual action was emphasized less than within alternative existing theologies that advocated greater freedom and responsibility. Evangelicals within the muscular Christian movement were at a crossroads. Some still reflected a post-millennial optimism and believed the games themselves would foster change. Others more pessimistically and premillennially inclined felt that change would come only through conversion, thus their emphasis on games as a context for evangelism. Moody was earlier convinced that only changed people would change society. McBurney held that reforming social structures such as schools, churches, and games would change people. This was a recurring debate throughout the nineteenth and twentieth centuries, but it reached a climax in the first three decades of the twentieth century.

John Mott, a product of the Northfield conferences, reflected this debate when he addressed the Student Volunteer Convention of 1920. He indicated that the vision of a new world required students to attack industry, commerce, and finance, "to apply the principles of Jesus Christ to these great energies and to wield them in the interest of His Kingdom." In national and international politics, he continued, student volunteers should attempt "to Christianize the impact of our Western civilization upon the non-Christian world."[5] A student leader at the convention argued that students should become "the ambassadors for Christ to the social, industrial unrest of the day." By attacking those issues, he suggested, they could "give themselves to save the world."[6] As recognition of social problems sharpened, students began asking whether they should strive for social rather than personal salvation. The church had been too slow, another student argued, in realizing that there was a "social system which could damn men's souls before they were born."[7]

Mott tried to moderate the tensions between the two groups. He had come to appreciate "both the social and individual aspects of the creation Gospel and likewise their essential unity." They were not mutually exclusive positions. Both were necessary to build the kingdom of God. For Mott that kingdom was both present and future; it was to be ushered in by striving to improve the social environment by means of bringing individuals to a personal commitment to Christ.[8] The

73

debate between the two positions reappeared even as late as the 1970s, when Billy Graham appeared before the national council of the YMCA. He spoke of the need to "change men's hearts first" as a prerequisite to changing society.[9]

Shortly after inventing basketball and after receiving his medical degree, Naismith became athletic director and director of the chapel at the University of Kansas—a role he felt was made to order for a muscular Christian. At the university commencement in 1900, Chancellor Snow, who had brought Naismith to campus, indicated that Jesus Christ "bids each move heaven and earth to achieve for himself a worthy manhood." Each person was to work in the world, "seeking to advance the true, the honorable, the just, the pure, and the lovely which cannot help making the world better for your living in it."[10] The postmillennial hope that Christ's kingdom was returning to earth mandated that Snow and Naismith, as muscular Christians, participate in making the world a better place to quicken the coming of his kingdom. For Naismith, developing a better system meant developing better games. Through education, and a games philosophy in particular, Naismith hoped that society would improve in the coming millennium.

The Decline of Evangelical Muscular Christianity in Secular Institutions

What James Naismith and Chancellor Snow sought to accomplish at Kansas in the early 1900s must be viewed in the context of higher education in America, specifically at public universities. Historian Laurence Veysey has depicted the era of 1865–1900 as crucial for the rise of the American university, with that period divided at about 1890 into two parts, so that "the American university of 1900 was all but unrecognizable in comparison with the college of 1860."

In the earlier period (1865–90), attending college meant "confirming one's respectable place in society." Throughout the 1880s under the banner of "mental discipline," many colleges also "sought to provide a four-year regimen conducive to piety and strength of character."[11] Clearly, this was the collegiate context for the initial adaptation of muscular Christianity and for the YMCA movement on American campuses. Similarly, it was the setting for many of the early Northfield muscular Christians, especially those from private, eastern campuses.

What existed in latent form, however, rapidly took on new meaning around 1890. For public universities, it was an "era of rapid expansion, rising prestige for university education, correspondingly large business support, and proliferation of university-related structures. . . . Dependent on social, economic, and market forces, universities soon became remarkably alike and could not be guided by abstract ideals."[12] At a more subjective and personal level, the meaning of a college degree also was being redefined as the "mark of the social mobility of one's parents and of the hopes for further movement. . . . An academic degree was like an insurance policy against downward mobility."[13]

All this expansion, redefinition, and bureaucratization was hardly neutral for practitioners and institutions of religion. Several examples from the early 1900s illustrate how varied, but generally negative, were the effects on religion. In 1905 the Carnegie Foundation for the Advancement of Teaching (and predecessor of today's TIAA-CREF) was established to offer "attractive retirement programs for faculty members of colleges and universities," but only to faculty of those schools that were nonsectarian in religious matters. Many colleges quickly severed denominational ties to demonstrate that their religious heritage "played little, if any, part in the religious or intellectual life of the student body."[14]

In 1909 *Cosmopolitan* magazine ran a series of articles on what was being taught in American colleges. Author Harold Bolce's exposé pointed to the departure of the professoriat from traditional theological affirmations. While endorsing a secular worldview, the professors uniformly rejected a Christian theology of salvation, instead "declaring that the fall of man is a myth; that it was a Judean peasant, not a God, that was crucified on Calvary; and that shameful tragedy had absolutely nothing to do with remission of sins and the reconciliation of an erring race to an outraged God." Then in 1915 the American Association of University Professors was formed, allegedly to ensure academic freedom. For individuals and colleges of religious persuasion, however, the result was significant. "Schools that aspired to a national standing would have to concede that particular religious traditions could not have normative standing in shaping academic policies."[15]

What these examples suggest is that national forces were redefining and marginalizing the place of religion-based teaching and scholarship. Education was being standardized along increasingly secular lines, and religion within an educational setting was redefined as propaganda. The contrast to the days of the Beechers, when religion and education converged as a foundation for American evangelical muscular Christianity, is apparent. If muscular Christianity was going to survive and flourish in the twentieth century, especially within educational settings, it would be on terms quite unlike those of the late nineteenth century.

Therefore, as James Naismith began to serve God as director of athletics and of the chapel at Kansas, the world of education was radically changing. Chapel at the university followed the secular model. Although chapel attendance was required in the early years of the university, by 1890 it was no longer mandatory. During Naismith's tenure, fewer than one hundred out of more than a thousand students attended. Voluntary devotional exercises were conducted daily until 1913–14, when they were reduced to twice a week. Chapel services were replaced by convocations the following year.[16]

Although such developments were significant, perhaps of greater importance for muscular Christians were changes on the individual level. During the gradual separation of religious affairs from the operation of secular institutions, Naismith felt compelled to make distinctions between his personal piety and the public practice of his faith. When teaching his classes, he modeled Christianity without verbal exposition. Only in church services would he articulate his faith publicly.

The changes in chapel and in Naismith's role as a religious leader on campus reflected the critical changes in higher education. The dynamism of the YMCA movement, the student volunteers, and other missionary organizations in the latter two decades of the nineteenth century was slowly breaking down. The students' enthusiasm for religious renewal was channeled into other efforts at the beginning of the twentieth century. Yet, although his strategies of evangelism changed, Naismith held to his concepts of sportsmanship and gamesmanship. All activity was part of God's larger classroom, and Naismith hoped that the game environment would provide a Christian educational experience.

Because of this stance, Naismith and his invention were to become victims of the very forces that he and others had hoped would transform the world. His failure to pursue an activist role as a muscular Christian may have helped disengage sport and religion. A later generation of muscular Christians did not hold the beliefs or the personal faith in the system that Naismith and his peers did. As sport developed in increasingly secular ways, muscular Christians drifted to a system in which principles, either scientific or moral, would be coached rather than internalized merely by participation. Events of the twentieth century transformed basketball and all of sport. Diminished was the spirit that had prompted Naismith and other muscular Christians to dream of a game that would provide personal and moral growth. No longer did those who led the sports movement believe the arena held unalterable divine or natural laws that provided a positive social environment for transforming both the game and the players.

Billy Sunday and Complete Disengagement

The forces that had helped launch modern American sport in the late nineteenth century continued to forge changes

Billy Sunday was a successful professional baseball player in the 1880s, known for his speed and daring.

in the early twentieth century. Urbanization led to mass markets conducive to developing spectator sports. Technological advances promoted the construction of stadiums as well as the creation of improved sports equipment. Professionalism allowed athletes to focus their attention on the sport without being distracted by other demands. Capitalism provided a base for enhancing consumerism related to the business of sports. These social processes forced secularizing changes in sport and in the attitudes of muscular Christians. Evangelical muscular Christians, who had earlier embraced sport to accomplish God's redemptive purposes, now found themselves trapped by the values and structures of an institution rapidly moving in a different direction.

Even more important than these changes in social forces was the lack of leaders who would endorse sport. Unlike the nineteenth century, when evangelists, preachers, and Christian workers such as Dwight L. Moody, Henry Ward Beecher, and Robert McBurney were active, the twentieth century saw no spokesman of national prominence among muscular Christians. Especially where muscular Christian representatives such as Naismith and Stagg followed secular culture, the Christian witness was muted in the arena.

Add to this the erosion of an 1800s-style evangelical consensus, and muscular Christianity began to lose its evangelical identification. Naismith, Stagg, Gulick, and others moved in diverse directions. Most glaring of all, Billy Sunday, the most likely successor to the leaders of the nineteenth century, ironically helped dismantle the broad coalition that supported muscular Christianity.

As a revivalist successor to Finney and Moody, and as a noteworthy professional baseball player, Billy Sunday was in line to move muscular Christianity forward.[17] Yet he did the reverse. His baseball career lasted from 1883 to 1892, the same period that was so critical for the development of sport generally and for the engagement of sport and evangelical religion in particular. He spent most of his career in Chicago and established strong roots there. And it was in that city in 1886 that Sunday converted to evangelical Christianity.

The changes in Sunday's behavior and in his involvement in baseball were significant. He gave up drinking, swearing, gambling, going to theaters, and playing baseball on Sunday. He quickly joined the muscular Christian movement and began giving talks to boys at the YMCA in cities where the Chicago White Sox played. His talks emphasized two themes—sport and military drill. Sunday saw these efforts as a way to challenge the soft life in America and to return Christians to a more manly way. Not one to "turn his cheek," he was even willing to fight to prove the strength of Christianity. "I'd like to put my fist on the nose of the man who hasn't got grit enough to be a Christian," he said, demonstrating an aggressiveness he felt was important for society and for Christianity.[18]

Sunday's participation in professional baseball stamped a starlike quality on his life. His career covered nine seasons, and for a time he held the record of ninety-five stolen bases in a season, which Ty Cobb broke in 1915. Because of his reputation, men and boys came to hear Sunday's baseball stories when he spoke in the associations. A Pittsburgh newspaper compared him "favorably with the majority of young clergymen in the city pulpits."[19]

For Sunday, the greatest test came in 1892 when he solidified his desire to enter Christian ministry. Since he had recently signed a contract with Philadelphia, Sunday prayed for guidance. He set March 25, 1892 as a deadline; if he was not released from Philadelphia by then, he would assume God wanted him to play baseball. Sunday got his release on

March 17, and moved into full-time work at the YMCA in Chicago.[20]

Little more than one year later, he had worked out a rationale for his action. In a brief article titled "Why I Left Professional Baseball," in the July 27, 1893 issue of *Young Men's Era,* the official organ of the YMCA, Sunday provided ten reasons why he had left baseball:

1. Because it is a life which has an undesirable future.
2. Because it develops a spirit of jealousy and selfishness; one's whole desires are for personal success regardless of what befalls others.
3. Because it tends to indolence as shown by the fact that few use the five months of unemployed time for study and self-improvement and preparation for future pursuit.
4. Because it is better to benefit mankind than to simply amuse them.
5. Because, after one attains to a certain standard of efficiency, there is no more room for development.
6. Because it does not develop one for future usefulness, as illustrated by the fact that many ex-ball players are engaged in the saloon business.
7. Because it is a life in which morality is not an essential to success; one might be a consummate rogue and a first class ball player.
8. Because reflections in the past "grand stand catches," "great slides to the plate," "stolen bases," and the echo of applauding multitudes are very poor food for consolation.
9. Because I felt called of God to do His service.
10. Because of the anticipated contentment (now realized) which comes to any man who finds himself in the right place.[21]

Sunday's reasons consist of eight negative reactions to the culture of professional sport and two positive attractions to a career in Christian service. The contrast between these two groups of reasons marks a separation of Sunday's personal position from any underlying philosophy of muscular Christianity. He had enthusiastically participated in the "athletic

Sundays" and other YMCA speaking opportunities as a muscular Christian celebrity after his conversion in 1886. But by 1893 he had come to view participation in baseball and Christian work as mutually exclusive endeavors. In general theological terms, Sunday's ten reasons reflect a premillennial emphasis on "otherworldly" Christian service at the expense of involvement in "this present world."

More specifically, rather than seeing participation in athletics as a means to manliness, morality, and virtue (as muscular Christians from Thomas Hughes to James Naismith had), Sunday viewed the values of professional baseball as incompatible with those of Christianity. Perhaps the seventh item captures his rejection of previous muscular Christian commitments to the ideals of character and morality development through sport. Personal morality and success in sports were unrelated in Sunday's eyes. One might infer that Sunday perceived the very attitudinal ethos of professional sport to be antithetical to continued Christian commitment. He came close to claiming that one could not simultaneously be a professional athlete and a Christian.

Sunday seemed to be anticipating Naismith's 1914 NCAA address, Gulick's fears, and more recent analyses by Donald Mrozek, Andrew Miracle, Roger Rees, and others that the values structure of sport at the turn of the century was increasingly oriented to winning to the detriment of character formation. "All other things being equal, if you win you are morally better than your opponent."[22] Whether or not Sunday's views were correct, he both articulated a rejection of the existing muscular Christian ideology and anticipated an approaching disengagement of evangelicals from sport.

Sunday concluded that the only alternative for him was to dissociate from the world of sport. Had muscular Christian ideals continued strong and viable, Billy Sunday might well have been its primary spokesperson as evangelicals entered the twentieth century.[23] Instead, Sunday undermined the muscular philosophy. As indicated earlier, many of the first generation physical educators and athletics personnel specifically entered the profession to serve as "ministers of the gospel on the athletic fields." Sunday directly challenged this view by indicating that his call to evangelism was different from and higher than a "call" to sport. He articulated an emerging premillennial and separatist philosophy, which for the next fifty years took evangelical muscular Christians out of the mainstream of athletics.

In 1893 Sunday left the YMCA to work as an "advance man" for an evangelist-friend of Moody, J. Wilbur Chapman. Then in 1895 Sunday moved to full-time evangelism. A group of ministers from Garner, Iowa, invited him to lead a revival campaign, which Sunday interpreted as a sign from God that he should finally divorce himself from athletics. That revival was the first of hundreds Sunday would lead over the next forty years.[24]

Billy Sunday came to embody a new version (and a perversion) of the muscular Christian tradition which increasingly viewed sport simply as a means to the end of religious conversion and, secondarily, as a means for the enhancement of a cultural idea of masculinity. Sunday often incorporated baseball and other sports imagery into his sermons but never developed a conceptual framework for a twentieth-century muscular Christianity. He used his fame as an athlete only to attract and entertain an audience.[25] He did nothing to engage religion and sport in a meaningful way. In fact, Sunday played a key role in the disengagement of religion from sport.

As a revivalist, his goal was to attract listeners and convert them to Christianity. He constantly preached against the ills of modern urban life. As the leading spokesman for the emerging fundamentalist branch of evangelical Christianity, Sunday solidified the model for twentieth-century evangelical Christians who would emphasize a set of narrowly defined theological principles. Sunday also became the mouthpiece for the disengagement of sport from Christianity. In a 1920s sermon he declared, "It is an entirely good and Christian thing to give a down-and-outer a bath, a bed, and a job, [but] the road into the Kingdom of God is not by the bathtub, nor the gymnasium, nor the university, but by the blood-red hand of the cross of Christ." He argued that the way to help the poor in the downtown slums was to convert them, not to educate them. "The trouble with the church, the YMCA, and the young people's societies is that they have taken up sociology and settlement work but are not winning souls to Christ," he concluded.[26] Sunday became a key advocate of a "Christ-against-culture" philosophy at odds with the engaged muscular Christianity forged in the 1880s.

While the disengagement of muscular Christianity from sport appears on one level to have been engineered by fundamentalists like Billy Sunday, it would be imprecise to say that Sunday or anyone else was the sole determining factor. Nevertheless, Billy Sunday may have been the critical catalyst.

In fact, the gradual separation of conservative Protestant evangelicals from culture may have provided the environment for disengagement. Religious studies scholars David Moberg and Timothy Smith, among others, have identified a "great reversal" in evangelical social action late in the nineteenth century. They hypothesize that as the synthesis between evangelicals and culture ceased, evangelicals retreated from the social arena.[27] This appears to be born out by C. T. Studd's experience. Although he was a prototype for using sport as a platform to present the gospel on the mission field, he gave early witness as to how and why a separation might take place. Writing from China to his younger brothers, Studd explained, "I cannot tell you what joy it gave me to bring the first soul to the Lord Jesus Christ. I have tasted almost all the pleasures that this world can give. . . . I can tell you that those pleasures were as nothing compared to the joy that the saving of that one soul gave me. . . . Formerly, I had as much love for cricket as any man could have, but when the Lord Jesus came into my heart, I found that I had something infinitely better than cricket. My heart was no longer in the game; I wanted to win souls for the Lord.

I knew that cricket would not last, and honor would not last, and nothing in this world would last. . . ."[28]

It appears that evangelical Christians broke away from the dominant culture of sport as it professionalized. This movement then fragmented into two parties—social activist sportsmen and pietistic sportsmen. Some scholars such as Douglas Frank have suggested that the pietists' move away from American culture grew out of a consciousness that they no longer controlled it.[29] It is possible, however, that the separation resulted from a much more complex set of circumstances. Evangelical sportsmen could have been caught in "a great sport doublecross." Not only were they stymied by a culture they thought they were leading, but they were also caught carrying the baggage of unfulfilled idealism of what sport could do in and of itself. The burden became too great, and many muscular Christians may have abandoned social agendas for strictly spiritual ones.

For maturing muscular Christians involved in the YMCA and the SVM, the separation of muscular Christians from sport in the early twentieth century reflected changes in their theology. Ironically, their emphasis was shifting from using sport as a means "to make bad people good" to an emphasis on separating oneself from the evils of the world, including sport, until Jesus returned. Two distinct parties, the premillennialists and the postmillennialists emerged. As premillennialism became part of the litmus test to describe evangelicals, aggressive fundamentalists brought ideas of social and theological boundaries to Protestant orthodoxy. After the turn of the century, most premillennialists opted out of the emergent sports system. Presumably, as sport became professionalized and secularized, it became a symbol of the increasingly evil culture.

Two brief examples of fundamentalists' attitudes toward sport make this point. First, despite its increasing appeal, boxing embodied all that was wrong with sport, especially because of its association with violence and gambling. A broad, church-based opposition—larger than merely fundamentalists—reacted negatively to the Jackson-Jeffries fight in the summer of 1910. George Rockwell of Cincinnati created a national organization of businessmen and church people to prevent the staging of this event. Rockwell printed one million postcards with the message: "Stop the fight. This is the 20th century." After the fight, attention focused on its brutality as a reason for not distributing films of the event. The tract contained a muscular Christian connotation of moral protection for youth, arguing that "millions of upright and decent young people stood in need of protection against the agents of the pugilistic world."[30]

Fundamentalist opposition to boxing continued well into the 1920s. When a popular fundamentalist preacher from New York, John Roach Straton, viewed the 1921 Dempsey-Carpentier fight, he declared it "a relapse into paganism which glorified brute power, a 'moral carbuncle,' which 'naturally came to a head at the weakest spot in our body politic—the state of New Jersey, with its pro-liquor, anti-Constitution, anti-Sabbath governor.'" In 1927 fundamentalists declared the Dempsey-Tunney fight an "exaltation of the body over the soul and an alarming revival of paganism."[31]

Fundamentalists, however, were opposed to more about sport than boxing. They used the pages of the *Moody Bible Institute Monthly* in the 1920s to express this broader opposition. They opposed "clergymen [joining] a movement to procure grounds and organize base-ball clubs in order to increase [church] attendance. . . . Does not the Christian life call for an entire separation from the world?" They opposed "the insidious efforts to nullify Rest Day laws by the introduction of athletic games and sports on the condition that no admission fee is charged." Instead, they urged Christians to "proclaim a better way to spend Sunday and persuade the leaders of the community to adopt it."[32]

Meanwhile, many mainstream Protestants and many who had counted themselves as evangelicals remained in the sports system but began to conclude that the world was not getting better, despite widespread efforts. While many of them endorsed the Social Gospel movement, some became disillusioned about the power of sport to influence society. As sport took on increasingly secular meanings, character-development attributes became more difficult to sustain.

The schism between premillennialists and postmillenni-alists—or between private and public parties—would eventually erupt into full-scale warfare within Protestantism. Some issues were cultural, some theological. The private-party premillennialists sought both to preserve aspects of a threatened culture and to guard Christian orthodoxy. In the end they would be renamed "fundamentalists," with some of them forming a World's Christian Fundamentals Association in 1919. Meanwhile, the public-party postmillennial-ists continued to endorse innovations within modern culture and changes in theology. The Federal Council of Churches became their organizational identity in 1908, and the label of "modernists" was theirs to wear into battle. What was lost in the process was any underlying support approaching a consensus—either cultural or theological—for what only two decades earlier had seemed the basis of a most promising future for evangelical muscular Christianity.

Nowhere was this tension and eventual schism better illus-trated than in the YMCA of the early 1900s. As long as Moody and McBurney were alive (both died in 1899) and as long as Gulick guided the YMCA Training School (formally departing in 1903), the YMCA was able to chart a midcourse between the extremes of religious sectarianism and social activism. But without these leaders, the YMCA moved away from the more evangelical of its supporters. "The sympathies of most local Association workers," Howard Hopkins observed, "were long with the conservatives while national leadership almost imperceptibly gravitated toward liberalism."[33]

YMCA Bible study programs peaked in the first decade of the twentieth century and dropped to half the number of participants by the 1920s.[34] Earlier emphases on evange-lism and mission outreach were replaced by a Social Gospel activism that increased markedly after World War I. A 1926–27 study confirmed a "serious trend toward failure and break-down" in the YMCA's original Christian commitment,[35] and by 1931 its evangelical orientation had given way to a "purpose of building Christian personality."[36] The upshot of these transitions is that the YMCA forfeited by design and default its earlier role as an "organizational carrier" of the muscular Christianity of the late nineteenth century.[37] While some mainline churches continued to develop programs that included recreation, there is little evidence of a conceptual integration that held the sports experience as integral to bringing forth Christ's kingdom. Exceptions did exist within individual congregations, such as the development of the Sports Bay at the Church of St. John the Divine, and the participation of Wheaton College's basketball team in the 1904 Olympic Games in St. Louis. Generally, mainline denominations continued sports-related programs in their churches, but these served the needs of the churches' constituencies rather than functioning as significant means for evangelism.

Given the alternative reasons for and versions of disengagement of religion from sport, it is easier to understand how James Naismith could continue to work in sport over the next forty years and yet divorce himself from coaching and managerial aspects. It appears that the muscular Christian movement changed from being inclusive to being exclusive of Christian athletes. High-profile athletes such as Christy Mathewson, Major Taylor, Glenn Cunningham, and others were identifiable Christians. But unlike earlier or later muscular Christians, this group acted out their professional roles without much sense of muscular Christian identity.

The change in emphasis, reflected in the use of the word Christian as an adjective rather than as a noun, was repeated throughout American culture and paralleled the preceding shift in eschatological positions as well. The emergence in the twentieth century of Christian athletes as well as Christian colleges, Christian businessmen, and Christian music, seems to indicate that muscular Christians did not succeed in making society "Christian," that is in making the bad of society good. Evangelical Christianity failed near the turn of the century in its attempts to create a kingdom of Christ on earth. As is evident by the secularization of the academy, including physical education, by the fragmenting claims of athleticism, and by the Social Gospel movement itself, the sports field had not become the playground of heaven where exposure to games would transform the lives of participants. Many evangelicals moved away from social processes that included sport. Without their idealistic, community- and character-developing influences, an important element in the development of sport no longer existed.

As another generation of muscular Christians emerged after the turn of the century, many moved to the sidelines. They left to others the responsibilities of addressing the role of women in athletics, of prescribing ethical behavior in sport, and of defining the use of sports by institutions such as schools, the military, and the government. This new generation appears to have become a lost generation in the "golden age of sport." As sport shifted into second gear and gained momentum in American society, evangelical Christians shifted into neutral and were no longer a part of the dynamic that drove the institutionalization of sport.

Implications of Disengagement

Even at the height of the evangelical muscular Christian movement in the 1880s, new forces outside the walls of Christendom were forging inroads into these strongholds. As Amos Alonzo Stagg led athletics at Northfield, social and economic changes were shaking the foundation and perspective of many in the muscular Christian movement.

Much of what was occurring culturally has been captured by American religious historian Robert T. Handy in the phrase "the second disestablishment."[38] Throughout the nineteenth century, a quasi-established religion of culturally supportive

Protestantism provided a significant measure of the "cultural glue" that held Americans together. But in the aftermath of World War I, more and more Americans realized that "the center no longer held." Changes within Christianity and in the larger culture led to disestablishment of the two. Whereas the initial legal disestablishment of religion from government and the state was guaranteed by the First Amendment, Handy argues that this second disestablishment was more cultural in nature. Within religion, the earlier cultural Christianity had become too fragmented, partly because of new immigrant groups bringing in diverse forms of religion and partly as a response to other nonreligious changes in American life. Handy further argues that "the direction of social change, demographic trends, and urban patterns was against the dominance of an acculturated Protestantism with its partly exorcised notions of Anglo-Saxon superiority and its rural nostalgia. . . . By the twenties the force of a public conscience informed by religion was in fact diminishing, especially in the cities, even though it was still maintained in theory. . . . The 'second disestablishment' of religion was well along. The continued use of the rhetoric of a Christian America was increasingly out of place."[39]

In its most overarching connections, evangelical muscular Christianity implicitly depended on the kind of cultural consensus that Handy describes as waning after World War I. Muscular Christianity historically was not only an evangelical Protestant phenomenon but was an indigenously American adaptation of the British original. The unstated assumptions and values of its American setting were not seriously challenged or called into question in the 1920s. They simply lost their strength, as a plurality of values and assumptions grew in number and potency. Thus at an overarching level, evangelical muscular Christianity simply lost its ties to the culture and so was also "disestablished" and disengaged in the process.

One strand of social action continued within the YMCA and within mainline Protestant churches. While church recreation programs and the activities remained, the emphases of their leaders were quite different from those of muscular Christians of the 1880s and 1890s. The YMCA moved away from endorsement of high-level competition and endorsed more cooperative sports activity. For example, although the YMCA fielded the strongest basketball teams early in the twentieth century, by 1910 it had mandated a reduction of emphasis on high-level teams.

There appears to have been a direct correlation between the disengagement of muscular Christianity and the concern of Christian workers who perceived that sport was teaching values that were being transferred to society. When the American model based on naturalistic assumptions that sport would build character was called into question, considerable confusion arose among evangelicals. This position was further clouded by some muscular Christians who held aspects of a Christian worldview but did not necessarily interpret the development of sport on the basis of those Christian commitments. Moreover, part of progressive education's emphasis on character development appears to derive energy from this secularized version of muscular Christianity, which blended the playing of sports with other cultural themes, including patriotism, group loyalty, and national pride.

In this sense, President Theodore Roosevelt served as a contemporary counterpoint to Billy Sunday. Roosevelt personified a secular man of action and reflected a cultural, secularized muscular Christianity. His model caught on and flourished, while Sunday and many of the evangelical muscular Christians receded into the shadows, at least as far as their overt witness on the playing fields was concerned.[40]

Within popular culture this secularized version dominated muscular Christianity during the 1920s. And in some circles it projected a glowing aura for society. As early as 1922 the "golden age" metaphor for the cultural significance of the time between World War I and the Depression (1918–29) also was applied by the *Literary Digest* to depict "a new golden age of sport and outdoor amusements."[41]

Nevertheless, given the reality of what was occurring in the decade, perhaps the overlapping nadir of muscular Christianity and the emergence of a golden age is not incongruous. Despite the admitted advances within sport during the 1920s—new stadiums, record-setting gate receipts, technological innovations, and the elevated status of sports heroes—this unfortunate metaphorical extrapolation has consistently overlooked a series of deeply rooted problems, many of which remain today. Structural problems including racism, gender inequity, educational deficiencies, politicization, and commercialization characterized big-time sport in the 1920s. If the decade really was the golden age, it was only golden to the privileged participants and their cheerleaders—the media.

As early as the 1930s John Tunis reflected that thinking. Writing in *Harper's Magazine* Tunis asserted, "That it was the boom period of sport in this country is not, however, true. There was more noise and shouting, more exaggeration and hyperbole, more space in the newspapers devoted to sports or what passed at the time for sports; but there were fewer persons actually playing games. . . . To-day there is a more intelligent appreciation of the values of real sport, there are more persons of average ability competing, there are more participants who are interested in the game for the game's sake, more people playing than ever before in our history."[42]

Foremost among social problems during the golden age was the status of African-Americans. Whatever promise the Civil War had held for their freedom and equality, the Jim Crow structures late in the nineteenth century removed this vital segment of society from participation in mainstream social affairs, including sport. Certainly African-Americans played sports in traditionally black colleges, on various segregated teams such as the New York Rens, and in a host of other activities. Yet in the early 1900s, none of the professional teams and few colleges held African-Americans on their rosters. This stood with a few exceptions until after World War II.

The separation of women from the sports arena was even more pronounced. Although some women had participated earlier with men or had participated in "men's sports," the 1920s was a period of institutionalization of the separation of women from men in sport. The development of the National Amateur Athletic Federation—Women's Division demonstrates this. Women's attempts to become involved in the Olympic Games were met with considerable resistance, and a separate women's Olympics during the twenties became a reality. But perhaps most revealing was the elimination of girls from youth sport. Given that the legitimation of sport in the United States in the late 1800s was possible because of the supposed character values associated with participation, it is interesting that by the mid-1920s, the arena was perceived to be for boys only.

The famous Margaret Gisolo case, which established the framework for exclusion of girls from youth sport, is instructive.[43] In 1928, as the American Legion baseball program was evolving, Margaret Gisolo played on a team from Blandford, Indiana, which reached the finals of the national regionals and played at White Sox Park in Chicago. Over the protest of some of her opponents, the commissioner of Major League Baseball, Judge Kenesaw Mountain Landis, ruled that the girl should be allowed to participate. She was an excellent player at second base, was one of the team's leading hitters, and produced hits in situations that brought victories to her team. Yet the following year the male leadership of the Legion, with the blessing of professional baseball, decreed that American Legion baseball would be open only to boys. That decision effectively established the structure for girls to be restricted from youth-sport organizations in the United States.

At the time of racial exclusion and gender separation, some educators revolted and attempted to alter the managerial system established by Stagg, Camp, and others. The management model had installed the coach as primary gatekeeper for organization and control. But in several parts of the country and on several levels, including high schools and colleges, a movement to eliminate the coach from actual competition developed.[44]

Some educators felt that it was appropriate for sports to be a part of the curriculum and for a coach to help young men learn rules and strategies. But they perceived that the "Stagg system" had led to abuse. To reduce the role of the coach and elevate the role of the player, these reformers attempted to force the coach to sit with the fans during the game. The movement reflected a growing concern among educators about ethical problems related to collegiate and interscholastic sport revealed in the Carnegie Commission reports of the 1920s.[45]

These protests did not produce the desired results. Instead, coaches and athletic organizations established a separate organization outside the authority and control of educational institutions. As coaching became institutionalized in the twentieth century, American sport moved to quantitative comparisons of performances (wins versus losses) and forfeited much of the qualitative and educational elements. Emphases on the size of stadiums, advances in technology, and the economic impact of the sporting goods industry overshadowed any efforts toward character development and related issues of the earlier muscular Christian agenda.

What the golden age metaphor camouflages is that most in American society did not enjoy a golden age. The inaccuracy of that myth is reflected in its incorrect depiction of the state of sport. Blacks were excluded from mainstream teams, and their performances were excluded from most national press reports. Women and girls were relegated to programs that were separate and unequal. And the efforts to make sports more educational and to accomplish reforms in intercollegiate arenas were rejected.

Nevertheless, sport became woven into the fabric of American society and the direction of sport was determined by business decisions and dominated by a male cultural perspective. Indeed, problems in the sports culture (cheating, rule violations, ego exaggeration) came to fruition in the 1920s and affected sport for the remainder of the twentieth century. This is not to say that the disengagement of evangelicals from sport created these problems. A causal relationship would be impossible to document, if not unwise to assert. Nevertheless, without a clear connection between muscular Christianity and sport, the emerging social phenomenon had no solid philosophical underpinning. And although various organizations involved in sport, such as the American Physical Education Association, the Sportsmanship Brotherhood, the Carnegie Commission, the NCAA, and the American Legion, among others, attempted to define a coherent philosophy of sport, none was successful in developing a framework that would work in all levels of sport and society. One need only reread Naismith's address before the 1914 NCAA convention to see that little had changed.

Perhaps the most significant of all was the lack of leavening influence from the Christian community in the development of sport in the United States. Not only did the withdrawal of evangelical muscular Christians eliminate any kind of witness in society, it eliminated input from them to influence the ethos of sport. Whether the moral outcomes would have been different with their continued participation is impossible to answer. Perhaps they would have been no more effective than other agencies and institutions. As we shall see in chapter 4, this was a period of extreme depression in American society. That depression extended not only through the economic fabric but to social areas such as sport and religion.

Toward the Reengagement of Evangelicalism and Sport

A young fundamentalist Protestant revivalist returned to his native North Carolina in November 1947 to begin a series of evangelistic meetings. Several years earlier, after graduating from a Bible institute in Florida, he had moved to the Chicago area to finish his undergraduate education. While there, he also narrowed his career choices, which led to his speaking in churches and before other youthful audiences and then trying his hand as a pastor.

In 1945 he joined forces with a newly formed organization called Youth for Christ, traveled 135,000 miles as its first full-time evangelist, and spoke to groups in forty-seven states. In 1946–47 he spent six months in the British Isles, speaking in over 350 meetings. While in London, he received an invitation from a group in Charlotte to conduct a citywide revival campaign that eventually continued for eighteen meetings.

Billy Graham Introduces a New Tom Brown

Billy Graham went to Charlotte in the fall of 1947 determined not to fail, and he spent an incredible amount of energy and money on publicity and preparations for his homecoming. In addition to preparing his own sermon for each night, he assembled a variety of musical warm-up groups to share the meetings with him—a Salvation Army band, a brass quartet from Bob Jones College in nearby South Carolina, a child piano prodigy, and the "world's foremost marimba player."[1]

But for the opening night, Graham provided a special attraction by inviting the reigning American mile champion, Gil Dodds, to join him at the podium. Before the sermon, however, Graham had Dodds and a local runner from the University of North Carolina run a pseudocompetitive six laps around the audience on a makeshift track. After winning the "race," Dodds challenged his listeners, "I wonder how many of you here tonight are doing your best in the race for Jesus Christ." Later Graham's associate Grady Wilson recalled, "I sat there that Saturday night watching the thing, the whole audience quiet with those boys just streakin' around and around and I remember it came to me, *This is awfully silly. This is really a little absurd.* But you know, when we gave the invitation that night, we had an incredible number of young people to come forward. That just showed us, God can use just about anything."[2]

The likelihood ten or even five years earlier of predicting such a scene as this one was virtually nil. In 1937 Billy Graham was a student at the Florida Bible Institute, and Gil Dodds was a freshman at Ashland College in Ohio. By 1942 Graham was starting his final undergraduate year at Wheaton College in Illinois, and Dodds was a first-year seminarian in Boston, where he was identified for the first time by the national press as a promising world-class miler.[3] But even then there was little indication that somehow a "reengagement" of religion and sport was in the offing.

Even more remarkable is the transition that took place after sports journalist John Tunis complained that "deadly serious sport" was supplanting traditional forms of religious expression and becoming the new American religion.[4] In the 1940s—less than twenty years later—Billy Graham and his Youth for Christ associates realized that sports might provide exactly the means their brand of religion needed to attract an audience ready to listen to a religious message. Graham and Dodds—two country boys born in 1918—personified that reengagement, one of them the world-traveling preacher who longed to be an athlete, and the other the world-class athlete who frequently tried his hand at preaching. Together, they accomplished one small but necessary step. But how does one move from the disengaged and antithetical relationship between religion and sport of two decades earlier to the rediscovery of their potential for mutual aggrandizement and benefit? The answer lies in the relatively unknown story of how evangelical religion again found sport as a potential ally during the 1940s.

A Time of Depression

The whole of American life, including religion and sport, fared poorly during the 1930s. Cultural historian Warren Susman invokes the concepts of "culture" and "commitment" to capture the essence of this decade. He plays with these two terms to make a powerful point—that once Americans discovered the idea of culture and emphasized conformity to an American cultural way, many of them sought to further define their individualistic forms of commitment to that culture in the 1930s. "If there was an increased awareness of the concepts of culture and its implications as well as a growing self-consciousness of an American way or a native culture of value, there were also forces operating to shape that culture into a heightened sensitivity of itself as a culture. . . . Individualism can exist only if the culture permits it, that is, if it can have a necessary function within the structure of culture itself."[5]

If Susman is right, one long-term but indirect effect of disengagement was the emergence of a new cultural understanding of the American way and the American dream. The American dream now "meant something different"—"the commitment to irresponsibility as a cultural stance, extreme antinomianism, glorifying in the experiences of the self and saying to [h——] with everything else." Or in terms reminiscent of the views of neo-orthodox theologian Reinhold Niebuhr, "There is no essential morality in any group, party, or class. Ultimately man was alone in his struggle within culture."[6]

For religious historian Robert Handy, what made this new cultural understanding conceivable was the unraveling of the underlying vision supplied by Protestantism. "The direction of social change, demographics, and urban patterns was against the dominance of an acculturated Protestantism."[7] The contrast between two observations made by sociologists Robert and Helen Lynd provides a sense of this declining significance.

When the Lynds first studied "Middletown" (Muncie, Ind.) in the mid-1920s, they incidentally noted a potential problem for organized religion. "In theory, religious beliefs dominate all other activities in Middletown; actually, large regions of Middletown's life appear uncontrolled by them." When the Lynds returned to Middletown a decade later, the problem was more real, so that no one thought about theory. "The gap between religion's verbalizing and Middletown life has become so wide that the entire institution of religion has tended to be put on the defensive; and the acceptance of a defensive role has tended to mean that it is timid in jeopardizing its foothold in the culture."[8] To the degree that any single community can represent the whole of American life, this transition suggests that both the larger culture and the religious institution were in difficulty. Culture was changing, and commitment was up for grabs.

The Lynds were only verifying what representatives of American Protestantism had long suspected—they were not doing well. In the religious press, a self-examination took the form of "Why No Revival?" with the confession that "we might as well be frank about it. This depression has lasted too long for Christian leaders to continue to assert that because religion has always experienced revival in past depressions we are sure even yet to witness a like phenomenon in this. That is mere wishful talk."[9] Similarly, the secular press asked "Is Religion Dying?" and then observed that "Protestant Christianity must put on spiritual passion. We lack that something. . . . In too many cases the world doesn't even know that [Christians] are around."[10] Handy has suggested since then that the spiritual depression actually preceded the economic depression, so the depressed economy had a compounding or reinforcing effect on the decline in religion. Historian Winthrop Hudson contends that "the astonishing reversal in the position occupied by the churches and the role played by religion" was evidence of an "evaporating" religious enthusiasm during the 1920s.[11]

If the nation's depression transcended the economic sphere and if the churches seemed incapable of a concerted response, how were things in sport? The answer is probably less troublesome than for religion, but still not good. For one thing, Tunis may have been prophetic in stating that sport was creating a religious-like aura and myth, thereby filling a cultural need following the "second disestablishment" of religion from culture. While "a sort of demystification affected all areas of culture save sport, . . . during the long American Depression the headlines on the newspapers were a continuous record of man's failures; the sports pages recorded his triumphs."[12]

In most ways, however, the fate of sport was more closely tied to the depressed economy than was that of religion. While Protestants puzzled over why economic depression had not led to spiritual revival, the picture was a bit clearer in sport. The forms of participation that relied on discretionary spending fell off precipitously—at least up to the mid-1930s, when a slow economic recovery began. While private golf and tennis clubs went bankrupt, while the sale of sports equipment declined markedly, and while attendance at college football games dropped off, beneficiaries of the depressed economy included professional baseball with its transition to night play, plus amateur urban softball and bowling leagues.[13]

At least two changes occurred in sport against which the church was unable to mount unified opposition. The first was the trend toward Sunday games with the repeal of Blue Laws and other prohibitions. "The first breaches in these Sabbath laws were made by changes in economic life. . . . The immediate motive power behind these changes has been the result of the depression on tax income. Legislatures have seen . . . the increased amounts of taxes that can be raised from Sunday amusements."[14]

A second change was the movement toward legalized gambling, including sports gambling. Governments saw it as a likely source of additional tax revenues, and depression folk were eager for a big return on a small bet. This activity also was reinterpreted in terms of a more individualistic commitment to a new civic moral culture a la Susman. "Betting on the races, after so many years underground, suddenly, to its pleased surprise, finds itself, like beer, basking in the sun of comparative civic approval. It has become increasingly public-spirited, not to say patriotic, to back your judgment at the track with a modest wager. . . . Doubtless, as has been argued in this connection, we are growing more liberal in spirit, less ready to see sin in the more jovial diversions."[15]

Thus, two major issues of concern to the church during the disengagement of the 1920s—Sabbath participation and gambling—were pretty much decided by the mid-1930s. Unfortunately for the church, those issues were resolved largely on the grounds of economic necessity and not because of any overarching theological or ethical agreements between the church and sport. Instead, acceptance of Sunday play and of gambling illustrates the declining strength of the church and the increasing secularity of sport within American life.

In 1929 President Herbert Hoover commissioned the Research Committee on Social Trends to "throw light on the emerging problems . . . which may be expected later to confront the people of the United States." When the committee finally issued its report in 1933, it observed that "many of the amusements once so vigorously banned are now accepted by the church. . . . There is no evidence that the church is exercising control over recreation in any way comparable to the censorship that it once exercised. . . . The failure of law enforcement agencies to suppress Sunday amusements . . . seems to indicate a definite turning of the tide of public opinion away from the earlier ideas of Sunday observance."[16]

In the context of Susman's thesis about culture and commitment, what occurred in the 1930s aftermath of the disengagement of religion and sport is significant. Religion, which had enthusiastically provided support and legitimacy to sport a half-century earlier, occupied a less influential place in American culture. The old Protestant establishment was weakened and splintered, while fundamentalist Protestants turned their backs on sport as a symbol of what was wrong with American culture. Meanwhile, sport moved farther away from an alliance with religion, within a cultural context that enabled an even more autonomous and secular existence. It was very unlikely that individuals would maintain commitment to both religion and sport.

If the picture was bleak in the 1930s, and if reengagement was improbable, then the appearance of fundamentalist Protestants to lay claim to the arena of sport was even more unexpected. In the early twentieth century, Protestantism was an uneasy alliance of increasingly divergent points of view. By the 1920s two opposing camps—modernists and fundamentalists—had emerged. These camps roughly parallelled the two parties Martin Marty identified as forming after the Civil War. Modernists controlled the historical Protestant denominations. They were represented by publications such as *Christian Century* and preachers like Harry Emerson Fosdick, who threw down the gauntlet in a famous 1922 sermon, "Shall the Fundamentalists Win?" Meanwhile, fundamentalists had organized the World's Christian Fundamentals Association in 1919. They seemed ready to accept the modernists' challenge, having formulated conservative positions on selected cultural and theological issues, although they did not have ready access to resources of power and influence.[17]

Modernists were generally supportive of the directions American culture was taking, while fundamentalists attempted to preserve the traditional forms and expressed suspicion of the modernists and the changes they embraced. Fundamentalists also responded more individualistically to the culture, inadvertently confirming Susman's ideas about individualism, although the increasing challenge posed by modernists induced a measure of coherence among fundamentalists.

One major test of the relative strength of the two positions came in 1925 in Dayton, Tennessee. There, the soon-to-be-world-famous Scopes trial was testing a law forbidding the teaching of evolution in public schools. "Although the outcome of the trial was indecisive and the law stood, the rural setting and the press's caricatures of fundamentalists as rubes and hicks discredited fundamentalism and made it difficult to pursue further the serious aspects of the movement."[18] The modernists may have lost the battle, but they easily won the larger war within American Christianity.

One unfortunate result for the next three decades of American religious history was the assumption that the discredited fundamentalists disappeared or, at best, were relegated to the margins of American life. So *Scribner's Magazine* in 1933 would "rule out" any possibility of "the religious hope of the world" rising out of fundamentalism. And *Christian Century* would interpret the death of Billy Sunday in 1935 as a sign of "the desperate and hopeless condition of the evangelical type of piety."[19] To the modernist Christian community, fundamentalism was dead—figuratively and literally. With the burials of Sunday and of fundamentalism, the vestiges of nineteenth-century muscular Christianity were also put to rest.

Evangelical Entrepreneurs: Innovative Fundamentalists

In reality, what many fundamentalists did after the Scopes debacle was to undergo "realignment, as [they] relocated and built their own networks of separate institutions." Having been shut out of most major denominations and excluded from any significant cultural dialogue, they displayed their "vigor at the local level [which] ensured that this segment of American Protestantism was one of the few that was growing during the 1930s."[20] Nonetheless, fundamentalist activity was largely unnoticed by secular and religious commentators for nearly a quarter century. In 1958 *Life* magazine would detect that fundamentalists composed a major element of a "third force in Christendom." Religious historian William McLoughlin examined this idea more systematically in 1967, conceding only then that "many American churchgoers were ready" to listen to the evangelical successors of the 1930s fundamentalists.[21]

In one sense, by the late 1930s two distinctive but "paradoxical impulses" were operating within fundamentalism. One was more militantly opposed to cultural change and modernist religion. The other was given to the historic evangelical themes of revival and saving souls, even when that meant working alongside suspect denominations. This second option often included "building institutions that were in practice separate," but without going so far in theory as repudiating all of mainstream Protestantism.[22] This brand of fundamentalism would even find supporters within the modernist denominations, and from this second fundamentalist impulse more open to cooperative efforts would come the impetus for the reengagement of evangelical religion and sports.

Fundamentalists developed a variety of innovative means for revival and saving souls. Two of those are significant for this study—the use of radio for religious outreach, and the targeting of youthful audiences.

In the first area—radio—fundamentalists already had a strong background going back to the early 1920s. Radio enabled fundamentalists "to take their message straight to the people. Radio reached into homes, automobiles, and even bars and pool halls. Anyone could tune in. Denominational barriers seemed irrelevant."[23] Fundamentalists' use of radio "was a means of creating a national evangelical identity, locating and promoting symbolic leaders and legitimiz-

103

ing particular values and attitudes. . . . Along the way they helped transform conservative Protestantism into a more acceptable—and more American—style of evangelicalism."[24]

The second major area of fundamentalist innovation was among adolescents and young adults, and it served as a separate but overlapping impetus. In the 1930s several nonaligned preachers in Philadelphia, Dallas, New York, and other cities targeted impressionable adolescents with their religious messages. In some cases the weekend rallies were also tied to a radio program. The master of this format was a young insurance salesman and former dance band leader in New York named Jack Wyrtzen.[25]

These activities coincided with a spreading national concern for the moral well-being of American youth. Civic and religious leaders were concerned with an increase in criminal behavior, and "reports came in from the cities that teenage gangs were terrorizing the streets." J. Edgar Hoover of the FBI wrote frequently on this subject and on the role the church might play in addressing these moral needs.[26]

Groups such as Christian Endeavor and the Epworth League had preached to youthful audiences for decades. But one assessment suggests, "Denominationally sponsored youth fellowships appear to be on the border of stagnation. The program had become institutionalized . . . [with] a gradual de-emphasis on traditional Protestant values."[27] What was new were entrepreneurial (often nondenominational) fundamentalist preachers presenting messages that combined traditional revivalism with moralistic warning, either on the radio or in weekend rallies or both, but in a "packaging" that reflected the attractiveness of an early "youth culture."

One of the first radio and rally youth evangelists was a Canadian named Percy Crawford. He launched The Young People's Church of the Air in 1931, vowing that the religion he presented would never be dull. Crawford was proud of being "master of the seven minute sermon," as his "broadcast paved the way for the twentieth century youth movement."[28]

In the mid-1930s one regular listener to Crawford's programs was a young New Yorker, Jack Wyrtzen. Following Crawford's advice "to go into youth evangelism with radio as his pulpit," Wyrtzen took his idea of a weekly program to Brooklyn station WBBC in 1940. Calling themselves the Word of Life Fellowship, Wyrtzen and several friends presented live music and preaching.[29] In 1941 they moved the format to 50,000-watt WHN, New York, and on October 25 accomplished the first combined broadcast and Saturday night youth rally from Times Square.[30]

Pearl Harbor provided an impetus to these early efforts. Wyrtzen began a series of Victory Rallies in 1942 with military personnel among his guest speakers. By 1943 the size of the rallies warranted a move to Carnegie Hall, and on April 1, 1944 Wyrtzen rented Madison Square Garden for the first of seven rallies there; it attracted over twenty thousand youth.[31] By then the secular press was taking notice, and the *New York World Telegram* described the "young man [he was thirty-one] with a round face and curly hair" pleading with his listeners, "Let God come into your hearts." *American Magazine* predicted with certainty that "the religious revival which Jack Wyrtzen has started among the nation's youth will spread much farther."[32]

Wyrtzen's Saturday night rally format already had spread far beyond New York. The fundamentalist leaders from the 1920s were succeeded by a younger cohort of energetic leaders displaying a more moderate tenor toward the culture and their Protestant kin. Under the leaders, awareness of Crawford and Wyrtzen's appeal among youth had spread to Washington, Boston, Indianapolis, Detroit, St. Louis, Chicago, Minneapolis, and points beyond. Yet there was no organizational structure or formal link between these locations.[33] Instead what the rally leaders had in common was a subcultural version of Susman's emphases on culture and commitment, that is, their shared commitment to reach an emerging youth culture with a modern version of revivalist Christianity and a willingness to try new methods and formats. Historian Joel Carpenter has summarized how a "new 'youth culture,' with its own fashions and celebrities, and a new 'young people's evangelism' seemed to be the instinctive response of young preachers and laymen who had grown up with this mass-media-generated popular culture. They emulated the entertainment world's stars and restyled gospel music to the 'swing' and 'sweet' sounds then popular. And like the radio newsmen, their messages were fast-paced, filled with late-breaking bulletins, and breathlessly urgent."[34]

The key geographical transition came in May 1944, when a young Chicago minister, Torrey Johnson, pulled up the curtains on Chicagoland Youth for Christ. The initial rally at Orchestra Hall drew more than two thousand young people. After weeks of packing out the hall, Johnson moved to the Chicago Stadium in the fall for a rally that attracted twenty thousand.[35]

In November 1944 leaders of the larger rallies around the country met informally in Detroit. It was a significant step toward developing a routine youth rally format, with the scheduling of a subsequent meeting for July 1945. Forty-two delegates of the first-ever Youth for Christ International leaders' conference met then at Winona Lake, Indiana, and elected Torrey Johnson as their first president.[36] *Newsweek* magazine already had identified Johnson as a "natural leader" and the "religious counterpart of Frank Sinatra. He, too, has a Voice and curly hair, wears bow ties, and speaks the language of bobby soxers." Clearly Johnson was a logical choice to lead the new organization.[37]

Youth for Christ also attracted the attention of William Randolph Hearst. "Apparently because he liked its patriotic emphasis and felt its high moral standards might help juvenile delinquency," Hearst sent his Chicago editor a telegram with two words, "Puff YFC." On July 1, 1945 all twenty-two Hearst newspapers carried a front-page story on the Youth for Christ movement. The article titled "Youth's New Crusade" included these excerpts describing the new phenomenon: "The Youth for Christ movement . . . offers a constructive and powerful antidote to the poison of juvenile delinquency. . . . The only novel aspect of all this is that it should have taken some of us so long to discover it. . . . The Youth for Christ movement seeks to provide the correct motive, and is doing so with great deftness of understanding. . . . What better direction, then, than to guide and stimulate youth toward the true purposes of religion?"[38]

Not everybody was enthralled with Youth for Christ, however. In *Christian Century* Harold Fey concluded, "When one compares the milky abstractions of Youth for Christ with the solid meat of Jonathan Edwards, . . . one is entitled to doubt that the current resurgence will endure very long." Fey saw Youth for Christ as providing "competition" for the churches by "cutting across sounder programs of Christian education."[39] One denominational executive, Leslie Conrad Jr., later accused Youth for Christ of beginning "to lure active youth from their church moorings" and found it "unacceptable" with "objectional features [that] overshadow the commendable" ones.[40] Outside the church, suspicions centered on the movement's blatant patriotism, and some accused it of anti-Semitism. But with an increasing list of supporters, including President Harry Truman and the governors of Washington and Illinois, the early leadership pushed ahead.[41]

Torrey Johnson's choice of speaker for the initial Chicagoland Youth for Christ rally in 1944 was one of his most important decisions. Johnson invited a young pastor and recent college graduate from the Chicago area, Billy Graham, to speak at the Orchestra Hall rally. The rally was a huge success, and Graham began regular appearances in the Chicago rallies. By early 1945 Johnson had prevailed upon Graham to become a permanent member of the Youth for Christ team and serve as staff evangelist and representative. This position was formalized at the Winona Lake organizational meeting.[42] That was the year Graham traveled 135,000 miles and spoke in forty-seven states. Youth for Christ International went truly international in 1946 with Johnson, Graham, and others heading for Europe with the youth-oriented ministry.

Later that year, Graham received the invitation to speak in his home area of Charlotte. By 1947–48 Graham had developed his own organizational identity, although he remained on the Youth for Christ board and made six trips abroad on its behalf within a three-year period.[43]

What Jack Wyrtzen, Torrey Johnson, Billy Graham, and the dozens of other youth leaders developed in the 1940s was an innovative revivalist strategy and methodology for reaching youthful listeners. Until the 1945 organizational conference of Youth for Christ, these visionaries had little formal structure. Yet they shared great energy and an entrepreneurial spirit that filled an apparent vacuum as the moderate fundamentalist party moved out of its depression to face the post–World War II reality of a nation in transition. Perhaps the relative isolation of the movement stimulated it to consolidate and become stronger. In any event, by the end of World War II the movement was ready to move back toward mainstream culture.

Gil Dodds: The Embodiment of a New Tom Brown

Sometimes the reality of an individual or group's accomplishments coincides with the myth surrounding them. That is true of the American mile champion of the 1940s, Gil Dodds. In contrast to the fictional Tom Brown, who existed only in his fans' imaginations, Dodds brought real accomplishments to enhance his fans' fondest dreams.

Gil Dodds was reared in rural Nebraska, the son of a Protestant minister. Arthur Daley of the *New York Times* relished recalling the story of how Dodds met the man who would become his part-time high school and college coach. When Gil was about thirteen years old, he became bored one day while fishing and began throwing pebbles at passing autos. One irate motorist chased him down and "administered to him an inglorious kick in the pants." The driver turned out to be Lloyd Hahn, retired American and Olympic mile champion during the 1920s, who lived on a neighboring farm.[44]

Dodds competed as a runner while in high school. However, Falls City High School had no track team, so Dodds was untrained except for occasional instructional visits from Hahn. Yet over three years of high school competition, he was undefeated.[45]

Gil Dodds planned to attend the University of Nebraska in the fall of 1937 and to continue his running there. However, his father insisted that he attend Ashland College in Ohio, a liberal arts college sponsored by the Church of the Brethren, his father's denomination. Ashland had about three hundred students but no track team; nevertheless, the Dodds myth grew. Continuing to receive instructions from Lloyd Hahn by mail, Dodds ran a two-minute half-mile as a freshman, though he lost to an experienced collegian in his first defeat ever. After Dodds set a conference record in cross country as a sophomore, a local sportswriter got him an invitation to run in New Orleans at the Sugar Bowl meet in 1939.[46] He lost the two-mile race by a step to the Big Ten champion, but his performance earned him an invitation to the Millrose Games in New York and then to the Boston Amateur Athletic Union meet. The Millrose run was a disaster, apparently because of the smoky atmosphere. According to Daley, Dodds was lapped by two runners "before falling ignominiously on his face while the crowd roared in derisive laughter."[47]

In 1940 Dodds won the NCAA cross-country championship in record time, then posted the second-best college mile time at the Beloit Relays in Wisconsin. In 1941 he placed third in the NCAA two-mile race and was named an All-American.[48]

After Dodds graduated from Ashland in 1941, Lloyd Hahn persuaded him to go to Boston to train formally for the first time with Hahn's former coach, Jack Ryder. Dodds also learned of a nearby seminary, the Gordon School of Theology and Missions (now Gordon-Conwell Theological Seminary), which he could attend while training with Ryder at Boston College, beginning in December 1941.[49]

Within three months the results were dramatic, and the national press noticed Dodds for the first time. After pushing Greg Rice to the second-fastest two-mile ever, Dodds ran against Leslie MacMitchell, who had won nineteen consecutive mile races. *Time* reported that "the man who outran him [MacMitchell], bespectacled 23-year-old Gilbert Dodds of Falls City, Nebraska, had never run a big time mile before. . . . Matching strides with miler MacMitchell, Mr. Dodds proved that he had learned a lot since his correspondence-schooling. . . . Mr. Dodds beat him by two yards. His time: 4:08.9. World's indoor record: 4:07.4."[50]

Later that year, Dodds ran a 4:08.5 mile, then won the AAU outdoor 1,500-meter race. *American Magazine* cited him as one of its "Interesting People" in a brief photo-essay: "He's faster than the devil."[51]

After these initial successes, the 1943 season was something of a disappointment. Dodds won the Bankers' Mile in Chicago and again won the AAU outdoor 1,500-meter race, but his real success that year was in races he finished second. During the summer, the AAU sponsored the Swedish world champion, Gunder Hagg, on a national tour. Dodds furnished the competition in several races—minus Jack Ryder—and he never did beat Hagg. But along the way, he ran a 4:06.5 mile, the fastest ever by an American.[52]

Dodds was awarded the 1943 James E. Sullivan Memorial Trophy as the outstanding American amateur athlete of the year.[53] In 1944 he began a string of thirty-nine consecutive victories and three undefeated seasons. First he won at Millrose. Then he ran a 4:07.3 indoor record mile in New York. He followed that with a 4:06.4 Bankers' Mile in Chicago and another indoor record. But as the 1945 season approached, Dodds was planning his departure from running. On January 27 he took his last exam at Gordon, ran his final two-mile race, then flew to Los Angeles to begin a new era. *Time* reported, "For eight seasons, short, bespectacled Gil Dodds has been something of a track oddity. He usually knelt and prayed before each race. On trips, he often carried bread and honey sandwiches in a paper bag. . . . Last week, . . . Dodds said he had received the Call to begin full-time gospel work. The news knocked the breath out of indoor track. . . . Now

Gil Dodds was eager to comply with requests from admiring fans for his autograph, often writing "Phil. 4:13" after his signature.

the man who prefers gospel teaching to mile records joins Torrey Johnson's Evangelistic group."[54]

Clearly Dodds went out at, or immediately prior to, the peak of his running career. He told reporters, "Right now, something inside of me tells me not to run in competition. I intend to follow that inner feeling because I believe I have the greater challenge in my religious work than I have ever had in my running." In fact, Gil Dodds had not suddenly become interested in "religious work." He had been active since his college days, opening closed churches in Ohio, and speaking in various places, "using his testimony as a runner to bring out the Gospel story."[55]

Dodds was known for refusing to run on Sundays and for adding a Scripture reference when signing autographs, especially for teenagers. A favorite verse was Philippians 4:13, "I can do all things through Him who strengthens me." Dodds would sign, "Gil Dodds Phil. 4:13." At least one fan apparently thought he was referring to having run a 4:13 mile recently in Philadelphia. Similarly, when *Newsweek* reported on his winning the Sullivan Award, it described how he "told startled sports writers: 'Don't get the idea that I won this race on my own. The Lord helped me.' Currently, the parson of the cinderpaths is appearing in New England pulpits. His sermons: 'It takes a man to be a Christian.'"[56]

By early 1944, Minneapolis sportswriter Mel Larson helped spread the Dodds myth by means of a popular biography. Dodds had also met Jack Wyrtzen and visited the rallies in New York, apparently even on nights when he ran competitively. When Wyrtzen rented Madison Square Garden for the first rally there on April 1, 1944, Dodds was on the program. He was a "hot" item, having set the world indoor record on March 11 and then broken it a week later with the 4:06.4 mile.[57]

In the summer of 1944, when his first son was only four months old, Dodds began a sixteen-state speaking tour that lasted nearly four months. He spoke in churches, on army and naval bases, and before dozens of youth rallies and conferences, for a total of 158 times to more than fifty thousand people. In at least fifty-five of those meetings, he appeared with Wyrtzen on the East Coast. He also appeared in St. Louis, Indianapolis, and Chicago. When Wyrtzen returned to the Garden on September 30, 1944 for a rally that attracted twenty thousand people, Dodds was there to talk about his faith and his running.[58]

Thus it is not surprising that Dodds should retire from running to devote his energies full-time to the ministry upon completion of his seminary work in January 1945. The previous seven years of full-time running had included part-time ministry, so the transition was appropriate. In the following months, he spoke often, including a Memorial Day appearance in Chicago. That Torrey Johnson–led rally at Soldier Field attracted more than sixty-five thousand people. *Newsweek* reported that he "raced a mile around the field clad in a track suit. 'Running is only a hobby,' the bespectacled athlete-preacher said. 'My mission is teaching the gospel of Jesus Christ.'"[59]

When Torrey Johnson convened the first Youth for Christ leaders' conference in July, he announced that in addition to Billy Graham and two other men, Gil Dodds would be a full-time representative of the new organization. Later that summer, Dodds and his wife and son moved to the Chicago area. There he entered a master's program at nearby Wheaton College and served as Wheaton's assistant track and cross-country coach. His full-time work, however, consisted of speaking for Youth for Christ rallies.[60] In retrospect, Youth for Christ's decision to employ Gil Dodds was a significant early step in the reengagement of religion and sport. Neither the organization nor Dodds appears to have been aware of that. To Youth for Christ in 1945, Dodds was a nationally known sports hero who had created something of a stir by retiring from competition at age twenty-six to enter religious ministry. The obvious assumptions on the part of his YFC superiors were that his fame was compatible with their mission and that they could forge a new kind of "symbiosis" between Dodds' lofty cultural status and their goals of reaching American youth.

One of the unintended discoveries Youth for Christ had made in its innovative programming was the value of "the sports appeal" in its work.[61] Billy Graham assessed this aspect simply: "We used every modern means to catch the attention of the unconverted—and then we punched them right between the eyes with the Gospel." To that end, Dodds was often accompanied by Bob Finley, a former collegiate boxing champion also known for his religious commitment. Dodds' strategy was to arrive in a "town early in the afternoon in time to have a workout with the local high school trackmen. While there he invites the fellows to the evening service, and they usually come in droves."[62]

The next eighteen months were hectic for Dodds. He pursued his graduate studies, coached several successful teams, and traveled extensively for Youth for Christ. By October 1946, when his second child was born, he was beginning to feel again the call of the track. He explained the possibility of running again in relation to a revised sense of his ministry. "Running in competition is going to keep me close to

113

people. It'll allow me to prove that living for Christ isn't something apart from regular daily living."[63]

Time, Newsweek, and *Life* all covered his triumphant return on January 27, 1947, when he ran a 4:09.1 mile, the fastest ever in Boston.

"'The Lord was with me all the way. . . . There is more than one way of doing His work. If I can set a good example by clean living, I can influence a lot of youngsters and some grownups, too.'"

"His old coaches had begged him to try running again. Finally he agreed. Explained earnest Gil Dodds, 28, 'I prayed about it, of course. And my wife consented.'"

Life called him "king of the mile" once again.[64]

After receiving his master of arts degree in June, Dodds resumed his comeback. He also continued his work for Youth for Christ and in the fall appeared in Charlotte with Billy Graham. With his sights set on the 1,500-meter run in the 1948 Olympic Games in London, Dodds kept his victory streak alive and gave an outstanding performance on January 31, 1948 at the Millrose Games. When Dodds ran a 4:05.3 mile, the fastest ever indoors, *Newsweek* complained, "A fresh story lead was getting pretty hard to come by these days, in stories about any 1-mile race that had the Rev. Gilbert H. Dodds of the Boston AA in it."[65]

Dodds' hopes for the Olympics came crashing down prior to the Olympic trials in Evanston, Illinois. On July 3, 1948 he won the 1,500-meter AAU championship in Milwaukee. The next week, with part of his leg in a cast, he promised he would be ready for the trials just days away. But by Friday, July 9, he had to withdraw because of a strained Achilles tendon. "As I say in the pulpit, . . . may God's will be done."[66] Journalist Joseph Sheehan questioned whether Dodds' "constant willingness to oblige worthy causes" might have contributed to his "eleventh-hour breakdown." Because Dodds had appeared with Wyrtzen in a Yankee Stadium rally less than two weeks prior to the Milwaukee race, Sheehan may have had a valid point. The *Sport Annual,* however, merely called Dodds "the hard luck kid."[67]

With the possibility of climaxing a comeback at the Olympics gone forever, Dodds became Wheaton's full-time coach and threw himself into his Youth for Christ work with a new emphasis—spreading the Word outside the United States. From 1949 to 1954, Dodds made four trips to Europe, two to the Orient, and one around the world. Many of these endeavors were on behalf of Youth for Christ.

Beginning with Torrey Johnson and Billy Graham's trips to Europe in 1946, Youth for Christ had discovered the opportunity in carrying its rally-revivalism to other countries. Some of this vision came from American GIs who had returned from the war impressed with the potential Europe held for Youth for Christ's evangelical vision. In 1949 Dodds was part of a three-person Youth for Christ team that spent a month in Sweden, Norway, and Denmark.[68]

Dodds went to Japan for a week in the spring of 1950, then on to Korea for six weeks with another Youth for Christ evangelist, Bob Pierce. Rallies were "held in the largest stadiums and athletic fields. Running is a major sport among the Korean youth, and Gil Dodds is one of the best known American athletes in the country." In August Dodds was a delegate to the Youth for Christ World Congress in Brussels. Besides speaking there, Dodds ran exhibitions in Brussels, Stockholm, and along the Riviera.[69] In 1951 Youth for Christ experimented by sending a basketball team composed of small-college players to Europe to play exhibitions. The team was coached by Don Odle, the innovative basketball coach at Taylor University, a church-related college in Indiana. Taylor students rallied "behind the team in a financial way to raise the needed funds" for the trip.[70]

The following year, 1952, marked the last step toward the reengagement of evangelical religion and sport. Dick Hillis, the Youth for Christ leader in Taiwan, was familiar with the success Dodds and Pierce had had in the youth rallies in Korea. He requested a team. "Preachers or missionaries could not gain entrance into the schools and army camps for evangelistic purposes, but since basketball was the number one game, a team from the United States was very welcome."

Venture for Victory basketball teams in 1952 originated the format of presenting evangelistic messages in competitive settings. The man in street clothes standing behind the speaker is Bud Schaeffer, the first executive of Sports Ambassadors.

Specifically, Hillis asked for "a good basketball team which could play exhibitions with leading Formosa teams . . . and in addition hold mass evangelism meetings."[71]

Bud Schaeffer, friend of Dodds and a former small-college All-American basketball player from Wheaton, headed up the team with Odle as the coach. The first Venture for Victory team had basketball and revival successes beyond their expectations. On July 2, 1952 Hillis wrote to his American supporters, "Yes, it is a new thing to use a basketball team for evangelism—but God is blessing. The Chinese newspapers write about the 'formidable, non-smoking, non-drinking, good-preaching and hard-playing basketball team.' To his glory I can say that the team has prayed, preached and played before 65,000 people."[72]

Eight weeks later, the basketball team was on its way home, and Hillis wrote again, "Through them over one quarter million have heard the gospel . . . in the 160 meetings and 79 basketball games. . . . President and Madame Chiang presented to each team member a beautiful photograph of themselves. Madame wrote us 'Their sportsmanship and preaching is [*sic*] spiritual inspiration to our people.' . . . My deepest appreciation for making possible their visit to Taiwan."[73]

The players' experiences on Taiwan stand as another turning point in the reengagement of religion and sport. Dick Hillis eventually left Youth for Christ and founded an independent mission group, Orient Crusades (now OC International). One emphasis of the new mission was the Venture for Victory–style of sports evangelism, subsequently designated as the Sports Ambassadors branch of Orient Crusades.

Explaining the Reengagement

The reengagement of evangelical religion and sport was a trial-and-error experiment that occurred over a decade between the early 1940s and 1952. With radio and the youth rallies, Percy Crawford and the early Youth for Christ–style revivalists realized that they were "on to something." Yet they were more concerned about methods and strategies that would contribute to their immediate goals of revival and evangelism than about long-range planning or theological exactitude. Whether they felt forced to work outside normal Protestant denominational structures or simply chose to because of their own styles and preferences is probably a moot issue. In either case, they left themselves open to criticism, especially within the church, and some of it likely was justified.

In part, their approach probably can be understood as the response of a subculturally marginalized religious minority adapting to the religious and cultural realities of the pre–World War II era. By the early 1940s, however, the suggestion that fundamentalists were taking two directions, reflecting paradoxical impulses toward culture, seems substantiated. In the 1930s those impulses were manifest either as cultural and religious separatism or as a desire to revive the church, even if that meant accommodation to culture and to other segments of the church. By the early 1940s the two impulses took on organizational accoutrements in the forms of the American Council of Christian Churches—the separatists—and the National Association of Evangelicals—the accommodationists.[74] The larger story of that schism is beyond the purpose of this study, but Youth for Christ, Torrey Johnson, and Billy Graham gradually identified with the accommodationists (although Jack Wyrtzen probably did not). It is likely that in the 1940s, not all fundamentalists approved wholeheartedly of "secular" sports heroes such as Gil Dodds and Bob Finley—even though these men were practicing Christians—as appropriate representatives of the more separatist style of fundamentalist Christianity.[75]

The Youth for Christ–style accommodationists were driven by the persisting desire for revival and a pragmatic sense of doing "whatever works" to achieve that goal. Sports worked. Early on, sports worked most specifically in the person of Gil Dodds. Because Dodds simply took for granted, as a minister's son and a high-school track star, that religion and sport could intersect, he personified the earliest stage of their reengagement. The "myth" of the kid from Nebraska who trained by correspondence only perpetuated the public's interest in Dodds, particularly upon his surprising retirement in 1945 to join Torrey Johnson and Youth for Christ.

But sports also "worked" in a second way as a cultural legitimizer. It was heady stuff for the Youth for Christ leaders to be noticed by the president, by governors, by the Hearst newspapers, by *Time* and *Newsweek,* and by other cultural elites. The reasons behind the attention were mixed. But sports became a powerful means of legitimizing the previously marginalized, accommodationist fundamentalists. Cultural elites and their media representatives measured the increasing acceptability of disenfranchised groups in numerical terms, so when youth rallies attracted twenty thousand at Madison Square Garden and sixty-five thousand at Soldier Field, "something" must be happening. At a minimum, it meant thousands fewer potential juvenile delinquents on the streets, and that was good for American life. For J. Edgar Hoover, that was probably all that Youth for Christ rallies meant, but for the YFC leaders basking in the glow of Hoover's and others' endorsements, it meant far more.[76]

When Gil Dodds ran in Charlotte in 1947 at the early Graham crusade, the reengagement moved to another phase—something apart from mere youth rallies, something of importance that had lain dormant for years in the United States. Until Charlotte, what "Gil Dodds" meant was that the reengagement of religion and sport worked among high school adolescents, particularly males. That is what Jack Wyrtzen and Youth for Christ were good at, and Dodds re-created the manly images of muscular Christianity that had not been witnessed since Northfield. The reengagement originated within an emerging youth culture, but Billy Graham redefined the reengagement in more adult terms and with increasingly more adult audiences. Again, Graham probably never intended that to occur.

What Billy Graham needed in Charlotte was a crowd of people, or he would have been branded a failure among the homefolk.[77] There was no guarantee that Dodds' appearance would attract a crowd, and there is no way of measuring *post hoc* how much of Graham's success was because of Dodds' presence. At a minimum, however, Dodds' appearance did not keep people away, and, to paraphrase Grady Wilson on Dodds' running around the crowd, "It may have been absurd, but people responded." What Graham learned was that athletes on his platform (along with Hollywood personalities and former gangsters) provided one way to attract an adult crowd.[78] Graham's persistent use of athletes was significant as a model for evangelical muscular Christian activity over the next five decades.

Youth for Christ next learned that the reengagement of religion and sport could work outside a North American setting as well, even if it was couched largely in North American revivalist terms and symbols. With little sense of whether its approach was appropriate for other countries, Youth for Christ sent Dodds to Europe and then on to Asia. Arguably, the response in Europe was less emphatic and lasting than in Asia. The Youth for Christ representatives in Asia also made a further kind of transference, assuming that if a single runner attracted listeners, perhaps a basketball team would work even better. And it did.[79]

Of greater importance to the evolving reengagement in the 1950s than either the transition outside of the United States or the expansion into team sports was the organizational evolution of evangelical religion's use of sports. Until Dick Hillis formed Orient Crusades, reengagement occurred only within an existing religious organization—Youth for Christ. But Orient Crusades' Sports Ambassadors became a final, significant step in the story of reengagement because it was a first—the original organization whose purpose was using sport for evangelical purposes. Granted, this occurred in Taiwan, but the base of support, as well as the religious and cultural symbols, came from North America.

A brief comparison of this reengagement and the original engagement in the 1880s is appropriate. First, each era had its personifications of muscular Christianity. Initially there were C. T. Studd and Amos Alonzo Stagg and then Billy Sunday. In the 1940s it would be Gil Dodds and then Bob Finley. Perhaps the best comparison is of the roles of Stagg and Dodds. Each was an all-American, amateur-sport hero. Neither was a particularly adept public speaker. Neither was theologically sophisticated, although both had deep religious convictions and some formal theological training. Each attracted audiences among young males in educational settings. The critical difference was that Stagg never affiliated with organized evangelical Christianity as Dodds did. Stagg's lifelong commitment was to athletics and to coaching, which Dodds tried and eventually found wanting. Dodds really was a religious professional operating within fundamentalism, with sports his means to muscular Christian ends, not unlike what might have been anticipated for Billy Sunday nearly a half-century earlier.

A second parallel is between the roles of D. L. Moody and Billy Graham. In the succession of evangelical revivalists beginning with Edwards and Whitefield, Moody and Graham are two of the biggest luminaries. Both were driven by a premillennial and revivalistic sense of "winning the world in his generation" that eventually transcended their evangelical contexts, so they became cultural icons. Each expanded his confining theological boundaries that might also have limited his use of sports and their heroes. Each liked to play sports—although not particularly well—and to affiliate with successful athletes. Each had an organizational base—Moody in the existing YMCA, and Graham in the newly founded YFC—but each quickly emerged from those limiting structures to establish an enduring organization of his own. The primary difference between Moody and Graham was in longevity. Moody died within fifteen years of the initial engagement, while Graham continues to be active at this writing, more than forty years after the reengagement. Graham passed on his own uses of sports to two new generations of institutionalized muscular Christians.

This latter contrast suggests a third comparison of 1885 and 1945: the roles of the YMCA and YFC. Each organization fit into the cultural-influence purposes of evangelical Christians, but with a significant difference. Because the YMCA never operated from a creedal basis, it readily adapted to changing cultural influences as interpreted by its leaders. Youth for Christ, however, was more firmly located within revivalistic fundamentalism. After dabbling with juvenile delinquency issues and anticommunism crusades, it never wavered from the fundamentalist vision dictated by its accommodationist founders. What it did was forsake a larger "cultural mandate" that the YMCA had pursued two generations earlier. Both groups discovered "the sports appeal," although they operationalized their responses quite differently. Both have since survived significant changes in evangelicalism and in culture, and neither is closely identified with muscular Christianity today. What YFC did, however, was spawn a succession of articulate, young male leaders, provide them a "training ground," and send them out to develop more keenly their muscular Christian intentions, particularly through Orient Crusades and Campus Crusade for Christ in the 1950s. From those leaders eventuated the institutional differences that made the reengaged muscular Christianity the enduring phenomenon that the YMCA never even intended to set in place a half-century earlier.

By 1952, then, evangelical religion and sport had reengaged in ways unpredicted fifty, twenty, or even five years earlier. The marginalized fundamentalists and their youth-rally entrepreneurs serendipitously discovered the sports appeal to accomplish their goal of youth revival. Their experiment had taken on a life of its own, and as earlier, they could never have dreamed of what the future held for evangelical muscular Christians.

5

Institutionalizing Muscular Christianity since the 1950s

A popular journalist recalled in 1984 her fascination when, as a nine-year-old in the early 1960s, she sat in her small Texas church listening to the "biggest celebrity to hit town" that year. It was pro football's Bill Glass, who was appearing on the revival circuit during the off-season.

> Glass, a part-time seminarian who was then a starter on the Detroit Lions, had appeared as valiant as Samson to a dreamy young girl in a small town where pep rallies weren't much different in spirit from worship services and football players were pampered like gods. . . . Glass's huge body, its heroic massiveness looming over the pulpit, had seemed a bulwark against doubt and pain. As he described the sweat and blood of the crucifixion, the supreme sacrifice, his shoulders hunched as if in anticipation of the snap of the ball from center, he seemed strong enough to have borne the agonies of Golgotha, strong enough to have deflected a legion of Romans. Glass merged with my Sunday school image of a mild and merciful Jesus, and I saw an invincible redeemer who not only understood my weaknesses but who could fight my battles for me.[1]

Bill Glass had completed his high school football career as an above-average lineman in 1953—within months of Venture for Victory's successes in Taiwan. His brother Vernon had excelled as a quarterback at Rice University, and many of Bill's coaches and friends assumed he would follow in his brother's steps.[2] However, a challenge from his Baptist pastor caused him to hesitate. Glass's conversion had occurred a year earlier after he heard a youth evangelist speak. The pastor then encouraged Glass to take a more active role in influencing his friends toward Christianity. For this reason, Baylor University—a Southern Baptist school in Waco, Texas—attracted him. He "came to feel that Baylor was the school that could offer what I needed for spiritual growth." Glass's choice also made sense because Baptist churches in and around Waco often asked Baylor athletes to fill speaking engagements. "Many of these doors were opened as a result of my football career. As I gained ability and confidence in playing football, more opportunities were granted me to speak." By the summer following his sophomore year, Glass's appearances expanded to week-long revival meetings, as he began taking on the role of a traveling Baptist revivalist.[3]

After attaining All-American status in his senior year, Glass added schools and civic groups to his audiences. By his own estimate, he had only four or five nights free during the spring of that year. "I felt obligated to take advantage of this new-found athletic popularity for God's glory." Glass was married in March before his 1957 graduation. Then came his first major career decision, not unlike decisions faced by his predecessors, C. T. Studd, Billy Sunday, and Gil Dodds. "The most obvious thing for me to do would be to pursue a theological education. At the same time, I had opportunities to play professional football. How could I continue a theological education and play professional football at the same time?"[4]

Glass's decision was further complicated by his selection as a first-round choice by both the Detroit Lions of the National Football League and the Saskatchewan Rough Riders of the Canadian Football League. He opted to play for the Rough Riders in what was an up-and-down season at best. At the conclusion of football season, Glass and his wife moved back to Texas, and he enrolled in Southwestern Baptist Theological Seminary in early 1958. That spring Detroit again wooed him, and Glass signed for the 1958 season.

Moving to Detroit brought Glass in contact with veteran sportswriter Watson "Waddy" Spoelstra. Several months earlier Spoelstra had converted to Christianity during the traumatic illness of his daughter, who was suffering from a brain aneurysm. The two men forged a lasting friendship that negotiated an awkward, potential conflict of both men's interests. "We had to keep our friendship secret. As a sports writer, he [Spoelstra] was in a curious and somewhat delicate position. Neither of us wanted it to appear that I was deliberately playing up to a sports writer. That would jeopardize my relationship with my teammates. Waddy . . . went out of his way not to be partial to me in his writings in the paper. We sustained each other with our Christian friendship. Before games I would find out his hotel room number and go there for Bible study and prayer."[5]

Spoelstra was important to Glass for additional reasons. First, he expanded the Bible study and prayer meetings he and Glass shared to include other players. Second, he acted as "a sort of booking agent" for Glass, lining up speaking engagements. When the team was in another city preparing for a Sunday game, Glass often would appear before Saturday night study groups or Youth for Christ rallies as scheduled by Spoelstra. In the off-seasons, Glass continued his studies, as well as speaking in churches, including the one attended by his nine-year-old adoring fan in Texas.[6]

Glass was traded to the Cleveland Browns after the 1961 season. He first heard of the trade from Spoelstra. "I recaptured some of my old enthusiasm—something of the great desire for quality football which I had as a senior in college and something of the feeling that God was in my football career. My motivation was strong. God blessed my efforts." After the 1962 season, Glass was selected to play in the Pro Bowl all-star game, the first of his four appearances. In 1964 Cleveland shut out the highly favored Baltimore Colts, 27-0,

Bill Glass, an outstanding defensive football player, tackles fellow Christian Bart Starr of the Green Bay Packers.

to win the NFL championship. The same day, Glass flew to Chicago to speak the next morning at a youth convention "about the importance of standing for that which is really worthwhile in life. . . . A world's championship football game and proclamation of the good news of Jesus Christ were almost simultaneous events."[7]

Glass and two Browns teammates, Jim Ray Smith and Jim Shofner, and their wives became the core of a discussion and fellowship group that Glass and his wife led. Soon other professional teams, including Baltimore and the Pittsburgh Steelers, had chapel services or study groups or both for their players and wives. After finishing seminary studies in 1963, Glass continued to combine football with evangelistic ministry until 1967. Then from 1967 to 1969, Glass "conducted city-wide crusades in many cities," before retiring from football in June 1969 after a successful twelve-year career.[8]

Without realizing it at the time, Bill Glass provided the next necessary transition toward institutionalizing muscular Christianity, or achieving its goals through formal organizations. He connected evangelicals to sport far beyond the informal talks Gil Dodds and the Sports Ambassador basketball players had delivered in the 1940s and early 1950s. Unlike Studd, Sunday, Stagg, and Naismith, Bill Glass personified a reengaged combination of faith and athleticism conducive to institutionalization. He provided an early model for ministry among athletes that his fellow evangelical muscular Christians would soon perfect. How muscular Christianity has become institutionalized since the early days of reengagement, the pluralistic forms that the religion-in-sport movement developed, and the emergence of specialized sports ministries compose a complex story. It is a story that parallels, but is distinct from, what occurred in the decades following the initial engagement of religion and sport during the Northfield conferences.

Institutionalizing Sports Evangelism: The Big Three

Youth for Christ, Billy Graham, and numerous other conservative Protestant leaders maintained their existing relationships with athletes after the early 1950s. But with the founding of Sports Ambassadors in 1952, the possibilities increased dramatically for institutionalizing what had been a rather latent social and religious movement.

Dick Hillis appointed Bud Schaeffer the head of Sports Ambassadors, and their activities spread beyond Taiwan to Okinawa, Hong Kong, and the Philippines. Schaeffer continued to play with the touring North American teams, while Don Odle coached. In 1952 they experimented with combining an exhibition basketball game with personal testimonials and religious proselytizing by the team members. This format was routinized during the next summers. Schaeffer wrote to his supporters in 1955, "I wish you could have been with our Venture for Victory basketball team this morning . . . as we played and preached to over 5,000 soldiers. . . . Nearly every day we play two games, and sometimes three, in order to sing, testify, and preach at half-time, to an average crowd of over 4,000 people."[9]

Hillis and Schaeffer also broadened their base of support, some of which came from unlikely sources. Hillis received a letter from the daughter of James Naismith which read, in part, "My father, Dr. James Naismith, would be so pleased if he could know that basketball was being used for some good purpose and not to make a few people rich." Jack King of Sports Ambassadors wrote in response, "Thanks to your father's invention, Sports Ambassadors is designed to give people in the sports world the opportunity to become really 'rich' through receiving the Person and message of Jesus Christ as presented by Christian athletes." In 1977 Sports Ambassadors restated its mandate, "Sports Ambassadors is a ministry of Overseas Crusades [the mission's name at the time] that utilizes international sports for evangelism and that equips Christian coaches and athletes for effective growth and service for Christ."[10]

Sports Ambassadors played an important role in instigating and routinizing sports evangelism as one major thrust of evangelical muscular Christianity. It continues to be important for two main reasons. First, it gave its imprimatur, and tacitly that of American evangelicalism, to the strategy of using an athletic contest as a legitimate context for presenting the Christian message. Its parent organization, Orient Crusades, was an heir to the 1940s Youth for Christ–style fundamentalism. As such, it was one of dozens of independent, nondenominational mission organizations that developed within modern evangelicalism, as moderate fundamentalists made peace with culture after World War II. Dick Hillis was one of several spokespersons for third-world mission activity. By including Sports Ambassadors within its structure, Orient Crusades gave credence to the strategy of utilizing sports, and specifically the venues of competitive events, as a means to religious proselytizing.

Sports Ambassadors went beyond the strategy employed initially by Youth for Christ or Billy Graham, who simply used athletic heroes to speak as part of their rallies or at a revival. Sports Ambassadors had the athletes speak about their religious views to a captive audience at the halftime of, or immediately following, a basketball game at the game site. Clearly, this tactic signaled a more complex level of accommodation and engagement between religion and sport than either that of the late 1800s or the 1940s.

Second, the Sports Ambassadors model eventually was imported back into the United States and was replicated by subsequent groups. Hundreds of North American athletes participated in the Sports Ambassadors tours, usually for several weeks during summers. The strategy worked, and conservative Protestants inferred that it was the way sports evangelism could and should be practiced. Such a certainty continues to be widespread to this day.

Although they were not deliberate imitators, two other organizations followed in the 1950s and 1960s as variations on the Sports Ambassadors approach. Together they became an early "Big Three" of modern sports evangelism. The second organization, and the first working specifically within the United States, was the Fellowship of Christian Athletes. The FCA was the dream of Don McClanen, a small-college basketball coach at Eastern Oklahoma A&M. As a college student in 1947, he participated in a panel discussion on the topic "Making My Vocation Christian" at his Presbyterian church. As he prepared for it, he asked himself, "How do you relate Christ to the athletic world and how do you relate the athletic world to Christ?"[11] His answer would come with great personal sacrifice over the next several years, but it would lead to the first important variation on the Youth for Christ and Sports Ambassadors model.

In 1954 McClanen met one of his personal heroes, a revered Presbyterian minister, Dr. Louis Evans. McClanen told Evans of his dream of "a ministry of coaches and athletes, [with] the harnessing of heroes to reach those who idolized them for a life for the Lord." Evans provided encouragement, and McClanen contacted Branch Rickey, the executive vice-president and general manager of baseball's Pittsburgh Pirates. Rickey also responded positively, and helped him raise ten thousand dollars to get his idea under way. Other volunteers, including Amos Alonzo Stagg, lent their moral and financial support as well.[12]

By November 1954 McClanen, Evans, and Rickey were ready to charter the Fellowship of Christian Athletes in Norman, Oklahoma. McClanen continued his fund-raising, and in January 1955 he organized three kickoff rallies in Oklahoma that attracted eighteen thousand guests to hear prominent athletes of the day—Otto Graham, Doak Walker, Carl Erskine, Bob Richards, and others.[13]

But the FCA also encountered its first significant crisis—a theological one—in 1955, and it reappeared over the next four decades. As the FCA came in contact with a wider circle of potential supporters, questions arose about the scope of its mission and specifically whether *Christian* was a divisive term in its name. In contrast to Youth for Christ a decade earlier, the FCA was more inclusive within the Christian community. Yet Evans was adamant in drawing the line. If *Christian* were replaced by *Religious,* as some were suggesting, he would withdraw his support.[14]

The original name remained, and in early 1956 McClanen went to Denver for three days of citywide rallies and high school assemblies with a twofold purpose: "One, to give young people the opportunity to meet and receive tips and advice from well-known athletes; and two, to have the athletes share their Christian witness and to promote fellowship and a feeling of oneness in Christ with all the participants around the common bond of sports."

McClanen took with him a roster of athletes, including Robin Roberts, George Kell, and Deacon Dan Towler, to make brief presentations.[15]

Sports Illustrated covered the Denver meetings and opined that the sports "stars turn to evangelism and score [a] hit with admirers. . . . [T]heir sincerity won them their listeners as few polished speakers could have done." The publisher of the

Denver Post was comparably impressed, wrote a check for one thousand dollars, and declared, "I consider this a frontal attack on juvenile delinquency." Within two months, the rallies had been duplicated in Houston and Indianapolis before a total of ninety thousand young people who heard athletes speak "about the importance of a Christian life and attitude."[16]

Largely on the basis of this positive response, McClanen organized the first of many summer conferences for Estes Park, Colorado, in August 1956. The purpose was "to confront athletes and coaches, and through them the youth of the nation, with the challenge and adventure of following Christ and serving Him through the fellowship of the church and in their vocations." President Dwight Eisenhower and Secretary of State John Foster Dulles sent telegrams of their support. The meetings were a success, with 256 coaches and athletes attending to listen to Doak Walker, Otto Graham, and others. *Life* and *Newsweek* covered the "muscular religious group." The latter quoted Branch Rickey as approving, "I have never faced a program which is so full of promise for so many young men in terms of service to God."[17]

In retrospect, 1956 was probably the pivotal year for the FCA. The summer programs have been duplicated in the years since then and have been evaluated internally as "the ministry's most effective outreach tool," with more than 16,000 campers enrolled in 161 camps in 1998.[18]

In the late 1950s and early 1960s, the FCA grew and moved toward formalizing its membership. It developed "huddle" programs among athletes on high school and college campuses in 1966. The huddles are meant to motivate athletes, coaches, and their friends "to find a better way of playing the game of life, add a purpose to coaching, and heighten the standards of campus and school life." By 1994 more than five thousand huddles and fellowships were meeting on high school and college campuses. Thus, within about a decade of Don McClanen's vision coming to fruition, the FCA developed the structure and programming that characterize it today. It has relied on professional staff plus local coaches and other volunteers. The two lasting programs have been the summer conferences and the huddles. The organization amended its purpose statement in 1977 to include: "The FCA model can be best implemented when coaches are involved in some type of a sponsor or supportive role resulting in coaches and athletes participating in their local church."[19]

From its inception, the FCA model was both narrower and broader than that of Sports Ambassadors. It more narrowly targeted high school and college athletes. But as a fellowship, the FCA has never been as creedal or ideological as a mission organization. Along the way, the FCA has had to assure the church that it was an ally, not a competitor, and it probably has varied in strength and effectiveness from one region to another. But it has persisted and grown for four decades.

The third of the Big Three is a combination and further variation of what Sports Ambassadors and the Fellowship of Christian Athletes originated. In 1951 a seminary student named Bill Bright began a ministry on the UCLA campus in suburban Los Angeles. He named his work Campus Crusade for Christ.

Like McClanen, Bill Bright was from Oklahoma. He moved to Los Angeles in the mid-1940s. Nominally a Methodist, Bright was intent not on things religious but on making money. But he began attending Louis Evans' First Presbyterian Church in Hollywood. There he was influenced by Henrietta Mears, who was well known in the area for her Bible teaching and for encouraging young men to attend seminary. In 1947 Mears and four men including Bright began an annual Bible conference that in 1949 would include among its speakers the young evangelist Billy Graham. Meanwhile, Bright was becoming a successful businessman, and after a brief time at Princeton Seminary in 1946, he had transferred back to California to attend Fuller Theological Seminary in nearby Pasadena.[20]

Bright was not yet thirty years old in 1951 when he got the vision of beginning an evangelistic ministry, "specifically through winning and discipling the students of the world for Christ. It was an intoxicating experience." He dropped out of seminary, sold his business, and moved with his wife to a rented

132

house a block from UCLA. They began recruiting leaders from among the students, and by early 1952, they had 250 attending their Bible studies. One of their first converts was Rafer Johnson, the reigning world decathlon champion. He was one of many athletes Bright sought to join Campus Crusade, with an initial emphasis on football players including Don Shinnick, Bob Davenport, and Donn Moomaw. Bright soon added six staffers to help lead the Bible studies that within another year had spread throughout California and nearby states.[21]

By the early 1960s Bright's movement included social ministries, campus lecturers, publishing, and then in 1966 the Athletes in Action affiliate. With Bright's encouragement, Los Angeles Rams football draftee, Dave Hannah, initiated AIA. In Hannah's words, "The purpose of this work is to introduce athletes to Christ, then to use the platform they have for evangelism. . . . This visibility is influential, because when spectators and athletes themselves hear the testimonies of our players and see the way they play, it makes an impression."[22]

Campus Crusade's contacts on college and university campuses proved invaluable in filling the rosters of the traveling basketball, wrestling, weightlifting, and track-and-field squads that quickly became an AIA hallmark. Within a decade AIA was the most visible of the Crusade affiliates, although many probably were unaware of the connection between the two.

When pressed to clarify the distinction between AIA and the more established FCA, Hannah emphasized a particular approach as characteristic of AIA. "FCA is primarily a *fellowship* of Christian sports men and women. We're a fellowship too, but our fellowship is grounded more in aggressive evangelism and discipleship training. We're activists, so to speak. And the particular strengths of AIA—unlike FCA—are our work with pro athletes, in competing teams, with the media, and internationally."[23] But because several athletes involved in the early days of Campus Crusade soon were numbered among the FCA's elite attractions, Hannah's distinction was not always apparent to participants. In relative terms, however, Crusade's aggressive approach more closely mirrored that of the Youth for Christ rallies a decade earlier than the lower-key style of the FCA in the 1950s and 1960s. What YFC had sought to establish with high schoolers was extended by AIA among college students.

Hannah chose not to address theological differences between the FCA and AIA, but the definition of *Christian* in FCA was broader and more inclusive than in AIA terms. The early FCA leaders represented a more broadly understood evangelicalism also present within mainline Protestant denominations. But many of the early staff members of Campus Crusade and AIA—although not Bill Bright himself—had closer ties to a more narrowly defined fundamentalism. For example, Billy Graham never was identified with the FCA to the extent that he was with Campus Crusade and AIA.[24] There was some overlap between the theology and the audiences of the two organizations. However, AIA implicitly positioned itself to the "right" of the FCA on the continuum of evangelicals potentially attracted by both groups' efforts.

The role of sport in American life was changing throughout the 1950s and 1960s. Because of the public's greater familiarity with sports, it is conceivable that their expectations were higher by the time AIA appeared. For one critic of AIA's teams, "Their effectiveness in converting teenagers seemed dependent on their ability to deliver points. Said an AIA basketball player, 'It's important to win, not because God wants winners, but because Americans do.' Players for the AIA, he said, were out to prove that Christians were not 'Casper Milquetoasts.'"[25]

In one sense, AIA combined the sports-venue evangelistic strategy and the organizational character of Sports Ambassadors—a muscular Christian affiliate within a larger organization—with the subcultural emphasis of targeting a constituency within sport that more characterized the FCA. AIA then readily built on the resources, style, and national platform that Campus Crusade had shaped during its first fifteen years. With some justification, the FCA probably felt that AIA was competing with it, particularly among college-age audiences. For different reasons, Sports Ambassadors saw what AIA did as a direct borrowing of its approach—in using the venue of competitive events and then in sending teams into third-world settings.

In another sense, the combined visions of Bill Bright and Dave Hannah mirror the combined visions of Moody, Drummond, Mott, and Stagg at Northfield. Bright, echoing Moody and Mott, wanted to "win and disciple the students of the world." Hannah realized "that athletes had been given an incredible platform"—which is why Stagg and Drummond seized upon sport to help build the kingdom.[26] The players and the circumstances changed, but the vision recurred.

As it recurred, it really was a singular vision shared by Sports Ambassadors, the FCA, and AIA—that of using sport for "making the bad of society good," with less sense of "making the good of society better." Only FCA has recently sought to reconnect these in a singular fashion. To that end, the Big Three employed a variety of means and sought to identify distinct audiences in domestic and third-world settings. Their strategies eventually overlapped more than was intended.

The result was that within twenty years of Gil Dodds' running laps around Billy Graham's audience in 1947, the reengagement of religion and sport not only was institutionalized by Sports Ambassadors but took on additional variations in the Fellowship of Christian Athletes and Athletes in Action. What the FCA and AIA particularly refined were constituencies among athletes and coaches with goals and strategies tailored more narrowly to those groups.

Expanding Institutionalized Muscular Christianity

Between 1952 and 1966 the reengagement of religion and sport took several directions similar to those found in the institutionalization of any social or religious movement. With the emergence of the Big Three, the organizational foundations of the movement were in place by the late 1960s. Further expansion and variation lay ahead.

The first trend was the development of specialized ministries within the larger sports subculture. One variation appeared in the late 1970s at a Billy Graham Crusade in Milwaukee. Graham's people announced a baseball clinic for young people, only to discover that none of their personnel was capable of leading it. An acquaintance put them in contact with Tom Roy, a former professional player from the area. Roy mustered his best skills, turned the clinic into an instant success, and rescued the crusade from embarrassment. He then founded Unlimited Potential in 1980 for the purpose of sharing "the Gospel of Christ through the platform of professional baseball players." Roy's clinics involved major- and minor-league professionals who paid their own travel expenses to participate. By 1984 the clinics had become a common means for Christian athletes to share their baseball expertise and basic Christian teachings with learners from Venezuela to Uganda to Russia and points beyond.[27]

Scores of smaller groups also emerged in the 1970s and 1980s to provide religious services to segments of a growing and fragmented sports marketplace. For example, the Fellowship of Christian Anglers Society uses Jesus' metaphor of making "fishers of men" as the basis of its group. The Race Track Chaplaincy of America "is dedicated to serving people in the horse racing industry—particularly those on the backside." And the Christian Motorcyclist Association provides support and fellowship for its members while challenging negative stereotypes of cyclists.[28]

These groups vary in size, style, and effectiveness. Yet they all represent a continuation of the original purpose since the days of reengagement—developing evangelism and fellowship opportunities among an increasing range of athletes and other sporting participants. Every major individual and team sport is represented by some kind of muscular Christian ministry, so that by the 1990s the total is easily more than fifty, perhaps as many as one hundred and fifty, and still increasing. The transition in the 1950s from Youth for Christ and Sports Ambassadors to the FCA and AIA indicated a shift from reaching a broad audience to targeting narrower audiences. The development of groups such as Unlimited Potential,

FOCAS, and the Race Track Chaplaincy is evidence both of the institutionalization and specialization within sport in the last third of the twentieth century. It also demonstrates the creative responses of entrepreneurs within the evangelical church and their innovative forms of ministry for reaching new audiences with the Christian message.

A second trend appeared in the 1960s and resulted in organizations such as Baseball Chapel and Pro Athletes Outreach. After the eras of Gil Dodds in the 1940s and the Shinnicks and Moomaws of the early 1950s, the number of evangelical Christians entering elite sport increased dramatically at the professional and major university levels. That growth was one of the largely unrecognized, but necessary, conditions for the expansion of the muscular Christian movement. Conceivably, the more culturally accepted attitudes—including widespread enthusiasm for big-time sport—among moderate fundamentalists composed another of those conditions. Two prime examples of Christian athletes who came onto the scene in the late 1950s were a pair of Southern Baptists—Bobby Richardson and Bill Glass. Each was tied to one of the subsequent new groups.

Bobby Richardson became a fixture as a second baseman for the New York Yankees in the late 1950s. After he succeeded Billy Martin as an everyday player in 1957, the Yankees won American League pennants in 1957 and 1958, and 1960–64. Richardson starred in the 1960 World Series, although it was won by the Pittsburgh Pirates. Becoming the series' most valuable player earned him a place among baseball's elite. Richardson then had excellent years in 1961–62 and recorded more than two hundred hits in 1962.[29]

Equally impressive was Richardson's reputation among his peers, especially for his consistent but quiet Christian commitment. One secular writer assessed Richardson's overall contribution to the team. He was "the spiritual leader of the Yankees, a religious man who was highly respected for his morality and clean living. . . . He had a strength and confidence in himself that he attributes to his belief in Jesus

Christ. . . . Bobby was religious, but he was not a holier-than-thou stuffed shirt. He abided by the rules, and the religious services that he held on Sundays were well-attended by the Yankee players."[30]

In 1961–62 Richardson also was noticed by *Youth for Christ* magazine. In four articles, it chronicled his presence as a Christian and as a significant contributor to the success of the Yankees.

But in the context of this discussion, Richardson was more important for leading Sunday services among his teammates. While chapel services on professional teams are commonplace now, thirty years ago they were a new development. They went beyond Amos Alonzo Stagg's signing autographs and being acknowledged as a practicing Christian. Individual athletes with the vision, skill, and stature of a Bobby Richardson were responding to a perceived need after having been assimilated into elite team sports. Groups such as Youth for Christ and Campus Crusade for Christ provided a base within evangelicalism from which individuals like Richardson could operate. The larger culture was increasingly accepting of their presence and eventually willing to give them a hearing. Richardson's efforts spread to other baseball teams, in part through the help of Waddy Spoelstra, the Detroit sportswriter (and the author of one of the *Youth for Christ* articles about Richardson).[31]

Within a decade Richardson's services resulted in the formation of Baseball Chapel and its goal of bringing Sunday morning worship opportunities to all major-league players and coaches. Since the 1970s it has branched out to offer a variety of religious services and Bible studies in all major-league and most minor-league cities. Richardson remains the president of Baseball Chapel, and he inadvertently provided the model for similar programs among basketball and hockey professionals as well.[32]

Perhaps more important than the leadership of Richardson was the role played by Bill Glass among National Football League players. As early as his freshman year at Baylor, Glass had begun to combine his striving for football excellence with winning the right to be heard as a Christian. "Coaches, alumni, and friends are more impressed by a good football player than they are by a mediocre player. They are more eager to hear what a good player has to say. . . . I wanted to have an audience for what I have to say concerning the Christian faith."[33]

Glass attended the 1956 FCA summer conference at Estes Park, where he was impressed with the need for stronger emotional and spiritual ties among Christian athletes. Meeting Waddy Spoelstra in 1958 and then forming the fellowship group with several Browns' players and their wives in 1962 were steps that further clarified the vision perhaps first stimulated by Glass's pastor in high school. In fact, Glass's experiences already were being mirrored by others. Buddy Dial of Pittsburgh, for example, started Sunday morning chapel services among his teammates at the beginning of the 1963 season.[34]

In the early 1960s Glass and the Baltimore and Pittsburgh players came in contact with Ira Lee "Doc" Eshelman, a Florida-based pastor and entrepreneur. Eshelman dubbed himself the Unofficial Chaplain of the Sports World. His contacts with Glass, Dial, Shinnick, and others brought him opportunities to speak to numerous NFL teams.[35]

The eventual organizational result of these chapel services and study groups would be Pro Athletes Outreach. Later in the 1960s, Miami Dolphins football player Norm Evans and several friends began serious discussions about the feasibility of such an organization. Doc Eshelman's son, Paul, together with Campus Crusade friends Eddie Waxer and Arlis Priest, set about the task of fund-raising. The athletes, mostly from the NFL, met in Dallas for their first conference in 1970. The PAO was organized formally in 1971 with the desires "to encourage each other in their faith and to reach out to other pros with the Gospel." Since then, their purposes have expanded to three general areas: "lead pros to a personal faith in Jesus Christ," "train pros to grow in their faith and personal life," and "recruit pros to reach others for Christ."

139

Evans continues as the president of Pro Athletes Outreach and has developed leadership training conferences as a major activity for the athletes. Other activities include practical marital and financial counseling.[36]

PAO represents a third generation of reengaged muscular Christians—Campus Crusade begot Athletes in Action, which begot Pro Athletes Outreach. Implicitly, however, these developments followed a sequence of increasing specialization and sophistication within evangelical muscular Christianity. Whereas Bill Bright sought out athletes in his early days at UCLA, they were but one group of campus elites he targeted for evangelization. Dave Hannah then expanded Campus Crusade's range of "services" to address one specialized subpopulation of Crusade's constituency. But the orientation to college and university athletes remained.

By the 1970s, however, Norm Evans, Paul Eshelman, and friends realized an audience existed among professional football players. But as PAO's target audience narrowed, its range of services broadened. PAO personnel also realized that the status of professional athletes and the social meaning of the professional athletic subculture were evolving rapidly in ways not being addressed by conventional religious institutions.

The issue was partly one of numbers; Pro Athletes responded to an increasing number of athletes who were open to evangelical Christianity in the 1970s. But the issue was also one dictated by changes within elite professional sports. To be a professional athlete in the 1970s and 1980s created demands on players and their families that lower-level institutions were incapable of addressing. Norm Evans—and more recently Claude Terry, a former American Basketball Association all-star player—used the worlds of sports, evangelical religion, and American life to develop the organizational structure to meet these distinctive needs.

PAO spends relatively less time on evangelism than did earlier groups such as Sports Ambassadors and AIA. Ironically, while serving a narrower subcultural slice of America, PAO presents a more holistic approach to the Christian ministry not unlike that advocated by some of the YMCA-influenced muscular Christians at the turn of the century. Despite that similarity, however, the YMCA always has served a broad constituency. What has made the situation distinctive recently is that PAO's positioning is a response both to increasing specialization among muscular Christian organizations and to the developments within elite sport and its relationship to American culture.

Since the mid-1960s, when the Big Three of Sports Ambassadors, the FCA, and AIA were in place, further institutionalization within muscular Christianity has taken two primary directions. First, dozens of smaller and more specialized organizations have arisen to address audiences oriented to specific sports and athletic activities. Then, as more evangelical Christians have moved into elite sport, organizations such as Baseball Chapel and Pro Athletes Outreach have offered a greater number of services to even more specialized audiences of muscular Christians.

Microlevel Institutionalizing: The Role of Sports Chaplain

If evangelical muscular Christianity was relatively established organizationally by the 1970s, then these developments took place on both smaller and larger scales among muscular Christians. The first of these was at a "microlevel," and it involved the origin and development of the specialized role of sports chaplain.

Since the days of Waddy Spoelstra and Doc Eshelman, the role of sports chaplain has become highly routinized. When Max Helton, for example, sought to develop the Motor Racing Outreach ministry among NASCAR drivers in the late 1980s, a pattern was in place. Helton left his suburban Los Angeles pastorate in response to a challenge by one of the drivers, and he easily adapted the strategies dozens of other chaplains had devised among parallel groups of athletes.[37]

141

Getting from Doc Eshelman to Max Helton, however, required that several "preconditions" first be satisfied. Two of these alluded to above—organizational and demographic—are now obvious. Two others, cultural and theological, were just as important and less apparent.

Sports chaplains needed the structure that organizations such as Athletes in Action, Pro Athletes Outreach, and Baseball Chapel furnished. Talented and well-meaning individuals such as Gil Dodds, Waddy Spoelstra, and Doc Eshelman unintentionally devised some of the strategies and procedures still followed by contemporary chaplains. But they typically had full-time occupations, and being a minister to athletes was a part-time endeavor at best.

Organizations such as AIA and PAO changed all that, in large part because of their narrower and more specialized approaches to elite athletes. Once those groups were in place by the early 1970s, their full-time employees already were perceived as Christian workers analogous to ministers or chaplains. Thus, one might think of sports chaplains as parallel to military or hospital chaplains, whose institutional and organizational support and expectations had been in place for a long time.

At the microlevel, what sports chaplains might do was an outcome of two similar preconditions. Organizationally, military and hospital chaplaincies helped to provide models for those among athletes. But interpersonally, the trial-and-error approaches of informal chaplains such as Waddy Spoelstra and Doc Eshelman helped tailor those models to the athletic subculture. If Spoelstra led Bible studies and Eshelman led Sunday chapel services among their small groups of athletes, then their institutionally situated successors logically could conclude that must be what chaplains do.

A second, obvious precondition was demographic: chaplains simply were not necessary, so long as there was no audience of athletes in need of their services. The athletes typically would have to come from fundamentalist and other conservative Protestant religious backgrounds. Through the

1950s and into the 1960s, the number of athletes from such backgrounds was relatively low. Men such as Bill Glass and Bobby Richardson were the exception more than the rule. But as college and professional opportunities in big-time sports expanded in the 1960s and 1970s, the evangelical presence in sport also expanded. By the mid-1970s this "critical mass" of new muscular Christians had arrived, with distinctive needs most readily served by the new breed of chaplains, who often had a background in AIA or PAO.

The upshot is that this demographic precondition paralleled chronologically the organizational precondition for sports chaplains. At about the same time AIA and PAO were becoming organizational "players," more and more athletes from evangelical Protestant and like-minded religious backgrounds were moving into big-time sport. A need for chaplains could be demonstrated.

Two further preconditions leading to sports chaplains were in supporting, but less visible, areas of cultural and theological readiness. Although it would be too much of a tangent to explore in detail, the cultural readiness for sports chaplains connected the overlapping areas of American culture and the religion and sports subcultures. Changes in post–World War II religion have been discussed in some detail, so brief attention will be made here to several parallel changes in American life and sport. The era of the institutionalizing of muscular Christianity was also the era of the Cold War. Most Americans held a polarized worldview—good versus evil, capitalism versus communism, and especially the U.S. versus the U.S.S.R. It was the era in which W. Lloyd Warner alerted Americans to the cohesive power of cultural events such as Memorial Day observances.[38] It was the era of making "In God We Trust" the official motto on coins and currency and adding "under God" to the Pledge of Allegiance.

The 1950s brought the era of President Dwight Eisenhower's famous proclamation that "our form of government has no sense unless it is founded in a deeply felt religious faith, and I don't care what it is."[39] In other words, the functional religion for most Americans was "the American Way of Life." As sociologist of religion Will Herberg explained, "The American Way of Life is, at bottom, a spiritual structure, a structure of ideas and ideals, of aspiration and values, of beliefs and standards; it synthesizes all that commends itself to the American as the right, the good, and the true in actual life. . . . The very expression 'way of life' points to its religious essence, for one's ultimate, over-all way of life is one's religion."[40]

Later, historian Martin Marty would contend that this was really an "attitude toward religion" that had risen as a fourth "partner" alongside Protestants, Catholics, and Jews. This attitude could incorporate readily the new postwar expressions of American culture.[41]

Paralleling these changes in attitude and ethos were changes in American sport. It was a time of expansion, professionalization, and redefinition. Prior to the early 1950s, elite sport was largely confined to the northeastern United States. But with the postwar baby boom and the suburbanization of America, professional-sport franchises shifted into the West and South with new leagues and new teams. All of this was reinforced by the exposure and money available for the first time through television. Sport was adapting to a new era, which in turn redefined sport. With expansion and new money came an increasing acceptance of *professional* sport as culturally legitimate, a response necessitated in part by what sport historian William Baker has labeled "the demands of the marketplace."[42]

But more important, sport's meaning was undergoing a redefinition that paralleled and reinforced the religion of the American way of life. This was particularly noticeable in the expanding role of sport in the political arena. Decathlete Bob Mathias captured the new, politicized meaning of sport held by many of his U.S. Olympic team colleagues in 1952. "There were many more pressures on American athletes because of the Russians than in 1948. They were in a sense the real enemy. You just loved to beat 'em. You just had to beat 'em. It wasn't like beating some friendly country like Australia. This feeling was strong down through the entire team, even [among] members in sports where the Russians didn't excel."[43]

Although the use of sport as a political tool was not new in itself, the significance of sport was new for many athletes and common citizens alike. President Eisenhower held a "belief in sports as an important aspect of life," which led some sport scholars to call him "the most sports-minded President to occupy the White House since the days of Theodore Roosevelt."[44] *Sports Illustrated* appeared in 1954 and rapidly developed a broadly based mass audience. It unintentionally served as a highly effective, legitimizing tool of sport, especially during international competition. Then in 1958 network television captured the Baltimore Colts' thrilling overtime defeat of the New York Giants in an NFL championship game. This occurred shortly after the Soviet Union had launched Sputnik. In the aftermath, fascination with sports reached new heights in the context of reinterpretations of the cultural significance of sport.

What resulted was a widespread recognition of sports as effective means of socializing the populace to the importance of the American way of life. The power of television in the process was obvious. Sport took on the characteristics of a folk religion that conveniently overlapped the religion of the American way of life.[45] This new religious understanding of culture led journalist Robert Lipsyte to observe in 1975, "Sometime in the last fifty years the sports experience was perverted into a SportsWorld state of mind in which the winner was good because he won; the loser, if not actually bad, was at least reduced, and had to prove himself over again, through competition." Lipsyte continued that SportsWorld "has surpassed patriotism and piety as a currency of communication, while exploiting them both. By the end of the 1960s, SportsWorld wisdom had it that religion was a spectator sport while professional and college athletic contests were the only events Americans held sacred."[46]

Numerous changes within institutional sport in the late 1960s to mid-1970s reflected the cultural unrest of the period between Vietnam and Watergate, but those changes also created a different context for muscular Christian activity. The threatened boycott and the Black Power protests at the 1968 Olympic Games in Mexico City, followed by Jim McKay's live and breathless coverage of the terrorist attacks at the 1972 Munich Olympic Games, dramatized new political meanings for sport.[47] Title IX legislation (the Education Act of 1972) juxtaposed with the pseudoevent of Billy Jean King's defeat of Bobby Riggs in tennis in September 1973 before a national television audience in excess of forty million, signaled a new era for gender in sport.[48] And the carefully orchestrated presence of the Super Bowl as an annual cultural event surrounding a football game demonstrated the new economic and media realities for sport in the final quarter of the century.

Arguably, these overlapping changes in culture and sport were perceived intuitively by the evangelical Protestants who were institutionalizing muscular Christianity in the 1950s and 1960s. Discarding their suspicions about the worth and spiritual value of sports, they quickly took advantage of the populist, folk-religious status of sport within the cultural acceptance of the religion of the American way of life. They realized what an alliance with big-time sport might accomplish for their social status and their evangelistic purposes.

By the time Newsweek asked "Are Sports Good for the Soul?" in early 1971, the task of explaining why "religious fervor has become so much a part of the U.S. sport scene" was relatively simple. Newsweek cited Billy Graham's insights "that 'sports keeps us busy; athletes, you notice, don't take drugs.' Billy also believes that coaches build character for life, and that the discipline that comes with competition naturally leads many coaches and their players to accept evangelical Christianity. The object of both, Billy contends, is to win. 'There are probably more really committed Christians in sports, both collegiate and professional . . . than in any other occupation in America.' Graham may be right."

On the other hand, *Newsweek* also suspected that "so long as competitive sports have stars and spectators who pay to see them, there will surely be religious promoters willing to use sports to sell their faith."[49]

Enter the sports chaplains. What the evangelical Protestants had needed all along were knowledgeable individuals who could move between the subcultures of sport and religion. These individuals also needed to combine the evolving acceptability of both subcultures to articulate a new vision of evangelical religion and sport sharing a place in American culture. It fell to the chaplains as the organizational representatives and legitimizers of muscular Christianity to fuse the overlapping interests and rhetoric of religion and sport.

One final precondition, however, had to be met—in this case a theological redefinition—before sports chaplains could practice their new role. When President Hoover's Research Committee on Social Trends published its findings in 1933, it noted the legal prohibitions on work and play on Sunday, "legislation of this kind, in so far as it applies to sports and amusement, is generally regarded as obsolete. . . . The failure of law enforcement agencies to suppress Sunday amusements has never been more widespread than at the present time and seems to indicate a definite turning of the tide of public opinion away from the earlier ideas of Sunday observance."[50]

This was probably true of American culture generally, but among many conservative Protestants, Sabbatarianism remained alive and well for at least a decade after World War II. As British Olympian Eric Liddell had refused to run a Sunday event in the 1924 Games, so Gil Dodds had enough influence in the 1940s to insist his event be scheduled for Friday night or Saturday before he would compete in world-class meets.[51] (The authors also have a copy of a baseball contract that an older acquaintance signed with the Brooklyn Dodgers in 1945. Five lines above president Branch Rickey's name, a "Special Covenant" is typed in: "It is understood that player's services will not be required on Sundays."

147

It probably is no accident that this is the same Rickey who supported the founding of the FCA in 1954.)

Before evangelical Protestants could become prominent participants in the muscular Christian movement, this theological prohibition would have to diminish. Although the exact date of that transition is unclear, the career of Bill Glass provides a clue as to when and how it happened. After Glass completed his collegiate football career at Baylor in 1957, playing the next year in Canada—where most games were on Fridays and Saturdays—helped him avoid a direct challenge to the subcultural prohibitions on Sunday activity. Indeed, *Youth for Christ* magazine carried articles well into the 1950s that argued for "holding the line" on Sunday sports and amusements, a position affirmed in a 1958 book on Christian athletes.[52] Glass joined the Detroit Lions in 1958 and began his NFL career by playing in Sunday games.

Evangelical Protestants took issue with Glass for violating the Sabbath, so he wrote them, "We live in a sports-minded, sports-mad country, and people are interested in what the pro athlete has to say. . . . For Christians to neglect this area of life is to miss a wonderful opportunity."[53] As long as evangelicals held to their traditional Sabbatarian views, they had little access to the expanding world of elite sport—unless they received a rare contractual exemption. But a few "pioneers"—Glass, Buddy Dial, Don Shinnick, and Bobby Richardson among the most visible—challenged this position that the larger culture had long since discarded. They contended for a more pragmatic, but still theological, position predicated on the "opportunity" for evangelism through sports. This opened a door through which dozens of like-minded athletes would follow, setting in motion a minor revolution. From a few individuals in the late 1950s to dozens by the 1970s, Glass and his friends indirectly stimulated a need for chaplains, to which new organizations such as PAO and Baseball Chapel responded.

Chaplains did not become part of the elite sport scene until the 1970s, when a complex combination of preconditions had been met. Simply contrasting the muscular Christian scene in the mid-1950s with the mid-1970s supports this contention. The intervening years had seen the establishment of new organizations, the appearance of a critical mass of athletes with distinctive needs, the rise of a cultural context supportive of the sport-and-religion overlap, and the decline of theological impediments together with justification for "ministry" within the world of sport. Chaplains of the 1970s were like the muscular Christians who attended Northfield in the 1880s. They too sought to combine evangelical religion and organized sport in new ways that the culture was supporting with its changed attitudes. Their actions differed, however, in a direction captured by sport scholar Michael Oriard. "The shift from justifying sport in the nineteenth century by appeals to religion, to promoting religion by appeals to sport, reveals much about the changing status of both sport and religion in America."[54] To push the analogy even further, the chaplains were the new Tom Browns, only routinized in new roles prescribed by their organizational, theological, and cultural settings.

Sociologist of religion Robert Wuthnow has argued that the muscular Christian organizations are examples of a vast array of "special purpose groups" that "in the years since World War II . . . now appear to cast their imprint heavily on the character of American religion more generally." Wuthnow's argument is further predicated on the declining influence of American denominations during this era, so that, in effect, denominations were supplanted by scores of the newer groups "whose common interests focus on hobbies or avocations that can in some way be combined with religion. For example, one organization focuses on drag racers and their pit crews."[55]

Assuming Wuthnow is correct, one might conclude that the special purpose groups represented by the FCA, AIA, and PAO had little immediate precedent until sport was reengaged with religion after World War II. Similarly, there was little precedent organizationally for developing the role of sports chaplain. In one sense, the role of chaplain was a historical "throwback" to an earlier era with less emphasis on

149

formal training, certification, or credentialing. Initially, one became a sports chaplain largely by announcing oneself as a chaplain and then proceeding by trial and error.

In the early 1970s, sports chaplaincy also was a response that some religious special purpose groups made to their new-found affinity with American culture. From evangelical religion's perspective, sports chaplains came to occupy a crucial role at the intersection of two compatible subcultures which share values, symbols, and purposes. Sports chaplains have been practicing their trade on the institutionalized muscular Christian scene for more than two decades, and it is possible to envision a kind of ideal sports chaplain. The social scientific procedure for doing this is to observe many examples in the real world and then exaggerate common characteristics to construct the ideal.

Pat Richie comes close to being a typical sports chaplain. He has a background in Christian ministry and was a full-time employee of Campus Crusade. Richie combines his background in ministry and proselytizing with a personal familiarity with the sports subculture. His model for the chaplaincy is representative of that followed by other chaplains and now common in elite sport. It consists of three main elements that can be thought of as concentric circles of diminishing size but increasing intensity—weekly group chapels for the members of the San Francisco Giants and 49ers; small study groups that gather weekly or at other breaks in the sports schedule; and one-on-one "discipling" in the form of "mentor-trainee" relationships with the athletes.[56]

Richie and some of his peers also increasingly get involved in teaching "life skills" distinctive to the elite athletic subculture. Many Americans seek out their minister for counsel about relationships, marriage, finances, or problems at work, but for Christian athletes, these same issues typically have aspects that sports chaplains can more knowledgeably address.[57]

In a way not unlike Waddy Spoelstra's relationship with Bill Glass in the late 1950s, Richie acts as a kind of agent for the athletes, arranging appearances before religious and other cultural groups. He also prepares the athletes for their speaking engagements, advising them on content and delivery. Finally, Richie offers training sessions for would-be chaplains. His workshops have become a functional equivalent of more formal preparation for the sports chaplaincy.

Many of these activities are common to the role of sports chaplain, but other chaplains tailor their approach to their athletes' peculiar circumstances. In Max Helton's case, that means traveling with the NASCAR drivers and crews to all thirty-four sites of their racing season. Since the late 1980s, when Helton founded Motor Racing Outreach and became the semi-official chaplain of NASCAR's Winston Cup circuit, he has experienced an unusual response. About three-fourths of each Sunday's starting drivers (plus team officials and fans) attend his worship services two hours before race time. Helton came from an academic and ministerial background and initially was unfamiliar with auto racing. Then he met an elite muscular Christian driver who lamented not having access to regular church services and spiritual counsel. Helton resigned his parish, moved his family to Charlotte, and started Motor Racing Outreach. MRO has since expanded beyond the NASCAR circuit to include motorcycle and outboard boat racing, and Helton has added other full-time chaplains to his staff.[58]

Helton's approach is not unlike Richie's— a Sunday morning service at the track, weekly Bible studies for individual racing teams and larger groups, and many informal one-on-one conversations. However, two aspects make Helton's role distinctive. First, in the early 1990s Helton buried a number of his athletes and counseled several other victims of critical injuries. According to the Associated Press, "The racing community is so encompassing that Helton's organization helps someone cope with grief every week of the year."[59] Dealing with athletes for whom death is a possibility makes Helton's work more traumatic and perhaps more like that of a hospital chaplain.

In a second unusual role, Helton advises athletes who have moral and ethical concerns about representing products that are inconsistent with their evolving Christian perspectives. Several drivers have become convinced of the need to distance themselves, for example, from the alcohol and tobacco products advertised on their cars and uniforms. The cars' owners often do not share the drivers' reluctance to represent the products, which sponsors have paid dearly to have displayed. Helton advises the drivers on how to take ethical positions with significant legal and financial ramifications. He clearly faces issues that most chaplains know little about.

Historically and culturally, muscular Christianity has been a masculine domain since its inception, perhaps so by definition. Not only are there relatively fewer elite female athletes, but the total population of female sports chaplains might well be counted on one hand. One significant example, however, is Cris Stevens, chaplain for the Ladies Professional Golf Association. Her sponsoring organization is Alternative Ministries, and Stevens has her own version of Richie's three concentric circles of ministry and services.[60]

Not surprisingly, Stevens has developed an even larger number of services geared to the needs of traveling female golfers, many of whom take their young families with them. Stevens' role includes at least two additional features. First, she has organized several forms of "early childhood religious education" geared to the golfer-moms and their children. These include formal religious teaching and socialization, as well as fun times and puppet shows.

Another example is the formation of a Habitat for Humanity chapter among the golfers, largely at the instigation of Betsy King, clearly one of the tour leaders by example and performance.[61] The professionals take time off during breaks in the tour schedule or at the season's conclusion in late autumn. As a group they construct inexpensive housing in needy areas.

Stevens appears to operate from traditional gender role expectations common both to evangelical Christianity and to some of the sports subculture, while tailoring her services and activities to a constituency quite unlike the elite male muscular Christians.

A final variation on the sports chaplain model is Henry Soles, who works with the Chicago Bulls. The model for the sports chaplain role is based on a specific period in the post–World War II evangelical church's experience, and as products of that subculture, a clear majority of chaplains continue to be conservative, middle-aged, white, male, and Protestant. One would have to look far and wide to find a greater contrast than exists between the conservative world of evangelical muscular Christianity and the flashy, high-profile milieu created by the National Basketball Association.

Henry Soles is not unique, but one of his attributes is his facility in bridging these two worlds. Soles lives in the predominantly white, middle class, western suburbs of Chicago. Yet as an African-American, he really is at home with the Bulls in the United Center on West Madison Street. Soles's less formal programmatic approach to the chaplaincy mirrors some of the cultural differences between the dominant white heritage of sports ministry and the contemporary African-American church.[62]

Soles is a "victim" of the mobile world of professional basketball, which offers interesting explanations for less institutionalization of sports ministry in the NBA than in other sports. Is that lesser development a function of the largely white-oriented cultural assumptions and organizational structures of the muscular Christian groups, including their expectations of a sports chaplain? Or is it because the schedule of professional basketball provides fewer breaks and "home stands" during which the chaplains might perform their services? This circumstance has not escaped PAO as it has moved into the NBA,[63] but at this point Henry Soles still represents a less entrenched and more fluid, individualized version of the sports chaplaincy.

From the perspective of evangelical religion, sports chaplains make a great deal of sense. They were the means by which the evangelical subculture gained access to elite sport. Evangelicals also benefited from the cultural legitimation that the chaplains' association with sport and its version of the

American way of life provided, while at the same time carrying out the evangelistic mission articulated a generation earlier by Gil Dodds and Youth for Christ. Through a variety of spokespersons from elite sport, evangelical religion also derived greater cultural visibility and was able to "use" sport to proselytize and increase its numbers.

Given the nature of their organizational attachments, chaplains have enjoyed greater freedom to adapt their emerging roles than might be expected after twenty years of institutionalization. This has prevented the role from becoming static. Max Helton, Cris Stevens, Henry Soles, and others continue to exercise great personal discretion in achieving their goals.

Probably the greatest indirect purpose the chaplains have fulfilled is instilling a measure of control over potentially antisocial behavior among athletes. For every coach or general manager who has grumbled about his athletes losing their competitive edge once they "got religion," as many have been grateful for the counseling and other activities that have instilled personal responsibility and good citizenship in their athletes.[64] The contrast with the eras of Tom Brown and Amos Alonzo Stagg is marked. Rather than seeing values and morality instilled in the athletes as a result of participation in sports, modern chaplains work behind the scenes—in Bible studies and counseling sessions over a cup of coffee—to foster moral responsibility in the athletes. Given the negative publicity in the 1980s and 1990s resulting from athletes' off-field antics, management has been appreciative of the chaplains' efforts at "damage control."

This suggests an interesting dilemma, however, about any inherent role conflict within the sports chaplaincy. Simply put, should chaplains be experiencing more role conflict than they appear to? Chaplains are dependent on the goodwill and beneficence of sports management to gain access to the athletes. Does that reliance alter the potentially larger cultural understanding of elite sport? Does that restriction serve either religion or sport well? Does it mean chaplains act too "priestly" and not as "prophetically" as they might, so as not to incur the displeasure of management?

The situation for chaplains is one of operating within the symbiosis that first gave rise to the affinity by which elite sport and evangelical religion discovered each other in the 1970s. As with many symbiotic situations, the mutual benefits are not necessarily equivalent. Similarly, the benefits have come with some costs—examined in chapter 7—which also are not equal for the two partners. Still, the chaplains have stood at an interesting intersection of "mutual need-meeting." And they have become the muscular Christian organizational representatives at the microlevel, as well as the cultural interpreters between the worlds of elite sport and evangelical religion. They are the Tom Browns of the 1990s.

Macrolevel Institutionalizing: National and International Networks

By the 1980s evangelical muscular Christianity was well established organizationally and culturally. Sports Ambassadors, the FCA, AIA, PAO, and numerous smaller, specialized organizations were riding the crest of popular enthusiasm for both evangelical religion and big-time sport. Chaplains working with professional and major-college athletes had become commonplace. But with proliferation and specialization had come fragmentation, duplication, and suspicion. Behind the scenes, several concerned representatives of these organizations along with other churchmen (the masculine noun is used deliberately here) started asking whether anything could or should be done.

Those asking the questions appear to have represented at least two constituencies, with several overlapping interests and purposes. One group consisted of interested churchmen—clergy and laity—who shared a vision not unlike that of Moody, Mott, and others a century earlier, or that of Wyrtzen, Johnson, and Graham about forty years earlier. In the context of the resurgence in evangelical church activity in North America and elsewhere during the 1980s, these visionary representatives perceived a possibility of enhancing the use of sport as a vehicle for worldwide evangelization. What was different then from either the 1880s or 1940s was the level of global acceptance of sport, particularly during times of international competitions, such as the Olympic Games. Sport not only had become a "universal language" culturally but was widely accepted as a means of transcending divisive cultural and political boundaries. Bob Pierce and Dick Hillis had recognized this potential during the early 1950s in their work in Asia, and Sports Ambassadors was the direct result. The churchmen of the 1980s perceived something available on a much larger scale, given the intervening expansion and redefinition of sport worldwide.

Meanwhile, a second group with overlapping interests, although different concerns, was made up of representatives from established sports ministry organizations, particularly Sports Ambassadors, Athletes in Action, and the smaller groups also moving between North American and international settings. They probably shared the churchmen's vision for global evangelism via sport because that is what they already did, albeit with less of a grasp of the bigger picture. Their concerns were at least twofold and probably mixed.[65] On the one hand, they were concerned with the increasing duplication of "services" and the need for more effective communication among the groups and better operational efficiency, particularly in fund-raising. Evangelicals operating special purpose groups outside of denominational structures necessarily are sensitive to the availability of funds. As their numbers increased, the groups were "chasing" limited resources—financial and human—within the evangelical church. They were understandably motivated to increase efficiency.

On the other hand, an undeniable degree of suspicion and jealousy existed among the groups. During its twenty-year existence, for example, AIA had become the dominant muscular Christian organization. Some of the smaller groups were looking over their shoulders for the shadow of AIA looming nearby.[66] If the evangelical boom of the 1970s and 1980s was mirrored in the growth of Campus Crusade, AIA, and sports ministries generally, the other groups knew that fundraising was becoming more difficult, and the boom could not last indefinitely. Who would survive if AIA continued to grow?

A third smaller group acting as a stimulus for improved communication comprised muscular Christian representatives working outside the United States and with little direct tie to North American organizations. Probably there were two subgroups here. One consisted of missionaries supported by North American organizations who were proselytizing in other countries. They were adapting to the religion-and-sport reality in their settings with less formal, indigenous efforts at evangelism through sport. A second subgroup consisted of local church or outreach personnel who shared evangelical inclinations but were already adapting a Christian message to the sports scene, with no organizational ties to the North American groups.

In the early 1980s representatives of the American evangelical churches, the muscular Christian organizations, and the foreign-based ministry groups gradually discovered each other through a series of informal meetings and conferences. Shared concerns for evangelical ministry through sport in the larger contexts of expanding evangelical activity and the globalization of sport eventually gave rise to the International Sports Coalition. In action not unlike the Northfield conferences in the 1880s or the early Youth for Christ meetings in the mid-1940s, several individuals worked to merge the overlapping interests and concerns.

A key evangelical churchman was an Ohio pastor, David Burnham. Burnham had been a small-college All-American in football at Wheaton College in the early 1950s. His Sabbatarianism precluded his playing professional football, and he became a minister for the next thirty years, all the time maintaining a keen interest in sports.[67] Burnham became the pastor of an evangelical megachurch, and he was a familiar figure among evangelicals as a writer and conference speaker.

157

Ralph Drollinger, guarded by fellow muscular Christian, Swen Nater, in an exhibition game against NBA stars in 1979. Drollinger was a key member of Athletes in Action tours in the 1970s prior to his leadership of Sports Outreach America.

Two important representatives of the muscular Christian organizational interests were Eddie Waxer and Ralph Drollinger. They brought different but complementary strengths to the early discussions. Waxer had converted to Christianity as a tennis player at Michigan State University, worked for Campus Crusade for a time, and then joined the staff of a large Presbyterian church in Florida. His strengths were boundless energy and excellent fund-raising skills. Drollinger was an All-American basketball center at UCLA on four national championship teams coached by John Wooden. After forsaking a likely professional career to tour with AIA, Drollinger had become something of the muscular Christian movement's "resident conscience," ethically and intellectually, particularly through speaking and writing.[68]

A final representative—this time of the groups working in non–North American settings with no direct ties to the U.S. organizations—was Andrew Wingfield-Digby. Wingfield-Digby is "British to the core," and his work with Christians in Sport in Britain had included contacts with Formula One race drivers, and soccer, tennis, and cricket players. Wingfield-Digby is an independent evangelical churchman. He has adapted many of the muscular Christian strategies familiar to North Americans to support his conviction that "while many societies in the world are closed to the propagation of the gospel, they are open to sport. Thus the modern itinerant evangelist can say, 'With a football and a Bible, I can go anywhere and guarantee a crowd.'"[69]

These men helped to convene a series of informal meetings of like-minded muscular Christians in Hong Kong, San Antonio, and suburban Milwaukee during the early 1980s. The result was the formation of the International Sports Coalition in 1986 with the announced purpose "to promote unity and cooperation with local church and parachurch sports ministry servants so that together we might follow God's leading in worldwide evangelism and exhort each other to keep Christ first in our lives and ministries." Burnham resigned his church in Akron, Ohio, and for several years in the mid-1980s, he and Waxer virtually willed the ISC into existence.[70] Their crowning accomplishment was a weeklong gathering of more than five hundred delegates in Seoul prior to the 1988 Olympic Games for the World Congress on Sport. Evangelical missionaries and sportspersons from around the world discussed theology, philosophy of ministry, and global sport in the interest of increased understanding and cooperation in sports ministry.

The ISC convened a conference in Houston in early 1989 and another in Dallas the following year. From those meetings emerged the coalition's North American branch, Sports Outreach America, which has met annually since then in either Dallas or Atlanta. Both groups continue to act as "umbrella coalitions." ISC meetings are oriented more toward the internationalizing of sports evangelism. SOA conferences are geared toward North American and church-related concerns.

By the mid-1990s, the ISC and SOA had identified a group of mostly white men who are thoroughly evangelical in their theological orientation, conservative in their lifestyle, and passionate lovers of sports. A core of national and international practitioners of muscular Christian evangelism is more fixed than ever before. With the annual conferences approaching the end of their first decade, however, it is difficult to discern whether the movement has continued to expand as expected. There is some evidence of retrenching within the ISC, since a Barcelona-based congress on sport in 1992 did not measure up to what the response in Seoul might have suggested. David Burnham left the ISC as planned in 1989, and his presence as a charismatic leader has been missed. Eddie Waxer—the peripatetic organizer, facilitator, and fund-raiser—is as active as ever but may be spreading himself too thin in his worldwide activity.[71]

The prospects are probably less clear for SOA, with persisting questions about an absence of continuity in leadership and long-term *raison d'être*. Since its inception as the North American affiliate of the ISC, Sports Outreach America has benefited from a narrower focus on the role of muscular Christianity in the programming of local churches, denominations, and church-related colleges, which will be pursued in detail in chapter 6. Some of the suspicion of AIA has quieted, partly with a resurgence of the FCA during the early 1990s. The number of individuals and groups adopting an SOA-like philosophy continues to grow in North America, although SOA probably has not done as effective a job as it might in "marketing" its services to them.[72]

What the ISC and SOA likely have learned after more than a decade is that greater centralization and bureaucratization within any movement are often a mixed blessing. For much of their history, evangelicals have been characterized as "Lone Ranger entrepreneurs" who are not "good team players." Cooperative sports ministry is more easily conceptualized and discussed than practiced. The long-term prospects for SOA and the ISC are mixed, with a greater need than earlier for sensitivity to their team-members' needs, as well as to shifting cultural and subcultural contexts.

As might be expected, institutionalized muscular Christianity, now well into its fifth decade, is in a stronger situation at the microlevel represented by sports chaplains than at the macrolevel of SOA and the ISC. The exception to that generalization, however, exists within an interesting institutional intersection of religion, sport, and education that may offer the most promise for the future of SOA and the movement.

Interinstitutional Muscular Christianity

Church, College, and Sport in Modern America

On March 7, 1994 the men's basketball team of Liberty University in Lynchburg, Virginia, defeated Campbell University 76-62 to qualify for the NCAA Division I tournament for the first time in its twenty-three-year history. When the NCAA pairings were determined the following Sunday, Liberty University was seeded sixteenth and given the privilege of facing perennial powerhouse University of North Carolina in its first game. Liberty lost to the Tar Heels, 71-51, after leading with less than ten minutes remaining.

Shortly after the NCAA tournament, Liberty University redesigned its promotional literature. A magazine advertisement pictured its chancellor, Jerry Falwell, cutting down the net after the victory over Campbell. Under the picture ran the following text:

> Chancellor Jerry Falwell cuts down the net following the Liberty Flames basketball team's victory at the Big South Championship. This accomplishment led to Liberty's first appearance at *"The Big Dance"*—the NCAA Division I Final 64 Tournament. The Flames captured the attention of the entire nation by taking the defending National Champion North Carolina Tar Heels to the brink of defeat!

March 18, 1994 was the day that the nation recognized Liberty as a premier contender in NCAA basketball. However, Liberty is not only renowned for an outstanding athletic program but also for our commitment to excellence in academics and a unique emphasis in spiritual growth.[1]

Nearly five years earlier to the day, Jerry Falwell had given two interviews to reporters from the *Chronicle of Higher Education* and the *New York Times*. The resulting articles were titled "Liberty U. Seeks Success in Football to Spread Fundamentalist Message" and "Liberty Builds from the Ground Up." Within several months *Sports Illustrated* would contribute a seven-page treatment of Liberty football as well.[2]

The *Chronicle* reported, in part:

> The Rev. Jerry Falwell . . . believes it is only a matter of time before the university, now in its 18th year, will compete academically and athletically with such religiously affiliated institutions as Notre Dame and Brigham Young University.
>
> Mr. Falwell insists that with football helping to trumpet the institution's name and to spread the message, Liberty is on course to become a respected national university for born-again Christians. . . .
>
> In building a major liberal arts university, "sports are as much a part of it as English and Biology," Mr. Falwell says. A sports program develops character and discipline among students, he says, and "helps a school build an identity around which students and alumni can join hands."[3]

The *New York Times* had a different emphasis in concluding its article.

> "While winning isn't everything, it's certainly a part of life," Falwell said recently. "We hope we're not training losers."
>
> The quality of that training is not without its critics. Liberty has an open admissions policy, meaning anyone can matriculate who has graduated from high school and can show proof . . . of a belief in Jesus Christ as a personal savior. One Liberty coach said that this lack of academic stan-

dards made teams from more selective universities unwilling to play his squad, the members of which must meet N.C.A.A. requirements.

A student legislative body at Liberty recently voted to request the adoption of minimal academic standards, a direction Falwell has resisted as an impediment to achieving his goal of a 50,000-member student body.

An editorial in the school newspaper earlier this month that the editor said was heavily censored by the administration hit upon a theme familiar on other campuses: It complained that the commitment to sports has not been balanced by improvement in academic facilities.[4]

Perhaps because of the high profile of its chancellor, Liberty University's emphasis on football and basketball and its capitalizing on qualifying for the NCAA tournament became more widely known. In the 1980s and 1990s Liberty represented a trend among Christian schools to use their athletic accomplishments to legitimize their academic and theological missions. Similarly, Pentecostal evangelist Oral Roberts two decades earlier had sought to forge a connection between basketball success and institutional acceptance at his university in Oklahoma.[5]

What Liberty and Oral Roberts and other colleges illustrate, however, is a less well-known but even more widespread interinstitutional convergence of church, college, and sport within evangelicalism. It goes well beyond the simple discovery of the sports appeal made decades earlier. The convergence suggests a greater symbiosis within the interinstitutional status of evangelical religion and elite sport than had been known previously.

The Dilemma of Voluntaristic Evangelicalism: "How to Be *of* the Church, but Not *in* It"

Most scholars of American religion would assert that denominationalism has exerted an incredible power over the way Americans have practiced their religion, particularly among Protestants, but also for Catholics and Jews. Andrew Greeley—a Catholic priest, sociologist, and novelist—for example, argued in his book *The Denominational Society* that "religion and the rest of society relate to each other through multiple quasi-equal ecclesiastical organizations which are . . . actually a social organizational adjustment to the fact of religious pluralism. . . . Denominationalism helps to maintain and to reinforce the remarkable stability and culture of the United States."[6] Besides denominations among Christians, one can think of divisions among Orthodox, Conservative, and Reformed Jews. In addition to their importance for religious identity and social adjustment, denominations say a great deal about their adherents' social status and historically are related to Americans' income, education, voting patterns, family size, and a host of other social minutiae.[7]

When thinking about contemporary evangelical muscular Christians, however, the problem with the denominational concept is at least twofold. First, as sociologist Robert Wuthnow claims (see chap. 5), the denomination continues to decline as an indicator of social status and behavior. It no longer works as it once did, especially with the parallel, rising strength of religious special purpose groups.[8] But second, much of evangelicals' identity, history, and social interaction exist quite apart from—sometimes in antipathy to—denominations. To make sense of the interinstitutional realities between evangelical religion and sport today, one must use some other sociological model.

Part of this need for another model is related to the interconnected modern meanings of the term *evangelical.* Clearly the term no longer means what it did in the U.S. or elsewhere in the 1890s or the 1790s. Today, evangelical is probably a combination of three elements:

1. a theological heritage that is tied to a set of orthodox Protestant, creedal affirmations;

2. a historical continuity through the private party of nine-teenth-century conservatives, but with a significant disruption from the fundamentalist-modernist schism in the 1920s and a further realignment after World War II; and

3. a sociological reality that emphasizes voluntaristic institution-building among conservative Protestants who share this theology and history but work outside traditional denominational structures.[9]

Evangelicalism has come to mean a religious movement with distinctive organizations and institutions such as colleges and media outlets. Sometimes these organizations intersect with Protestant denominations, but often they exist alongside them and, perhaps, in competition with them. Evangelicalism is also a subculture with its own values, norms of behavior, and symbols. It fluctuates in relation to other religious traditions and to the larger American culture and way of life.

Voluntarism is another characteristic of American religion, tied in large part to the First Amendment and the disestablishment of religion, so that Americans have no state church. Citizens have the freedom to establish their own religions as they see fit. All organized religions have an equal legal status, with none given preferential treatment. Historically, Protestants were the first to come to America, and they voluntarily sorted themselves in ways that merged their religious traditions—as new denominational preferences—with their nonreligious social statuses. But there were always dissenters who did not fit the list of acceptable preferences and who often voluntarily created new institutional forms and then set out to attract converts.[10]

Voluntaristic religion in America creates a fluidity and vitality not readily compatible with the normal institutionalizing processes. Voluntarism has often been expressed in revivalist terms, particularly among those on the cultural margins. Thus, popular Protestantism has attracted a host of resourceful entrepreneurs who of necessity have been "market driven" in their sensitivity to their followers' wishes.[11] In addition to the revivalists mentioned in chapter 1, D. L. Moody, Billy Sunday, and Billy Graham fit the model closely. So does the YMCA, although its story is more mixed. As Zald and Denton have demonstrated, despite its evangelical origins (probably not because of them), other contextual factors brought about a rapid transformation within its mission.[12] In a narrower theological sense, however, the YMCA was never as evangelical as it appeared, and as its contexts and markets shifted, its mission and theology were transformed quickly. As suggested in chapters 2 and 3, the emerging place of sport was more than incidental to those changes within the YMCA.

The situation was quite different by the 1950s and the reengagement of evangelicals and sport. Here Wuthnow's model is instructive but of limited value. For Protestant traditions or movements not following the denominational form, the Wuthnow "replacement thesis" of special purpose groups supplanting denominations does not work well. Instead, as suggested in chapter 4, the predecessors of the post–World War II evangelical movement were well on their way to developing earlier versions of special purpose groups in the late 1930s and 1940s, even as the existing Protestant denominational arrangement was still in place. When the fundamentalists split into the separationist and accommodationist parties in the 1940s—which in some cases generated new, competing denominations—the National Association of Evangelicals became an early clearinghouse for the network of accommodationist organizations and special purpose groups.[13]

In recent years, historians and social scientists have documented the "extended family" or network-like quality of postwar evangelicalism. It persevered and grew with expanding organizational linkages plus shared, redefined symbolic meanings and boundaries.[14] Anthropologist Mary Douglas' concept of "symbolic boundary" articulated by Wuthnow is helpful to demonstrate both the self-identity shared among evangelicals and the process of delimiting who is "in" and who is not.[15] For example, from the 1950s through the 1970s, "Where you stand on Billy Graham" distinguished separatist fundamentalists from accommodationists. That was succeeded by the "born again" symbol in the 1970s and 1980s; if one knew about being born again and claimed to be born again, then one was an evangelical. Being able to sing the same songs (usually from memory) also served as such a symbolic boundary. Specifically within sport, the evangelical redefinition of Sabbatarianism in the 1950s and 1960s is a case of a shifting boundary.[16]

Organizationally and institutionally, evangelicalism cohered around shared media outlets, conferences, Christian colleges, and shared acquaintances. In a classic study of early twentieth-century fundamentalism, historian Ernest Sandeen asserted that Bible institutes and colleges often acted as surrogate denominational headquarters among fundamentalists.[17] Among their post–World War II evangelical successors, a similar clearinghouse function was in place. Students or alumni of Wheaton College, Taylor University, Gordon College, Biola University, and similar institutions knew about each other, had relatives or friends from the other colleges, and granted a privileged status for each other in the network. When the early sports ministry groups came into being, Sports Ambassadors and Campus Crusade took advantage of these organizational ties and reinforced them.[18]

In this evangelical subculture, one personality type has always been valued more than others—the entrepreneur. Although evangelicalism is relatively well institutionalized, its structures and symbolic boundaries always have tolerated, even encouraged, the charismatic entrepreneur who possesses a "call from God." A Jerry Falwell, for example, working within loose, Baptist structures is valued as a visionary for his acumen in politics, education, sport, and media. Thus, he is able to carve out a niche in the evangelical "market."

The discussion that follows is an explanation of the threefold interaction of sport and evangelical churches and colleges that characterizes institutionalized muscular Christianity at the end of the twentieth century. The model is based on the assumption of shared functions and symbiotic

167

relationships between the three institutions, with attention given to examples of connections between the church and sport and between college and sport.

Interinstitutional Underpinnings

The key notions underlying the rise of interinstitutional muscular Christianity in the late twentieth century are "function," "symbiosis," and "elective affinity."[19] A functional interpretation assumes that new roles and structures develop in response to needs elsewhere in any social system. As needs change, individuals create new services or, perhaps, new special purpose groups. Institutionally, this means that the church-and-sport relationship, for example, arose from needs-meeting by both parties, and new responses to new needs continue.

Symbiotically, the interinstitutional relationships are seen as mutually beneficial but not necessarily of equivalent contribution or importance. With benefits also come costs. The relationship will continue as long as it is functional and provides reasonably more benefits than costs to both parties. The benefits are not only monetary but human, organizational, and cultural. Trade-offs are common in such a relationship. Similarly, the greater beneficiary may become the lesser beneficiary at a later time and vice versa.

Demonstrating an elective affinity between the parties is also important. It assumes that a strict, chronological, cause-and-effect relationship was not necessarily present historically. Instead, the parties to the relationship "found each other," with their affinity perhaps based on anticipated shared functions or a potential symbiosis.

In the case of the three institutions embodying contemporary evangelical muscular Christianity—church, college, and sport—they found each other over several decades. Today, what only occurred informally in the 1950s and then existed in preliminary connections in the 1970s is firmly in place institutionally. Their relationship resembles three interlocking

spheres, with each connection solidified by a specific organization. In two of the three cases, a significant overlapping
membership strengthens the linkages (see figure).

Interinstitutional Evangelical Muscular Christianity: Church, College, and Sport in the United States, 1990s

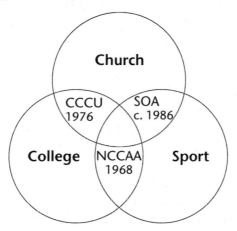

CCCU: Coalition of Christian Colleges and Universities (93 church colleges)
NCCAA: National Christian College Athletic Association (110 church colleges)
SOA: Sports Outreach America (scores of organizational participants)

Sport and the Church: Sports Outreach America

Chronologically, Sports Outreach America is the last of
the three connections in consideration here (it grew out of
the International Sports Coalition in 1986). Yet the linkage
between church and sport it represents is of primary importance and had been in place for decades. Much of the story
of that early connection has been related here, but examining it in terms of function, symbiosis, and elective affinity gives further meaning to the institutional reality today.
    The evangelical church and sport found each other in a
relationship of elective affinity partly because of the similar functions they perform in socializing Americans to gen-

erally conservative values. The evangelical church initiated the connection through the serendipitous discovery of the sports appeal. That initial relationship was built among young people, who were a concern because of crime and delinquency. But it did not take long for the church to realize that what worked among youth might also work among adults, in North America and abroad. Functionally, the church and sport found each other at two levels. Culturally, they were partners in stemming the tide of delinquency. Institutionally, the church appreciated the ability of sports to attract listeners.

Exactly how the evangelical church functioned initially on behalf of amateur sport is less clear, although not necessarily problematic. But a latent function quickly emerged with the expansion and redefinition of elite sport in the late 1950s and 1960s. Sport had taken on a political role in the 1950s, then profited from the expanding cultural role and further legitimacy its relationship with the church extended. According to Newsweek in 1971, "Coaches, owners and others with a financial stake in big-time athletics often welcome the aura of religiosity that has been draped around sports."[20] Bill Glass and Bobby Richardson—even more than Gil Dodds—were cultural heroes with well-known religious views and affiliations. The world of sport benefited from their clean-cut, moral images as increasing prestige and status were extended to it.

Once the church-and-sport relationship was in place, benefits and functions evolved for both parties. The increasing cultural legitimacy of sport extended credibility to the emerging evangelicalism of the 1960s and 1970s. Whereas the early Youth for Christ leaders enjoyed being noticed by President Truman and J. Edgar Hoover, the early FCA leaders received endorsements from President Eisenhower and John Foster Dulles. Billy Graham was often nearby as a kind of legitimacy broker or liaison, bestowing and benefiting from the sport-and-religion functional affinity.[21] Newsweek noted, "In selling evangelical religion, Graham sells sports as well."[22]

When Bobby Richardson moved to formalize the efforts of Baseball Chapel in the early 1970s, there was Bowie Kuhn, the commissioner of Major League Baseball, interceding on his behalf. Why Kuhn did this may never be known, although serving "the best interests of baseball" was a phrase he often invoked to justify his actions.[23] Kuhn probably reasoned that a dose of religion in the clubhouses could do little harm and might just do some good for the image and cultural influence of the American pastime.

The relationship between religion and sport was further cemented by the sports chaplains since the 1970s. For example, one might make the case that Andre Agassi's relationship to the men's professional tennis tour chaplain, Fritz Glaus, in the early 1990s[24] eventually reaped longer-term benefits for tennis following the departure of a cohort of previous star attractions. Clearly, NASCAR officials appreciate Max Helton's presence and have extended him unusual access to work among its performers. The presence of scores of elite athletes continues to give evangelical religion cultural acceptance and access to potential converts. When Orel Hershiser sang "Praise God from Whom All Blessings Flow" on Johnny Carson's *The Tonight Show* or when Dave Dravecky explained coping with cancer and amputation to thousands in live audiences,[25] the groundwork was laid for a broader cultural appeal on behalf of evangelicalism.

Enter Sports Outreach America in the late 1980s. The relationship between religion and sport that had evolved over four decades had now reached a new stage of interinstitutional affinity. The church continues to be the primary beneficiary of the services and perspectives SOA propagates. Attachments to sport enhance the church's mission by providing opportunities for service and evangelism. Denominational and local parish representatives are active participants in SOA conferences, exchanging ideas for improving ministry. How that is being extended by the multistaff megachurch will be further explained below.

Sport and College:
The National Christian College Athletic Association

In light of the history of muscular Christianity, one should not be surprised that a contemporary version of interinstitutional religion and sport exists. Rugby School was the scene of Thomas Hughes' *Tom Brown's Schooldays,* and the relationship between the British public schools and the ideal of muscular Christianity was taken for granted. Hughes placed Tom Brown at Oxford in his sequel, and it was at Cambridge through C. T. Studd and the Cambridge Seven that British muscular Christianity reached its apex.[26]

In the United States D. L. Moody had J. E. K. Studd tour college campuses, preaching to listeners accustomed to college campus YMCA activity. Then at Northfield, the muscular Christian alliance between athletics and campus life was fixed. For at least two decades it flourished. The departure of the YMCA from campuses and the rapid secularization of the higher education milieu changed all that, resulting in the disengagement cited in chapter 3.

But for a time in Britain and in North America, the alliance held. The story of function, symbiosis, and elective affinity between the two is quite unlike that of church and sport. Historically, the colleges were in place when sport gradually took on an institutional character and a cultural presence. British public schools and colleges saw in sport the possibility of a "functional ally." They anticipated a means for character formation, manliness development, and organizational cohesiveness. The character formation and manliness development functions quickly took on a mythical status, as proponents of sports-in-college selectively interpreted a causal relationship that went beyond mere elective affinity.

In the United States the character formation and manliness development tie between college and sport was extended by Higginson and the early YMCA supporters. This tie was evident as early as the 1860s, as cited in the introduction. But with the rapid development of intercollegiate sport in the 1870s and 1880s, what had been a latent function became more obvi-

The NCCAA honors Mid-America Bible College. The association has sponsored national championships in several sports.

ous. With the rise of institutional identity and prestige through intercollegiate athletics, the shift of emphasis from character formation to winning was virtually a *fait accompli*. For Andrew Miracle and Roger Rees, "athletic competition shaped character *because* [emphasis added] it gave opportunity for action, and as a result of this action, success and victory. . . . Americans were winners and showed their moral worth through victory."[27] The Northfield-based muscular Christians felt comfortable in their elective affinity with sport, as long as the cultural myth emphasized manliness and character building. Once the tide turned, however, to the more secular values, the Sundays, Naismiths, and Staggs went their disengaged and separate ways.

From this institutional symbiosis with the college setting, sport received instant cultural acceptance and a mythical certitude attesting to its value. It gained a base of support within upper-class and upper-middle-class America. From there, perceptions of its value would diffuse through the rest of society as new sports like basketball and volleyball were added to college programs and as baseball became part of the cultural myth of what makes America. All this would be tested at the end of the nineteenth century with the ascent of intercollegiate football and its associated antisocial attitudes and behaviors. The mythical value of sport was already so powerful as part of the American ethos that even rationally and empirically based arguments could not deny sports a place in the collegiate extracurriculum.

Things were different in the 1950s with the evangelical reengagement of muscular Christianity. Schools, especially colleges, were a secondary setting following the churches' initial use of sport for youth evangelism. By the time of the FCA and Campus Crusade in the mid-1950s, however, it was the college campus and the cultural role of elite athletes that religion found attractive. Character formation, manliness, and school cohesiveness were nonissues for the FCA and Crusade, but both knew that athletes in college (and high school, in the case of the FCA) had great potential as religious spokespersons.

In the 1960s Sports Ambassadors, the FCA, and AIA further realized how important college campuses were for their recruiting efforts. The idealism on campuses in the late 1950s and 1960s was beneficial as these organizations attempted to recruit recognizable speakers, build touring teams for competition-evangelism, and enlarge their full-time staffs.

Enter the National Christian College Athletic Association in 1968. The evangelical church had benefited from the twin forces of the baby boom and the rapid expansion of higher education from the late 1950s through the 1960s. When mainline church official Dean Kelley wrote *Why Conservative Churches Are Growing* in 1972, he pointed to the evangelical denominations and nondenominational groups represented by these muscular Christian organizations as experiencing the most rapid growth in American churchdom.[28] These same groups were also expanding a network of colleges, many of which were investing heavily in their athletic

174

programs. Many of those colleges were small, with perhaps none having an enrollment above two thousand. Some were members of the NCAA, and more were affiliated with the alternative National Association of Intercollegiate Athletics. But most had no affiliation for their athletic programs, despite the growth of their student bodies and of interest in intercollegiate sports among evangelicals.

In March 1968 six Christian colleges from New York, Tennessee, California, and elsewhere sent their men's basketball teams to Detroit to play basketball. From this invitational tournament would come the NCCAA. The story of the events leading to the formation of the association "sounds like a broken record" after the accounts of the engagement and institutionalization of muscular Christianity in chapters 4 and 5.

A number of coaches and athletic directors from small Christian colleges had for some time discussed the difficulties of competing within the NCAA or NAIA tournaments. Meanwhile one athletic director, Norm Wilhelmi of The King's College in suburban New York City, had organized recurring regional basketball tournaments. These early conversations and tournament experiences came together in Canton, Ohio, in 1966 as several men imagined a structure like the NCCAA.[29]

In 1968, with Wilhelmi's success as a model, another coach named Ron Hines rented a gymnasium in Detroit and organized the first national tournament. He persuaded acquaintances at several colleges to hold qualifying tournaments to identify participants. Other nearby colleges were invited to fill out the six-team field. One of them sported an 8-20 season record, and the college's coach recalls Hines's invitation, although he was not yet "an NCCAA member." "Bring $10 and join," Hines responded.[30]

Although the costs of the tournament were high, the long-term programmatic and promotional benefits for the colleges, their budding intercollegiate programs, and their increasing numbers of athletes—especially males—soon were apparent. The NCCAA adopted an initial constitution following the tournament, located its headquarters in Chattanooga, Tennessee, and for several years conducted only the annual basketball tournament. The initial "locus of power" gradually shifted from Wilhelmi and the northeast-midwest to Chattanooga's Tennessee Temple University and its neighboring southern colleges. National tournaments were added by 1973 in cross country, track and field, and soccer. In 1976 a Division II tourney for men's basketball at nonscholarship Bible colleges began. National tournaments for women's sports originated in 1981.[31]

Today the NCCAA has headquarters in Marion, Indiana, and a full-time executive director in Rob Miller. Its stated purpose is "to provide a Christian-based organization that functions uniquely as a national and international agency for the promotion of ministry and outreach and for the maintenance, promotion and enhancement of intercollegiate athletic competition with a Christian perspective."[32] Member schools' athletes have received numerous awards annually, including the Pete Maravich Memorial Award. In the mid-1990s the NCCAA had 110 members in two divisions—liberal arts and Bible colleges—which competed for valid forms of national championships in six men's and five women's sports.

In locating the NCCAA within its sport-and-college context, one can invoke much of the general description of evangelicalism in the late twentieth century as appropriate. Evangelicalism has accommodated significantly to selective aspects of American life since the 1950s. Thus, Liberty University's budget of one hundred thousand dollars in 1988 just for football recruiting raised few eyebrows, in part, because enrollment was more than 7,000 by then.[33] Most colleges affiliated with the NCCAA, however, have student bodies under 600 (the 1998 median enrollment was 531). Nearly one-third of its schools have fewer than 350 students. The association's annual budget is less than two hundred thousand dollars, not even double Liberty's football recruiting allowance. What the NCCAA schools provide athletically, however, is an opportunity for regional and national competition for 16 percent of their enrollment of 64,000.[34] This demonstrates the schools' attempt to incorporate sports into their extracurricula, despite their modest sizes and resources. Sports are an essential part of a Christian college in the 1990s.

Many of the larger schools in the association also maintain membership in the NAIA, which places the NCCAA in a tenuous position. NCCAA officials lament that their members use the association as a "stepping stone" to athletic legitimacy, in this case to gain a stronger attachment to the NAIA and succeed in its national competitions.[35] It is not an uncommon scenario for dual-member schools to bypass NCCAA tournaments for a chance to "win it all" in the NAIA. In 1995, for example, four of the best NCCAA men's basketball teams opted to play in the more prestigious NAIA national tournament. They rejected a more likely opportunity to win the NCCAA championship at nearly the same time. Meanwhile, the dual-member schools, despite their modest sizes, often provide athletic scholarships—in some cases up to a dozen twelve-thousand-dollar full grants for men's basketball alone—so they can compete more equitably with their secular NAIA peers. By contrast, among the smaller Bible colleges, which compose over half of NCCAA membership, allegiance to the Christian association is stronger, the competition is just as spirited, and they have no reason to look to the "greener pastures" of the NAIA.

The NCCAA has evolved to perform the "latent function" of providing a stepping stone for some of its member colleges, with all the attendant financial and ethical ramifications. At the same time, it obviously has a recognizably different organizational philosophy than either the NAIA or the NCAA. Attending an NCCAA event in the 1990s is probably not totally different from attending a Northfield meeting in the 1880s. The rhetoric and symbols of evangelical religion, intercollegiate sport, and small colleges intermingle. Although the meetings are dominated by adult athletic administrators, male athletes are present, as at Northfield, but now for the overlapping national tournament.

For the NCCAA in the 1990s, sports are only extrinsic means to an end, as proudly affirmed in its statement of organizational philosophy. That may not be much different from the NAIA or the NCAA, although their distinctive ends clearly vary. But the association differs from the others in its accidentally mirroring the twofold Northfield vision of making the good better and the bad good. Thus, a recent NCCAA plenary presenter spoke on "What Charles Barkley, Barney [from PBS television], and Christian Coaches Have in Common"—their opportunities to influence others. However, the speaker emphasized the differences between Barkley or Barney's influence and that of the coaches.[36] Christian college coaches as a group hearken back to an earlier era in their commitment to the belief that "the athletic experience provides a dynamic growth process for learning discipline, team work, leadership, and mutual respect where the student-athlete and his preparation for life is more important" than championships.[37] They want to make the good of society better, and they see athletic competition as the ideal context for achieving that purpose.

But they also want to make the bad of society good, and therefore another goal of the NCCAA is to "provide greater levels of support for NCCAA student-athletes for missions outreach endeavors around the world."[38] Granted, it is not unusual for NAIA teams to go abroad to play international opponents and to experience other cultures. But the NCCAA can tell its member institutions, "We'll give you that opportunity . . . plus something else—the chance to tell people in a third-world setting about Jesus, and we'll even cover some of your expenses to make it possible." The sports experience is an essential part of a Christian college in the 1990s, but in more than one way.

The NCCAA faces significant challenges as it looks to the twenty-first century. Its membership has leveled off. Small colleges join, but larger ones move on. It cannot come close to funding its national championships, and it would like to have ten or twenty times as much money available to support its student-athlete-missionaries. But it has carved out an identifiable niche, with distinctive functions, among a growing constituency interested in an expanding muscular Christianity.

Church and College:
Coalition of Christian Colleges and Universities

It is relatively easy to identify Sports Outreach America and the NCCAA as the organizations linking the church and sport, and sport and college, respectively. It is not so easy to identify a single organizational tie between the evangelical church and colleges. Part of the problem is the nature of evangelicalism as an amorphous, largely nondenominational or interdenominational movement that depends more on informal networks than on formal structures.

Another part of the problem is more historically linked to the fact that much of evangelicalism has only recently made peace with higher education and sought to forge formal connections with it. In the late nineteenth and early twentieth centuries, evangelicalism's fundamentalist predecessors reacted against the secularizing trends alluded to in chapter 3. "Many Protestant colleges and universities had now been under secular control for a generation or more."[39] Only a sprinkling of colleges acceptable to the fundamentalists existed and then survived the modernist-fundamentalist schism of the 1920s. Fundamentalists' reactions near the turn of the century spawned dozens of new Bible institutes and colleges that were more narrowly orthodox in theology, vocationally oriented in mission, and culturally marginal in their interaction with much of higher education. "Conservatives needed places they could trust for pastoral training. Bible institutes and Bible colleges filled that need."[40] In 1930 the weekly fundamentalist mouthpiece *Sunday School Times* published a list of fifty-one Bible institutes it recommended.[41]

Following the fundamentalists' split into separationist and accommodationist camps came another spate of small colleges. In addition, some of the Bible institutes and colleges that previously had been vocationally oriented gradually evolved into more culturally accepting and academically respectable liberal arts institutions. These institutions "of course had to develop new bases of financial support and student body

179

recruitment. The increasing number of independent churches and parallel independent agencies provided that."[42]

When the Carnegie Commission assessed the state of Protestant higher education in the late 1960s, it observed that "within the 25 years since the end of World War II more than 100 Bible colleges and institutes have been established in the United States. Some of these have become liberal arts colleges."[43] Of the eighty-eight Protestant colleges it surveyed in depth, the commission noted that "the fastest-growing group" consisted of those "associated with the evangelical, fundamentalist, and interdenominational Christian churches," with "the establishment of new liberal arts colleges taking place mainly under the sponsorship of evangelical Christians."[44]

These growth trends had not escaped the notice of some of evangelicalism's leaders in higher education. One result was the formation of a Christian College Consortium, consisting initially of ten of evangelicalism's older, more established liberal arts institutions, including Taylor, Wheaton, and Gordon. Among the consortium's stated purposes was "the more widespread promotion and explanation of the mission and record of the continuing Christian colleges." Then in 1976, "probably the single most important contribution of the consortium" was its founding of "the Christian College Coalition [which has recently changed its name to the Coalition of Christian Colleges and Universities] as a satellite organization with the specific task of protecting the religious and educational freedom of the Christian colleges."[45] According to one historian, the coalition has fulfilled two functions—"a lobbying group" and "a unifying and educational forum for Christian colleges."[46]

If any broad-based organization exists as a linkage among evangelically oriented colleges in the 1990s, it is the now ninety-three-member Coalition of Christian Colleges and Universities. In its twenty years of existence, the coalition has become more of a clearinghouse, while maintaining some of its earlier lobbying goals. It offers cooperative programs for students to spend a semester in Cairo or Oxford or Moscow, gaining study-abroad experience that their own small colleges cannot provide. It has underwritten a series of supplementary textbooks published by HarperCollins. It has provided professional development seminars for more than seventeen hundred professors.[47]

Recently the CCCU has begun dialogue with SOA and the NCCAA. The CCCU recently sponsored a seminar for professors of physical education and recreation, in which they exchanged ideas on philosophy and pedagogy, as well as on the Christian implications of their work. Coalition representatives also participate in the annual SOA conferences to enhance the opportunities for ministry and campus involvement that both groups address, although typically from differing perspectives. Presidents and athletic directors from CCCU and NCCAA colleges are also featured speakers at SOA meetings.

The CCCU-NCCAA connection exists largely through overlapping memberships as well as informal contacts. At last count, of the 110 colleges in the NCCAA and the ninety-three in the CCCU, forty were active members in both. If one eliminates the fifty Bible colleges in the NCCAA from consideration because they are not likely to belong to the CCCU, the overlapping membership is more striking. About thirty-five of the forty-seven liberal arts colleges in the NCCAA are also members of the CCCU.[48]

The three ties described here depict an interconnected set of relationships and functions being realized through cooperative programming and shared personnel. Conceivably, an increasing number of evangelical churches send their students to Christian colleges, where many participate in intercollegiate sports. They often spend a summer in a third-world setting through an SOA-affiliated group, "making the bad of society good" through sports evangelism. Following graduation, they take their places in evangelical churches as supporters of both intercollegiate athletics at Christian colleges and the muscular Christian sports ministry groups. The interinstitutional relationships truly are symbiotic. Church, college, and sport all benefit.

Sport in Christian Colleges

These overlapping functions and symbiotic benefits can be approached in a second, more cultural way. As a transition to chapter 7 and its interpretation of the modern myth of evangelical muscular Christianity, two case studies follow.

Magazine Advertising

The first is a more in-depth examination of sport in Christian colleges, particularly with how those colleges present themselves and their athletic programs through magazine advertising.

Christian colleges grew in number and enrollment during the 1960s and 1970s, then experienced the harsh reality of American demography. The baby boomers went off to college in record numbers, but they were succeeded by a smaller "birth dearth" cohort beginning in the early 1980s. Numerous Christian colleges faced declining numbers in the 1980s and 1990s, and not all survived.

Evangelical Christian colleges in the last quarter of the twentieth century are both similar to and different from their more mainline, religiously affiliated cousin institutions. Scores of liberal arts colleges are underfunded and tuition driven; are supported by fickle constituencies with often thin loyalties; are struggling to survive with few distinctives in a competitive market; and are generally career oriented in curricula, which reflect upwardly mobile, middle-class and lower-middle-class constituencies. Evangelical colleges share most, if not all, of these characteristics with their cousin institutions. They typically also possess a limited heritage in the liberal arts, as well as modest academic prestige.

Even more so, what the evangelical colleges have in common is their need for a "competitive edge" to distinguish themselves from others and to provide an image or identity. One further difficulty stems from Wuthnow's observation about declining denominational attachments in the past thirty years. Many evangelical colleges maintained denominationally strong, ethnically based origins for some time. But those loyalties have weakened, and the result is critical for the small colleges. One wonders, Where do they find their students, and how do potential students find them?

Intercollegiate athletics have come to the rescue. Scores of evangelical colleges present full-page, full-color advertisements in magazines and journals circulated among evangelicals. Many of these magazines, including *Christianity Today* and *Campus Life,* represent a broadly based evangelical audience. What is striking is how many of these advertisements feature intercollegiate athletics to inform potential students and their parents about the colleges.

Two examples suffice here. Trinity College (now Trinity International University) of Deerfield, Illinois, is affiliated with a small, originally Swedish-related denomination, the Evangelical Free Church. Trinity belongs to the CCCU, the NCCAA, and the NAIA. It began an intercollegiate football program in the late 1980s, about the time other colleges were eliminating theirs. By doing so, Trinity hoped to recruit more males to a student body of about six hundred. Within three years, "of the 70 players on campus, almost all say they would not be there were it not for football."[49] Trinity selected as its first coach former Chicago Bear Leslie Frazier. Trinity has run two advertisements featuring football. In one, four players in full equipment are pictured with Frazier and his close friend, muscular Christian Mike Singletary. The advertisement is titled "Play with the Pros in College," and it reads: "Leslie Frazier and Mike Singletary were teammates the year the Chicago Bears won the Super Bowl. Now Leslie Frazier, head football coach at Trinity College in Deerfield, Illinois, still gets help from his friend Mike Singletary. If you're in high school and want to play for a pro in college, call Trinity College, a four year Christian liberal arts college, today."[50]

A number of items stand out about the advertisement. The word Christian appears only once. Nothing is said about the college's academic programs. A second picture depicts

183

football action. The ad is obviously aimed at high school males. The juxtaposed phrases "play with the pros" and "play for a pro in college" form a unifying theme once unthinkable in a college context. The sequence of association from the Bears to the Super Bowl to Mike Singletary to teammate Leslie Frazier to coach Frazier to Trinity College to "play for a pro" to "call Trinity" is unmistakable and likely intentional.

Another advertisement presents Grand Rapids Baptist College in Michigan (now Cornerstone College). The college began as Grand Rapids Baptist Bible Institute and was sponsored by a small separatist denomination, the General Association of Regular Baptists. It had evolved to Grand Rapids Baptist Bible College by 1968, when its men's basketball team participated in the first NCCAA tournament. It is now a liberal arts college and is less culturally separatist. It belongs to the CCCU, the NCCAA, and the NAIA and is seeking to broaden its constituency while maintaining its ties to the GARB, which also sponsors several other colleges. It has fewer than seven hundred students and fits closely the "profile" of small evangelical institutions described above.

In the early 1990s it ran an advertisement that featured a half-page photograph of a baseball pitcher ready to pitch. The caption is "A Winning Tradition." In this case, the copy only mentions athletics once; the word Christian appears six times as an adjective, and Christ is mentioned once. "Liberal arts" appears twice, and phrases including "challenge your mind," "thorough liberal arts," and "academic excellence" proclaim an academic appeal. What is interesting, however, is that "winning tradition" is the central phrase, repeated three times. It attaches symbolically the photo of the baseball pitcher to the copy.[51] In contrast to Trinity's ad, Grand Rapids more obviously presents a combination of athletics, academics, and evangelical religion—the three necessary ingredients of nearly all these advertisements. But somehow it is never clear how the "winning tradition" sports metaphor should unite that threefold appeal in the minds of inquiring student-athletes.

Advertisements from more than a dozen evangelical colleges from all parts of the United States and a variety of denominational traditions have appeared. What do these advertisements mean for interinstitutional muscular Christianity and the church-college-sport connection? The first, most obvious meaning is that evangelical colleges have elected to use intercollegiate sport as a primary means to recruit students, particularly males. Some of the ads include female athletes—although none presents them solely. Azusa Pacific University in California featured an alumnus and 1992 Olympic bronze medalist, Dave Johnson, filling half a page in a two-page ad.[52] Whether anyone on this and other campuses questions the appropriateness or effectiveness of recruiting via sports cannot be determined from the ads. Trinity's addition of football arguably has not been a neutral occurrence, but one with meaning for the campus ethos and the remaining members of the college community.

Second, the advertisements mean that these colleges perceive sport as part of a legitimate philosophy of education and as an acceptable means to academic respectability. They apparently see no inconsistency between sport and their stated Christian commitment. One of the most secular aspects of American life at the end of the twentieth century is sport. Many of its underlying values challenge the development of a Christian worldview. Sport carries moral meaning, and some of it exists on the fringes of ethical responsibility. The apparent assumption among these colleges, however, is that sport fits well morally within their Christian and educational missions.

Third, these colleges have accepted the rhetoric of sport as a legitimate, shared means of communication, even for communicating about Christianity and their schools' positions. In addition to the Grand Rapids emphasis on winning, for example, Geneva College in Pennsylvania (Presbyterian) juxtaposed two phrases, "a winning tradition" and "a Christian perspective," in an ad with nine action photos of its athletes plus a list of four years of NAIA and NCCAA championships won by Geneva.[53] It further emphasized "Developing Winners in the Classroom and on the Field."

Winning is also prominent in an ad for Northwestern College (Reformed) in Iowa, with three of its athletes pictured as "winners" in athletics, academics, and "spiritual growth." Other sports terms such as "athletic excellence" and "success" also appear.[54] The symbols from sport take on different connotations when used academically and religiously. Only some of these connotations are consistent with their primary, sports-based meaning. The ads simply extrapolate the sports rhetoric into these other symbolic arenas.

Fourth, these Christian college advertisements have become significant, although indirect, means of socializing to and perpetuating a peculiar rhetorical phenomenon. The ads convey a merging of the colleges' spiritual, academic, and athletic missions that is articulated by the vocabulary and symbols of sport. This recently developed rhetorical system will be discussed in detail in chapter 7. So suffice to observe here that the colleges have become a primary means of familiarizing evangelicals with this muscular Christian symbol system.

Fifth, these colleges are deliberately taking advantage of the popularity of sports within their conservative Protestant subculture. The familiarity of Mike Singletary or Dave Johnson is another of the colleges' assumptions. The schools apparently take it for granted that seventeen-year-olds will respond positively to the images and associations of these sporting heroes. Thus, sports "work" for these colleges because sports work in a variety of ways in the evangelical subculture. How conscious the colleges are of the pragmatic value of sports when developing these ads one can only surmise.

Finally, in an indirect way, these advertisements further blur distinctions within the evangelical subculture and the potential student bodies represented by the athletes. Presumably, a high school athlete will ask herself in response to an ad, "Should I go there to play ball?"—without necessarily knowing anything about the denominational or theological heritage of the college. A pronounced version of this can be inferred from an ad placed by Atlantic Union College in Massachusetts. Atlantic Union is a Seventh-Day Adventist school, although that is not mentioned in the ad. Historically, Adventist colleges have not competed in intercollegiate athletics, nor have Adventists been perceived by evangelicals as "one of us." Some sort of "mutual legitimation" seems to be taking place between evangelicals and Adventists, in part via intercollegiate athletics—or even perhaps the legitimation is between Adventists and athletics via evangelicals—or both.

Even though Atlantic Union does not belong to either the CCCU or the NCCAA, it is a member of the NAIA, as the ad mentions in featuring its men's basketball and women's volleyball athletes.[55] Arguably, sports at Atlantic Union and *Campus Life* magazine's acceptance of the ad are means of redefining the boundaries by which evangelicals and Adventists determine who is in and who is not. Because the Atlantic Union ad states that "as Christians," getting to know members of visiting teams is "more important than our win/loss record," its intercollegiate athletic program presumably is a part of that redefinition and legitimation process. Perhaps evangelicals will respond positively to Atlantic Union's strategy of making the bad of society good—or at least becoming their friends.

In summary, Christian colleges are using sport as a powerful medium to communicate the evangelical muscular Christian, interinstitutional relationship between church, college, and sport. Having intercollegiate sport on its campus means that a Christian college—not unlike its secular counterpart—is a legitimate institution that provides an essential extracurricular experience in addition to an education with a distinctively Christian emphasis.

Debate at Asbury

A second case study of the connections between church, college, and sport considers one college's debate about the place of sports on its campus over the past fifty years. It also illustrates recurring themes in recent years as evangelical colleges have decided whether to embrace intercollegiate sport as part of their extracurricular programs and implicitly as part of their evolving service to the evangelical church.

Two brief caveats are appropriate here. One is that the diversity within evangelicalism, its churches, and its schools makes generalizations about their perceptions of sport difficult. Some evangelical colleges have endorsed sport for a century or more, while others still debate its role in the late-1990s. Acknowledging this diversity is important, but the overall trend toward embracing sport has accelerated only in the past two generations. A second caveat is that all case studies possess qualities that defy generalization to the whole of any population. Still, many of the distinctive arguments at one school have been faced at sibling institutions as well. The denominationally based distinctives among the colleges have given way to a more diffuse evangelical subculture shared by nearly all these churches and schools.

Asbury College, an undergraduate institution of nearly twelve hundred students, in Wilmore, Kentucky, is one such interesting case. In the mid-1990s, a committee of athletic administrators and coaches had proposed that Asbury phase in ten full athletic scholarships by the 1997–98 academic year.[56] That year would also be the golden anniversary of a front-page article in the college's student newspaper titled "President Opposes Intercollegiate Sports for Asbury College." In the article, President Z. T. Johnson laid out his rationale for Asbury's continuing rejection of intercollegiate sport.[57] How Asbury changed over those intervening fifty years provides insight into questions raised about the role of sport on evangelical campuses.

Asbury is part of the holiness and Methodist traditions shared with a number of other evangelical schools. Asbury has always represented conservative, and often minority, voices within the mainstream of Methodism. Part of this may be attributed to its location in small-town Kentucky, and much of it to a succession of conservative leaders. Its student body typically has not represented its geographical setting, but rather has come from pockets of conservative strength within Methodist and similar holiness groups. Although a liberal arts college and one of the early members of the Christian College Consortium in the 1970s, Asbury historically has seen its mission as preparing church leaders and evangelists.

After World War II, a number of nearby colleges from related holiness backgrounds gradually endorsed intercollegiate sports. Taylor University in Upland, Indiana, was an early leader in the reengagement. Colleges supported by the Free Methodist Church, including Greenville College in southern Illinois, developed intercollegiate programs, as did those sponsored by the Church of the Nazarene, including Trevecca College in Tennessee.

By November 22, 1947, Asbury's President Johnson had so many inquiries "from faculty members, students and constituents" that he responded on the front page of the *Asbury Collegian*. He took a three-pronged position to explain why he (and Asbury) was "definitely opposed to intercollegiate sports":

1. Programs of intercollegiate sport in colleges are "based more upon *'professionalism'* and *'the winning spirit'* than upon anything else." He cited a series of problems resulting from a sports program—athletic scholarships, program costs, alumni pressure, expectations of winning, and a succession of coaches if losing.
2. An "intercollegiate athletics program gives *the wrong emphasis*. It is based on the idea of training a few rather than the many." Johnson contrasted such a program with a strong intramural program that offered four advantages—physical exercise, participation, class-based competition, and a spirit of cooperation.
3. *"Asbury College is a unique institution."* Here the president cited religious training, evangelism, leadership, and doctrinal standards as defining qualities Asbury would forfeit if it added sports. His further judgment was that "when individuals or institutions imitate one another they usually imitate the weakest characteris-

tics rather than the strongest." He concluded by reiterating the problems listed above, with the likelihood of "smoking, drinking and rowdyism" coming onto the campus, plus the responses from constituents who would "be deeply grieved" and stop supporting Asbury if sports were added.[58]

Johnson's opposition—especially his first two areas—could have fit any number of American colleges at various times in their histories. His third reason is more ambiguous. On the one hand, he seemed to assert a case of "Asbury exceptionalism," but on the other hand, he framed Asbury's identifying qualities in the form of a relative, "strength versus weakness," cost-benefit analysis. To accept athletics would simply cost more than it would benefit Asbury. The costs had less to do with financial loss, however, than with skewed spirit, emphases, and institutional ethos and distinctiveness.

The next twenty years saw the rapid acceptance of sport among evangelical liberal arts and Bible colleges. Not much changed at Asbury, however, and the *Asbury Collegian* weighed in with a campaign on behalf of intercollegiate sport. Its November 27, 1968 issue included three articles— a report of a survey revealing the positive status of sport on five other Christian campuses (four of them holiness-related, plus Wheaton); an op-ed column in which past-President Johnson's 1947 article was reprinted alongside a column from a faculty member who listed eight advantages of adding sports; and a summary from the student sports editor arguing that "sports would help Asbury educationally, financially, and spiritually."[59]

By 1968 Asbury had an intramural program that the administration and board cited as more than adequate to meet student needs. Support from alumni and constituents was still a major concern, with the 1968 cost-benefit analysis framed in stronger financial terms than in 1947. Would the "conservative constituency discontinue their support if such a program were begun?" Those pushing for intercollegiate sport cited the "paltry $18,000" the alumni had given Asbury the previous year, in contrast to the potential benefits of attracting "prospective students, especially guys. . . . Empty rooms in the boys' dorms is [sic] money down the drain." Besides, some alumni might be heartened to learn that "Asbury isn't too bound by tradition" and would increase their giving.[60] Despite evidence of growing support for an intercollegiate program, little changed.

Over the next three decades, the debate recurred, and change was consistently slow, almost imperceptible. In 1976 an experimental schedule of intercollegiate men's and women's basketball was rejected for five reasons—inadequate facilities, absence of academic benefits, conflicts with existing events, negative spiritual effects (especially from visiting teams' fans), and inadequate funding. Then-President Dennis Kinlaw was also known for his opposition to sport on the grounds of misdirected priorities, endangering class-based intramural competitions, and an unwillingness to offer athletic scholarships. For some the financial concern became paramount in 1976. Needs in the library, dormitories, and faculty compensation were deemed higher priorities than intercollegiate sport.[61]

In the 1980s Asbury gradually increased participation in several inexpensive "minor" sports such as field hockey and track and field, while maintaining the intramural structure. Still, for many, being a college in Kentucky—the hotbed of basketball—without a men's basketball team had marginalized Asbury in the larger world of college life. So in 1987 the college's athletic committee proposed men's and women's basketball as cost-effective and culturally acceptable additions. "Choices must be made that reflect concern for the individual athletes, quality competition opportunities, and institutional support."[62]

Asbury finally added men's basketball in 1992. It also joined the NCCAA and the NAIA, and it developed a program of five sports for men and five for women. But it did not win consistently. In 1994–95 the men's basketball team lost all twenty-five of its games. And the loss of hoped-for benefits in public relations and attractiveness to potential athletes turned out to be something of an embarrassment.

So in March 1995 the athletic department proposed that ten full athletic scholarships be phased in over three years. A six-point rationale included the need for competitive equity, the ability to attract more athletes from diverse backgrounds, and the "ultimate goal . . . to increase our impact for the cause of world redemption through Jesus Christ." The campus community, however, remains divided into three factions:

1. Those opposing any expansion of intercollegiate athletics, arguing that nonathletic needs should take priority, especially now that a seven-million-dollar recreational facility is in place.
2. Those arguing for more adequate funding of athletics—but stopping short of scholarships—in the interest of enhancing campuswide morale and excellence.
3. Those supporting the scholarship program as the best means for achieving the levels of competitive excellence and opportunities for ministry that Asbury's students expect and deserve.[63]

If anything, the status of sport at Asbury is even less clear than it was during the 1960s and 1970s, and surely is more uncertain than in the 1940s. What Asbury has learned is that developing an intercollegiate sports program is not as easy as it sounds. The cross-purposes and competing demands are significant. Financial considerations are only part of the story, with theological and cultural attitudes often still an issue. Good reasons for and against sport can still be marshaled by equally well-meaning individuals. Unless an activist president or donor has the vision and the financial support to will the program into being, it may not occur; even if it does, the benefits may be less than anticipated. Finding the combination of educational, spiritual, and financial benefits that Asbury's sports editor imagined in 1968 is not easy for evangelical Christian colleges, most of whom are simultaneously seeking to enhance their position in the world of higher education.

In summary, what both the advertisements and Asbury's story indicate about Christian colleges' relationship to sport in the 1990s is a general widespread acceptance of sport on extrinsic terms, although the rhetoric portrays continuing ambivalence about its role and justification. Theological and cultural criteria have not disappeared, but they often play a lesser role than more pragmatic considerations. Still, the role these colleges attribute to sports programs in presenting themselves to their constituencies says a great deal about their enthusiastic acceptance of sport to "make the good of society better" as part of an evangelical, undergraduate experience.

Sport in Evangelical Megachurches

Evangelical churches have long supported the activities promoted by Sports Outreach America and its affiliates and have encouraged their youthful athletes to participate in intercollegiate programs at Christian colleges. Yet a relatively new phenomenon is represented by the commitment to athletics within local evangelical churches. Chronologically, this expanding role for sport has probably followed the similar increase in emphasis on sport in evangelical colleges.

Sports programs also have proliferated with the growth of the evangelical "megachurch" movement since the 1970s. Conservative Protestants have long built large churches, especially in urban centers, so what is new is neither their size nor their support for recreation and sports. The programming of churches in the Southern Baptist Convention has often included opportunities for recreation, typically aimed at the regular attendees. What is new is a redefined place of sport in the larger mission and programming of the church, together with a commitment to up-to-date facilities and full-time staffing by professionals in sports outreach and ministry. Much of this expansion has occurred since the 1970s with the sub-

193

urbanization of upwardly mobile evangelicalism in the form of megachurches that often boast congregations numbering from five to fifteen thousand adherents.[64] Much of this expansion mirrors the larger cultural interest in fitness and sports.

Since the first national meeting of SOA in 1991, the evangelical ministers of sports and recreation have become a permanent fixture in SOA and at its annual meetings—leading seminars, developing strategies, and exchanging ideas for increasing effectiveness.[65] Four brief examples of churches with extensive commitment to the use of sports follow. They could be replicated many times over, especially among Southern Baptists. These churches also illustrate the diverse geographical and denominational perspectives represented by the modern evangelical church-and-sport movement.

Grace Church of Edina, Minnesota, made a serious commitment to sports and recreation in the late 1980s. A change in leadership sparked a rethinking of the missions and evangelism programs in the formerly Baptist, now nondenominational, congregation. Dave Gibson, who had attended the church as a layperson while vocationally attached to the FCA, was invited to serve as the pastor of missions and outreach.[66] The foregone conclusion was that Gibson would develop a range of activities based in the church's underutilized, decade-old recreational center. Gibson is a master of innovative programming, and the church of three thousand is thriving as it implements his philosophy of using sport as a means to "relational evangelism." The evangelistically oriented celebrity golf tournament draws five hundred men. The day's activities culminate in a banquet talk from one of the PGA's muscular Christian, touring professionals. Similarly, a Rise with the Guys breakfast on Saturday of Holy Week features one or more sports heroes from the Midwest. When the Super Bowl came to the Twin Cities in 1992, Gibson, Grace Church, and the Billy Graham Evangelistic Association led the ecumenical efforts of Sports Outreach Minnesota to evangelize the area with the assistance of SOA and several professional muscular Christian heroes.

194

Perhaps Gibson's most successful program numerically has been Sports Plus. It uses a range of activities as an evangelistically oriented entree into the homes of unchurched families whose children have participated in Grace Church's recreational leagues. Gibson mandates that at least one-third of the participants in these leagues not be regular attendees of the church. What links these varied activities are the church's resources and commitment to sport, which Gibson can channel toward the goal of evangelizing in a wide range of settings.

Southeast Christian Church in Louisville would seem at first glance a much less likely place theologically and culturally to find a church-based recreation and sports program. Southeast is affiliated with the "independent Christian Churches," who both shun the label "denomination" and avoid the culturally accommodating tendencies of their more evangelical cousins. Nevertheless, this congregation that now numbers ten thousand members hired Eugene DePorter in 1986 as its first full-time staff person with primary responsibilities for sports and recreation.[67] When DePorter took over, the church had just grown past two thousand, had only a lay-staffed recreational committee, and offered informal recreational opportunities in softball, volleyball, and a white-water rafting trip. Within the next eight years, the church grew nearly five times as large. This was due in no small part to DePorter's developing a fivefold program of sports, fitness, recreational trips, creative activities, and family-oriented activities.

In the midst of this growth, the church relocated in the eastern suburbs of Louisville. DePorter's programming was one stimulus for the move and a primary consideration in designing the new building. The range of sporting activities open to Southeast Christian's members is mind-boggling; it includes aerobics, baseball, basketball, cycling, football, golf, marathons, racquetball, soccer, softball, tennis, volleyball, weight training, and more, along with first-aid and CPR training. The basketball program alone includes more than one hundred teams in a dozen leagues. As with Grace of Edina, Southeast Christian orients its programs toward both its members and the nonchurched, although more of its activities are directed to members. What Southeast demonstrates even more dramatically than Grace, however, is the crucial role that a local congregation's commitment to sports and recreation can play in the rapid growth of a megachurch, given the kind of leadership Eugene DePorter—one of thirty pastors at Southeast—brought to the development of the program.

Willow Creek Community Church in the Chicago suburb of South Barrington perhaps even better illustrates the newer megachurch approach to sports and recreation as part of the total outreach and programming potential. As a nondenominational congregation, Willow Creek began in 1975. It numbers more than fifteen thousand weekly attendees, nearly ten thousand of whom are involved in some type of church-based, small-group activity as well. In the 1980s, as it experienced its phenomenal growth, Willow Creek was relatively slower to move into sports ministry, with only informal programs in aerobics, biking, and volleyball attracting much lay-organized participation. Willow Creek launched a twenty-million-dollar expansion program in the late 1980s, and a gymnasium and fitness center were key parts of the plan.

By 1992 the gym was completed, and the church hired a college football coach, Len VandenBos, as its director of sports and fitness.[68] VandenBos enthusiastically shares the church's vision for building relationships as a means to enlarging the church, especially through small-group connections, and those emphases have driven his ministry. He has sought to make the facilities and programs accessible to larger numbers of participants at all skill levels, with most programs lasting a minimum of three months to allow relationships to develop. Meanwhile, sports and fitness compose a "self-supporting ministry," meaning that all activities exist on a "pay to play" basis. More than six hundred men are now involved in the basketball leagues, for example, but VandenBos's goal is to expand basketball in directions of forming small-group Bible studies and support groups. In 1995 fourteen men from the basketball league spent ten days in Spain under Willow Creek's International Ministries outreach with a sibling church there. A long-term goal is to develop a small international sports ministry along the lines of Athletes in Action. For VandenBos, the key has been fitting these developing activities into Willow Creek's emphases on evangelism and church-building through relationships and small-group opportunities.

Highland Park Presbyterian Church in Dallas is a final variation on the megachurch's use of sport. It is an older, more established member of the mainline Presbyterian Church USA denomination situated in an affluent neighborhood in Dallas. Highland Park's membership approaches six thousand, although its weekly attendance is less than half that. Jim Riley has served as its director of recreation since 1980, making him a dean among the SOA-affiliated sports ministers. Much of the evangelistically oriented vision for sports ministry at the church comes from the peripatetic Riley, who oversees a staff of four. He sees Highland Park's emphasis on recreation and special events as an exception to the typical PCUSA programming.[69] Highland Park's history, however, is one of growth in the early 1980s, particularly among young adults, at nearly the same time the church added a gymnasium.

Today Riley is adamant that the mission and program of any megachurch thinking about sports ministry must precede the brick and mortar of the facility. Conversely, the worst mistake a church could make would be providing "open time" in a facility with little notion either of who would staff it or how its use would be programmed. For fifteen years Riley has consistently preached the "gospel of sports ministry"—that sports and recreation must fit as a tool within the larger mission of the parish. It cannot be merely from a sense of "keeping up with the Joneses," or with a neighboring church already into sports. Riley also has been instrumental in organizing a group of sports and recreation ministers who, like himself, are singular in their vision of developing local sports ministries.

Not all sports ministry is occurring in the newer evangelical megachurches. Some denominations, notably the Southern Baptist Convention, have instituted denominational-level programs to enhance sports ministries in individual congregations. Similarly, numerous nonaffiliated churches have developed their own programs, often quite oblivious to any sports ministry "movement" in the evangelical world. One interesting example is the Centurion high school basketball tournament conducted each spring by the fundamentalist Marquette Manor Baptist Church in Downers Grove, Illinois, near Chicago. The tournament involves sixteen of the Chicago area's up-and-coming teams as part of Marquette Manor's community-level evangelistic concern. The event reflects the church's awareness of the keen interest in high school basketball immediately following each year's state tournament. The church hopes to build on that interest as a means of attracting community interest and new participants in the congregation and its programs. Quite on its own, Marquette Manor mobilizes dozens of volunteers and provides subsidies of more than ten thousand dollars annually to conduct this distinctive form of outreach via sports.[70]

On balance, however, much of the action at the local level in the 1980s and 1990s has been in the megachurches. What Grace, Southeast Christian, Highland Park Presbyterian, Willow Creek, and scores of similar churches have in common are the resources, vision, and underlying philosophy of ministry that find in sport a natural, culturally based ally for achieving their goals. Among their shared assumptions is also a persisting extrinsic view of sport—although not so forthrightly stated as by the NCCAA. They see sport as a most logical point of contact with the largely white, middle-class, nonchurched suburbanites who select a church much the same as they purchase other consumer products. For these churches, offering sports and recreational opportunities heightens popular awareness and perhaps gives them a competitive marketing edge, not unlike the process Christian colleges utilize among seventeen-year-olds choosing a college.

In summary, the organizational and institutional symbiosis among the evangelical church, college, and sport really goes well beyond the three circles of the NCCAA, SOA, and

CCCU. By untangling the contemporary interconnectedness of these three components, one can begin to grasp the relationships they have forged in the past quarter-century. Within the voluntaristic, competitive, and homogenizing world of evangelical Protestantism in the 1960s and 1970s, the growing acceptability of elite sport made it the perfect

On Super Bowl weekend each January, AIA presents its Bart Starr Award to a prominent Christian playing football. Cris Carter of the Minnesota Vikings received the award in 1995.

means to accomplishing a variety of ends for churches and colleges. Once groups like the FCA and AIA had helped to legitimize big-time sport among evangelicals, it was a small step for the churches and colleges to assimilate sports into their programs.

For churches and colleges, attracting members and students was a process not unlike that discovered by the revivalists and evangelists a century earlier. What worked for D. L. Moody and J. E. K. Studd could work for Cornerstone College and Highland Park Presbyterian Church as well. Not only would the unchurched listen to a famous athlete or to a revivalist using sports metaphors, they might also choose an evangelical church or college in part on the basis of its athletic programs. The twin goals of "making the bad of society good and the good of society better" were simply relocated within evangelical churches and colleges. Sport was still perceived as valuable, largely on the basis of its ability to provide the competitive edge necessary to the purposes of voluntaristic evangelical organizations.

Interpreting the Ethos of Modern Evangelical Muscular Christianity

Religion and Sport in New Patterns of Cultural Reinforcement

Muscular Christian Bill McCartney is an assertive and complex personality. For thirteen years, he was the eminently successful head football coach of the Colorado University Buffalos. Then he suddenly walked away from his post after Colorado's convincing victory over Notre Dame in the 1995 Fiesta Bowl. McCartney also has been a passionate muscular Christian for some time and has managed to spark controversy, deserving or not. Expressing his pro-life and antihomosexuality views got him into trouble with the university administration, and implicitly using religious criteria in recruiting got him into trouble with the American Civil Liberties Union. To two journalists, McCartney's "life has been a veritable battleground, the imperatives involved in running a big-time college football program clashing with those of a would-be spiritualist [sic]."[1]

Events of 1990 most readily illustrate both the passion and the potential cross-purposes in McCartney's muscular Christian career. Although Colorado won the mythical college football championship that year, for many the championship was tainted by Colorado's ungraceful victory in a crucial game at Missouri earlier in the season. On the final play of that game, Colorado scored the winning touchdown, but it occurred on a fifth down after the officials lost count. McCartney, the driven coach of a team striving for the national championship, was confronted with McCartney, the Christian activist well known for his convictions. McCartney the coach won.

What made that game result especially poignant was its occurring during the fiftieth anniversary year of a similar situation between Cornell and Dartmouth. Cornell was riding an eighteen-game undefeated streak and a number two ranking when it ran into a stubborn Dartmouth underdog on Saturday, November 16, 1940. Cornell won the game 7-3, but only after the officials inadvertently gave it five downs.

By Tuesday of the following week, Cornell coach Carl Snavely and President Edmund Ezra Day had taken action "unprecedented in intercollegiate football. . . . Cornell had the sportsmanship to yield a success it felt it had not rightfully earned. . . . Cornell was willing to make the correction in spite of the blow it delivered to its magnificent record."[2] The Cornell president explained, "If we hadn't made that decision, we'd have been explaining that game as long as football has a place in intercollegiate athletics—and I want no long count in Cornell's athletic history."[3] One journalist optimistically predicted, "The action of the Cornell authorities may invite claims for similar action by other colleges in the future."[4]

Bill McCartney and Colorado University president William Baughn took no similar action following their 33-31 victory on October 6, 1990. McCartney initially justified the victory by complaining that the Missouri players had gotten up too slowly after Colorado's offensive plays, and besides, Missouri's field was slippery. "We slipped and slid all day, or we would have put more points on the board."[5] In an interview for the *More Than a Game* cable television series on modern sport, McCartney laid out a more extensive justification, including a unique biblical interpretation.

> It just so happened that we were granted an extra down, and there are a lot of people who could have called attention to it. . . . Had we known and proceeded with it, I don't think we could live with ourselves. But . . . it was ten minutes after the game before I . . . came to an awareness that we had scored on fifth down. . . .
>
> I have to answer to my team. I can't answer to everybody out there. And there is a verse in Scripture; it's 1 Corinthians 4:4. And it says, "My conscience is clear, but that does not make me innocent. It is the Lord who judges me." And you see, only the Lord can judge a man's innermost thoughts. . . .
>
> I do not have any guilt attached to the decisions that we made. I felt like we earned everything that we got, and we operated within the rules as they were presented to us.[6]

Meanwhile, Bill McCartney the activist Christian was planning a meeting in the summer of 1991 for men concerned with assuming "a new level of spiritual leadership and vitality in [their] home, church, and community."[7] McCartney had been active in his local evangelical-charismatic Vineyard fellowship, especially with men having similar concerns. Eventually their group, which met regularly for prayer, fasting, and fellowship, grew beyond local bounds. They named themselves Promise Keepers. In the summer of 1991, the Promise Keepers held their first rally, and it attracted more than four thousand middle-aged men, most of whom were white. While his main concerns at that meeting were with issues of marriage and accountability, McCartney also was struck by the audience's homogeneity. "The absence of men of color somehow hit me between the eyes, and in that moment, the Spirit of God clearly said to my spirit, 'You can fill that stadium, but if men of other races aren't there, I won't be there, either.'"[8]

Through McCartney's capable leadership, Promise Keepers attracted larger and larger crowds, often with a significant multiracial presence. It also became "a summer ritual for churches large and small to ship busloads of men to its conference sites across the country."[9] McCartney's muscular Christian persona served as a powerful attraction. "What gives McCartney such influence . . . is his image as a championship-winning football coach who has taken a very public stand about his faith and about being a good husband and father."[10] But in the mid-1990s the rapid growth of such a group also fit logically into the context of the battles being waged on several moral fronts. More than anything else, the attraction of Bill McCartney, the "moral crusader," symbolized the recent transition of the ethos, or character, of evangelical muscular Christianity along both reformulated theological and new moral lines. Thus the final stage of the modern movement invites an interpretation of the most recent patterns of evangelical and cultural reinforcement.

Moral Crusaders in the Culture Wars

More often than not, the "moral dimension" of sport places it in a position of conservatively reflecting and reinforcing the existing norms and values of its cultural setting. During the 1950s and 1960s, as sport was being redefined in relationship to the American way of life, the assumptions of sport's worth as a character-building force brought it into a pattern of affinity with the prevailing mores of the day. One possible exception in which a change in sport preceded changes in the culture was Branch Rickey's moral motivation to racially integrate baseball, although even then his decisions also made good economic sense.

Then in the 1970s and 1980s with the advent of Baseball Chapel, PAO, and sports chaplains, the views of evangelical Christianity became more pronounced as part of this conservative moral and political alliance in sport. One example is evangelicalism's nonresponse to one of the most dramatic changes in sport over the past quarter-century—the increasing presence of girls and women at virtually every level of sport in the "post–Title IX era." Why "gender equity" and its moral implications have not gotten onto the evangelical muscular Christian agenda will be explained further below.

The 1980s and early 1990s, however, have been a time of cultural cross-purposes in America. On the one hand, twelve years of Republican politics and values, symbolized by Vice President Dan Quayle's challenge to the morality of television's Murphy Brown, indicated a traditional cultural mood. On the other hand, the themes of "political correctness" and multiculturalism reflected another cultural movement in an opposite, postmodern direction. The dramatic contrast between the positions of Dan Quayle and Murphy Brown—between the "priests" of cultural conservatism and the "prophets" of cultural change—was captured symbolically by sociologist James Davison Hunter in the metaphor of his book title *Culture Wars*. For Hunter the two positions are held by the "orthodox" and "progressive" extremes in society. Although a "middle" may exist between these poles, Hunter's point is that it rarely gets acknowledged in the midst of the media-driven rhetoric of the combatants.[11]

Implicitly, the world of sport probably has more in common with the conservative, orthodox position. It socializes well its youthful participants to accept society's values as articulated by their coaches and administrators. Subculturally, its values orientation and "creed" likely exist in a relationship of elective affinity to the larger patterns of culture—to the degree that any such consensus still exists.[12] Thus, "Stay in school" and "Just say no" and all the public service announcements sponsored on television by the NFL, the NCAA, and the NBA attempt to add a measure of the prestige of and identity with elite sport that support the American way of life. The persisting problem is that Charles Barkley, Tonya Harding, Mike Tyson, Dennis Rodman, and numerous other controversial sports figures have sent out dissonant messages as well. Meanwhile, evangelical muscular Christianity has elected not to address these mixed messages.

The values of the orthodox party typically have been reflected in personal moral and behavioral norms—not usually in terms of a more structurally based agenda—often not unlike those articulated by representatives of the New Religious Right. Examples of this recent elective affinity suggest that the conservative moral positions often verbalized by representatives of big-time sport, by spokespersons for evangelical Christianity, and by the orthodox party in the recent culture wars again have found each other. What has resulted, however, is a new group of muscular Christian moral crusaders with a quite different perspective from those taken by Tom Brown or Amos Alonzo Stagg, or even Gil Dodds.

Bill Glass, Joe Namath, and Prison Evangelism

This point can be made more decisively by a contrast with an individual "moral crusader" of a recent era but another ilk—Bill Glass. After Glass retired from the NFL in 1969, he shifted into a full-time pattern of evangelistic and revival meetings. In the late 1960s Glass added a moral dimension to his preaching. Some of his attacks were general jeremiads against the "new morality," which he labeled "the biggest lie ever propagated on the face of the earth," or against "expanding moral decay, [as] evil is expanding; there is a spread of curruptiveness [sic] now."[13]

But Glass also got increasingly specific in his moral pronouncements. His most frequent target was quarterback Joe Namath of the 1969 Super Bowl champion New York Jets. Namath was known for his hedonistic lifestyle, and to Glass, who saw Namath as "a moral ignoramus," he personified much that was morally deficient in the modern world—"free love"; "living with an unmarried woman, drinking—that's not the way to set an example"; "a whole new moral stance"; "popularized the Playboy philosophy more than Playboy has."[14]

In early 1971 Glass enlisted John Underwood, the respected writer with Sports Illustrated, to collaborate with him on a book. Underwood encouraged Glass, "Don't give it any particular order, just ramble around a little. So far we have an argument: the gospels according to Joe Namath, Jim Bouton, et al, are bad news. We need more than an argument. . . . We need a whole book. We have to maintain a theme for, say, 250 pages."[15] Although Underwood was a good writer and Glass already a published author, this book idea never came to fruition. Glass was still on the moral offensive in 1973 and still fuming about Namath, "He believes that as long as you have two consenting adults, everything is fine. He's throwing rocks at the biblical stance, which I think is wrong."[16]

In the meantime, Glass had received a challenge that diverted his attention from the behavior of Joe Namath and friends and infused him with an alternative muscular Christian moral vision. In 1972 an acquaintance who was a bank president encouraged Glass to begin a prison ministry. That changed Glass's goals in preaching and his entire career. As a senior at Baylor, Glass had visited an Indiana prison with a group that included the football great Otto Graham. The memories were so vivid and so negative that Glass determined "that I would never come back to a prison again."[17] But he did.

Since his first prison crusade at Marion in Ohio in 1972, Glass has conducted hundreds of Total Person Prison Weekends. What he learned in the early days in Texas Baptist churches still holds. "Professional athletes and entertainers who can draw a crowd of inmates who normally would be 'turned off' by religious activities, who deliberately perform in a secular manner but who close their performances with short Christian testimonies" are often effective as means to evangelism among the incarcerated.[18]

Glass's prison ministry is clearly evangelistic, and his involvement of other athletes is consistent with most muscular Christian organizations' goals. Yet he was perhaps the first of the modern muscular Christians to add a dimension of social activism to the more traditional forms of evangelism, not unlike Amos Alonzo Stagg's founding of the Yale Mission in the late 1800s. Prison reform may not be the primary focus of Glass's crusades, but his efforts on behalf of thousands of prisoners—men and women—for more than two decades have caught the attention of the prison establishment. At a minimum, that group perceives him as a "bridge" from the criminal justice system to the outside world at both individual and more systemic levels. He has benefited indirectly from an informal alliance with Charles Colson's parallel efforts in jails and prisons.

One variation Glass has incorporated into his prison weekend strategy is to involve dozens of laypersons, who act as unofficial counselors when prisoners respond to Glass's evangelistic appeals. Glass has sensitized hundreds of individuals and local churches to the human and social plight of the incarcerated in addition to their spiritual needs.

In terms of the culture wars metaphor, one cannot easily determine whether Glass's efforts better represent an orthodox or a progressive position. The point here is more a chronological one that places Glass's efforts in the 1970s, prior to the culturally divisive issues of the 1980s and 1990s. Joe Namath was an easy and controversial target for moral indignation in the late 1960s and early 1970s, and Glass's pronouncements fit into his larger evangelistic purposes at that time. But in both his moral outrage with Namath and his work as a prison evangelist, Glass was the individual muscular Christian moral voice, a man ahead of his time. He may have been an inadvertent prototype of the subsequent muscular Christian moral crusaders without necessarily placing his activities in the context of the more highly charged culture wars.

Bill McCartney, A. C. Green, and Personal Morality Wars

If the evangelical muscular Christian movement has joined forces with the New Religious Right on the orthodox side in the culture wars, their shared concerns should emphasize matters of personal and private morality. Sociologist Wuthnow has argued, however, that in the late 1970s and into the 1980s, the New Religious Right shifted the "symbolic boundaries" by redefining issues that previously had been matters of personal morality. These redefinitions reflected the distinction between private and public morality as well as the relationship among morality, religion, and politics. The "old boundaries that had separated religion, morality, and politics, or at least . . . how they were to be related, had become ambiguous. . . . It was useful to draw a close connection between religion and morality, especially by citing biblical injunctions in support of moral claims. . . . Conservative leaders also sought to legitimate their vision of morality as part of the broader political arena."[19]

By shifting these boundaries, the conservative leaders were able also to recast morality as a matter of faith "on which there was apparently broad agreement among various conservative religious groups, thereby mitigating the accusation that sectarian religion was involved in politics."[20]

At the same time, these private-public moral boundaries were redefined within sport. Attention was increasingly directed toward the moral lives of athletes and to the relationship between their on-the-field performances and off-the-field morality and ethics. Most of these athletes had little to do with the muscular Christian movement (although Steve Howe and Darryl Strawberry—both of whom struggled with drugs and other problems—were two who had been identified with it), but the questions raised by fans and the media were often tinged with Tom Brown–like assumptions.

That mainstream sport was becoming infused with the moral relativism of the progressive position became apparent as fans and sports officials alike grappled with the moral dilemmas of sport in the 1980s and 1990s. Perhaps the case of Pete Rose brought all of this to a head. Although Rose was a hero in the sense of accumulating more base hits than any other major league baseball player ever, should he be elected to baseball's Hall of Fame if he also had bet illegally on sporting events and possibly on contests in which he participated? Meanwhile, boxing champion Mike Tyson was on trial for the rape of a young beauty contest participant, and the matter of their having sexual contact was never in doubt. The question was whether the woman had consented. Steroid use seemed out of control in the NFL, and Olympic sprinter Ben Johnson's use of performance-enhancing drugs in international competitions raised further questions about sport's ability to police itself, let alone be a bastion of building character. Although his transgressions may not equal those of Tyson and Johnson, Michael Jordan—arguably the best basketball player ever—apparently wagered over a million dollars during his golfing expeditions and at Atlantic City casinos, "admitted under oath that he had lost the money," and then "was warned by the NBA to be careful" about his associations.[21]

The contexts, then, are overlapping, with concerns about morality from the larger culture, from evangelicalism, and from sport all coming together. As the larger culture dichotomizes along the orthodox versus progressive lines, the New Religious Right has pulled much of evangelicalism toward the "orthodox right" by redefining what had been private moral issues in terms of Christian responsibility within the public, cultural domain.[22]

Enter Bill McCartney, A. C. Green, and the new "moral crusaders." Unlike Bill Glass in an earlier era, their approach is based on a twofold rationale for assuming the mantle of moral and cultural spokespersons. This rationale is derived from their dual identity as evangelical Christians and sports heroes, resulting in an apparently overlapping "moral absolutist" position. In other words, their identity as evangelical Christians is bound to a particular hermeneutical understanding of the Scriptures, their normative teachings, and their ethical implications as being absolute and binding for all people at all times. Whether today's muscular Christians have been successful in applying these ethical standards consistently in their sports is a related but separate concern, as Christopher Stevenson has demonstrated.[23]

In contrast, the progressive view holds out for a more culturally relative and situational approach to ethical behavior.[24] In some cases, the moral crusaders concede that "secularists" may accomplish some short-term moral good, but the evangelical hermeneutic implies that those good deeds are built on relativism and therefore are inherently self-limiting. To evangelical muscular Christians, only an absolutist ethic derived from their literal approach to the Bible can withstand the slippery slope of ethical relativism and thus provide solutions to the moral uncertainties of the modern world.

Also, the moral crusaders invoke an implicit new version of the 140-year-old muscular Christian myth. If one really believes that sport builds character, then these crusaders have a second advantage not available to nonsporting individuals who may share their moral concerns. The supposed "lessons of the locker room," learned only through training and competition, are assumed to provide Bill McCartney and friends with insight and a perspective on moral issues that people from any other background simply do not have. For many Promise Keepers, McCartney's "image as a championship-winning football coach"[25] apparently is so overarching and valid that they assume he also possesses superior wisdom about being a good husband and father.

The new moral crusaders have fused a certitude about how to proceed on moral issues which comes from this combination of the biblically based, absolutist ethic and unique wisdom gained from participation in big-time sport. When A. C. Green and his Athletes for Abstinence carry their message about sexual activity to teenagers living in an AIDS-infested world, the certitude behind their message is similarly two-pronged: Just say no to premarital sexual activity because that's what the Bible says, and that's what I as an elite athlete know is best for you.

A. C. Green joined the Los Angeles Lakers in 1985 following a successful college basketball career at Oregon State. In Los Angeles he became convinced that God "chose me for a vocation of basketball and, in time, for an avocation of influencing the next generation." Initially that meant that "God would use my basketball career as a platform from which I could influence young people."[26] In 1989 that conviction led to the "A. C. Green Foundation for Youth to help build hope, confidence and self-esteem in young people. . . . I want to become the one who reaches out and helps others to reach out, such as corporations and small businesses."[27]

That foundation was well established, and Green was active in his outreach work when Magic Johnson stunned his Laker teammates and the entire sports community with his announcement on November 7, 1991 that he had tested positive for HIV. Johnson began appearing on television talk shows, "saying that condoms could have saved him from catching the disease." Green, however, "knew through my abstinence work that this wasn't true. Abstinence is the only 100-percent-sure way to keep from catching diseases, including AIDS."[28] The result was Green's forming AFA "to teach that the only 100-percent-sure way to avoid STDs [sexually transmitted diseases], unwanted pregnancies and a lot of the consequences of ending a sexual relationship is sexual abstinence."[29]

Green's position, perhaps even more than McCartney's, is derived from his more consistent application of the twofold moral absolutist view. In Green's case, combining what the Bible says about sex outside of marriage and his observation of the results of sexual promiscuity by fellow athletes constitutes the ultimate moral authority. "We need a higher standard by which to govern our sexuality. . . . The way I've chosen is the best way. I've been criticized and ridiculed, but I'm not afraid to stand alone on this issue if I have to. I've seen all the options, and I'm not going to back down."[30] Likewise, former Chicago Bears star Mike Singletary and former all-star pitcher Tim Burke have become spokespersons on behalf of supporting children, stemming child abuse, and promoting adoption. Their platforms are derived from the combined, perceived legitimacy of their biblical views and sporting experiences. Still, it is the Promise Keepers (whose dramatic growth is due in large part to McCartney's biblically and athletically based moral authority) who have catapulted to the forefront of the new moral crusaders in sport.

Most of the men refer to McCartney as "Coach," which seems appropriate given the inspirational, locker-room brand of pep talk he delivers. "We're calling men of God to battle—we will retreat no more," the coach declares. Many, like Gary Oliver, see McCartney as the spark igniting the Christian men's movement.

"The burden that God gave to Bill McCartney opened the whole thing up. It gave direction and clarity to it." The coach is someone with whom men can identify. Indeed, the essence of many a Promise Keeper's experience can be found in McCartney's own story.[31]

While this recent shift of evangelical muscular Christians into areas of public moral concern seems to go beyond earlier institutionalized functions and goals of the movement, there may be one historical precedent from the philosophical underpinnings of sport. Physical educators often use the phrases "of the physical," "through the physical," and "in the physical" to contrast differing philosophies for participation in physical activity. What the new moral crusaders seem to be combining intuitively are their own versions of the "through the physical" and "in the physical" philosophies.

"Through the physical" is embodied in the old, Tom Brown–like attitude of building character and manliness through sport. That still exists. What McCartney and the moral crusaders also assume is a confidence based on "in the physical." The inherent result of the sporting experience is a depth of understanding not available to nonsporting mortals.[32]

Using sporting experiences as a basis for making moral pronouncements goes significantly beyond the earlier uses of sport for evangelism or internationalizing the church's mission. The activity of individuals like Singletary and organizational spokespersons like Green and McCartney needs to be contextualized in the changing moral moods of sport, evangelical religion, and the culture wars of the 1980s and 1990s. The biblically based authority of the orthodox position together with the confidence placed in sports spokespersons provide muscular Christians the cultural legitimacy to make their moral pronouncements.

Recreating the Myth of Muscular Christianity on Modern Evangelical Terms

The broader cultural meaning of these morally crusading muscular Christians' efforts in the 1980s and 1990s can be understood best in terms of the current ethos and myth of the movement that approaches a half-century duration since the time of reengagement.

When Thomas Hughes wrote *Tom Brown's Schooldays* and *Tom Brown at Oxford,* he took advantage of an early form of the "myth" of muscular Christianity already in place in Britain. That myth has been the subject of much scholarly discussion, and Michael Oriard has traced its origins to "concern for physical health in the 1830s, gain[ing] momentum as sport was increasingly seen to be an agent for both the social control of the working classes (as 'rational recreation') and the character-molding of their future rulers, and reached its jingoistic extreme with the notion that cricket and rugby were ideal preparations for military and imperial responsibilities in ruling a colonial empire."[33]

For muscular Christianity to thrive in the United States, however, Oriard also asserts that as an "American athletic movement [it] *had* to have a religious impetus. . . . [T]hat muscular Christianity beginning in the 1850s arranged the marriage of sport and morality within the YMCA and other religious organizations makes obvious sense."[34]

The position of this book, however, has been that such an orthodox telling of the muscular Christian myth is still only half (or perhaps two-thirds) of the American story. Arguably, the Northfield participants were well on their way to constructing another peculiarly American version of the muscular Christian myth whereby sport might be valued primarily as a means to personal manly holiness and the "evangelization of the world in this generation." The prob-

213

lem is that such a reconstructed myth never was completely formulated. By the time of Billy Sunday just two decades later, the evangelicals-becoming-fundamentalists were already headed for a total disengagement from sport and from any previous or existing versions of muscular Christianity's mythical qualities.

Since the 1960s, however, the evangelical muscular Christian movement has attempted a modern reconstruction of the myth of muscular Christianity. In one sense, the modern evangelicals have started from scratch. That is, they appear virtually unaware of Charles Kingsley, Thomas Hughes, and Tom Brown. They all know something about Billy Sunday.

Given the popularity of the movie *Chariots of Fire,* some of them know about Eric Liddell in the 1920s. A few know about C. T. Studd and the Cambridge Seven.[35] Not many have heard much about Gil Dodds. All of this means that modern muscular Christians have constructed a new, ahistorical version of the myth which undergirds their now well-institutionalized efforts at evangelism and missionary activity. But they have little beyond their conservative Protestant roots in Billy Graham– and Bill Bright–related evangelistic activity to guide them.

The overriding characteristic of the myth of modern evangelical muscular Christianity is that it appears to have little to do with a theological foundation in specific beliefs. Perhaps that should not be surprising because evangelicals have not given much attention to the disciplined construction of a formal theological system. Instead, evangelicals are more concerned with "making the bad of society good" and thereby preparing for the coming of the kingdom of God. Evangelicals are about correct beliefs and theology, but primarily when those affect their larger concern with evangelizing the world. A reconstructed myth must connect the value of sport to the evangelical church's goals of evangelism and saving souls. Religious historian Nathan Hatch has argued persuasively that evangelicals in the twentieth century "have virtually organized their faith around the issue of communicating the gospel,"[36] so that any myth of modern muscular Christianity would have to be consonant with that commitment. In marked contrast to a core element of the Tom Brown myth of muscular Christianity that "sport builds character" or "sport builds manliness," the essential core of the modern myth must be something like "sport enhances the gospel" or "sport helps save souls."

Specifically, the myth of modern evangelical muscular Christianity appears to include five essential elements, some of which are articulated and some of which lie just beneath the surface of any activity oriented toward evangelism.

1. Pragmatic utility. The worth of sport is essentially determined by its utilitarian effectiveness as a means to Christian conversion. The contrast between the 1850s myth and the 1990s version is dramatized along an intrinsic-to-extrinsic continuum. For Charles Kingsley, Thomas Hughes, and some of the first-generation American muscular Christians, sport had inherent value. Participation was an end in itself, and the products of participation were some "good things," including manliness, health, and morality. Any other by-products were significant but not the primary purpose.

In contrast, most evangelical muscular Christians today can think of sport only in more extrinsic, utilitarian ways. If Hatch is correct, they do so because that's the way they have "organized their faith." The growing popularity of sports and the increasing numbers of athletes willing to accept the gospel of evangelical muscular Christianity then become *post hoc* verification that "God must be blessing Christians in sports." Likewise a published "History and Philosophy of the NCCAA" includes the overt statement, "The NCCAA believes: That athletics are a means to an end; not an end in themselves."[37] Eddie Waxer of the ISC has personified this element of the modern myth as much as anyone. He forthrightly contends that in the pragmatism of seeking any means to a competitive edge, muscular Christians find the elective affinity for reaching athletes with the Christian message.[38] If it works, then the message must be correct.

2. *Meritocratic democracy.* The meritocratic nature of American sports is an appropriate model for the democratic appeal of muscular Christianity. In meritocracies, individuals are accepted and evaluated on the basis of their own decisions and performances. Historian Hatch described why the "central dynamic" behind American evangelicalism is its "democratic orientation," which includes three aspects—audience centeredness, intellectual openness to all, and organizational pluralism and innovation.[39] While the first and third of Hatch's aspects capture the ethos of modern muscular Christianity, exactly why this works as well as it does mythically is the result of a further elective affinity.

One powerful point of the operant creed of American sport is that the world of sport is a meritocracy; that is, "if you're good enough, you'll make it." Americans view sport as one of the few "level grounds," where each competitor has an equal opportunity and can be compared to all others on the basis of objective, individual performances. This part of the sports creed is often invoked, for example, when contrasting the presence of African-American athletes in elite sport in 1950 and 1990. "If blacks are as good as whites, they'll make it." For the evangelical muscular Christian oriented to an individualistic and democratic biblical appeal, these Christian and SportsWorld versions of the myth of democracy and meritocracy find each other—on the playing field and in the chapel talk before the game.

3. *Competitive virtue.* Competition and winning are consistent with the teachings of Jesus and the writings of the apostle Paul. Ironically, although sports operate on the basis of a "zero-sum-game"—for every winner, there must be a loser—evangelical Christianity's gospel does not. It emphasizes an open appeal based on a "variable-sum-game"—God's grace is unlimited, and "whosoever will may come." Thus zero-sum competition and winning need justification. To many evangelical muscular Christians, the "culture wars" are really more like "spiritual wars," with the devil the ultimate enemy to be defeated. The proof of Jesus' competi-

tiveness is borne out in the gospel record of his temptation and victory over the devil. "The 'Wilderness Games' (the temptation) showed Jesus to be a competitor of discernment, diligence, and dedication. Today's competitors need to emulate his example."[40] Or in the words of Brett Butler of the New York Mets, "You can be a Christian and still be a hard-nosed player. If Christ were a ballplayer, he'd be the best there was. He'd take out the guy at second base, then he'd say, 'I love you,' pick him up, slap him on the butt and come back to the dugout. . . . God doesn't say you can't get mad or frustrated. Jesus flipped tables in the temple."[41]

Similarly, the Christian church has a long history of hermeneutical interest in Paul's use of athletic metaphors. To the modern muscular Christian, they are *ipso facto* proof that he believed "that the lessons learned through athletic competition can have carry-over value to the competition involved in the Christian experience." By contrast, "someone else would have to be the advocate for play. Paul is surely an advocate for competition—teeth-gritting, back-bending, leg-pumping, mind-setting, heart-willing competition."[42] What is new here is that the significance attached to Paul's athletic metaphors is located within the twentieth century American emphasis on sports as a zero-sum setting that extols the virtues of competition and winning, with little attention to the inherent value of participation.

4. Heroic models. Sport provides the predominant context for the heroes and role models American youth need, especially as a demonstration of Christianity's continuing relevance. The importance of heroes easily transcends both muscular Christianity and the world of sport. But a cursory glance over the shelves of a Christian bookstore or through the pages of *Campus Life* magazine verifies how powerful the heroic sports image is for the evangelical subculture.

With rare exceptions, however, such as the writing of Dave Dravecky as he recovers from cancer or of Dennis Byrd—the former New York Jets football player—as he seeks restoration from paralysis,[43] the heroic images projected by modern muscular Christianity reflect more closely the heroes of secular-ized sports than any biblical images. Sport historian Donald Mrozek, for example, has implicated the modern sports hero as "one identified not by his character but by his deeds."[44] Or in the words of the authors of *Habits of the Heart*, "'Being good' becomes a matter of being good *at things.*"[45] If evan-gelical muscular Christianity has borrowed its projection of heroic models from secularized sport, it also has not been able to provide the fuller range of character traits and behav-iors included in acting human, which is a truly biblical approach to presenting heroes, "warts and all." Onetime mus-cular Christian heroes such as baseball players Steve Howe and Darryl Strawberry simply disappear from view, with no effort to portray them realistically as Christians who stum-bled. Only a selectively truncated image of the muscular Christian models from big-time sport is presented.

5. *Therapeutic self-control.* Improved performance in sports is possible when one follows a disciplined regimen to achieve a level of self-control, like a mature Christian. This final ele-ment of the modern myth appears at first glance to share with its historical British counterpart an emphasis on moral and ethical virtue resulting from sports participation. In fact, what has occurred in the intervening 140 years is a "radical repsy-chologizing" of the values of involvement. Muscular Chris-tian rhetoric frequently extols participation for its pop-psy-chological worth, rather than for ethical outcomes. Without empirical support for the secularized version of the charac-ter-building power of sport, many muscular Christians instead draw a parallel between psychologized approaches to sports performance and maturing in the Christian experience.

One example of this is provided by author Wes Neal, orig-inator of the "total release performance" amalgam of ath-letic training tips, pop psychology, and biblical aphorisms. Neal is a onetime AIA staff member and deserves credit for his creativity in communicating his interesting ideas to a popular audience. He writes, "If you give a total release of yourself toward becoming like Jesus in your athletic performance, you will never look on a defeat from an opponent as a loss."[46] Elsewhere Neal exhorted, "Let me suggest one standard that not only demonstrates a Christian attitude, but also will help you as an athlete. . . . *Help other people succeed!* . . . Keep in mind that helping others succeed is part of the ethical code God wants us to have."[47] He followed this by quoting Philippians 2:3–4. Aspects of Neal's approach may be idiosyncratic. Yet muscular Christian literature is replete with discussions of motivation, toughness, endurance, and consistency from authors who similarly combine allusions to the Bible with a kind of folk psychology in making applications to sports performance.

Similarly, in contrast to the original Tom Brown myth, one is reminded that the Northfield emphases on power and victory have not disappeared. More powerful today, however, are the symbols from humanistic psychology that bridge biblical images and sports settings. Assuming that the value of modern sport is tied to both the methods of communicating the Christian message and the goal of converting individuals, most contemporary muscular Christians can assert that God has raised up culturally important modern sport for the advantage of the movement. Furthermore, one can infer some grand spiritual purpose in the elective affinity between evangelical Christianity and modern sport represented by these five elements—pragmatic utility, meritocratic democracy, competitive virtue, heroic models, and therapeutic self-control.

In the absence of a systematically theological approach among evangelicals to their mission and self-understanding, implicit and explicit expressions of this myth have arisen to constitute a kind of "folk theology of muscular Christianity." To the degree that any religious or social movement relies on a shared myth or ideology, evangelical muscular Christians have developed a folk theology built upon the five-point myth outlined above. In the mid-1980s, journalist Carol Flake summarized one version of this folk theology in operation: "The resurgence of evangelicalism in America had brought with it a revival of muscular Christianity and a return to the social

Darwinism of the athletic arena. Jesus the teacher had become Christ the competitor. . . . From the pulpit, preachers prayed for winning seasons, sprinkling their sermons with so much athletic symbolism that they sometimes sounded like color commentators on TV sports broadcasts."[48]

On the one hand, one might argue that such a folk theology is functional and therefore needed. In many contexts it communicates an underlying biblical "truth" by taking advantage of the SportsWorld rhetoric and symbols shared by evangelicals and the wider culture. The following example is from a missions conference in 1990 at a suburban Baptist church in the Midwest. In a sermon titled "His Coming and Our Going," the speaker employed an analogy from basketball to make an important point.

> I imagine if we have any basketball fans here, they are Bulls' fans. . . . Since Michael Jordan has come, I have gotten interested in basketball again in a very special way, and I like to watch it on TV.
>
> My wife will say, "Honey, dinner is ready." "That's great, Honey, but there are only two minutes left in the game. . . ." "Well, I guess it could wait two minutes." Five minutes later, "Honey, dinner is ready. Are you coming?" "Honey, there is only a minute and a half left." "You said there were only two minutes left five minutes ago." "I know, but . . . they have had three timeouts. And it's still another minute and a half." What had happened?
>
> You see, now in the last two minutes, it's gotten really serious. Now they're down to the very end. Now they're really working at it. Have you noticed how the complexion changes in just the last few minutes of the game? They really get serious.
>
> How would that game and many other games change, if only the referee knew when he was going to blow the final whistle? Every two minutes would be the final two minutes. We're always living on the edge of eternity.[49]

What makes this story work as a sermon illustration are the shared assumptions that this speaker can make in an evangelical church in the 1990s. He is able to borrow a broadly understood collection of details—about watching sports on television and about the conclusion of a game—to make his point. Most of his listeners know exactly what he is describing, and "if only the referee knew when he was going to blow the final whistle" makes perfect premillennial sense to them. He and they have no difficulty juxtaposing the athletic and theological connotations of his story.

Similarly, evangelical author Tim Stafford once crafted a provocative essay comparing his attachment to baseball with the Christian doctrine of the atonement. The essay assumes that although "the Bible teaches vicarious atonement," it is "how the Atonement works [that] no one quite understands."[50] Stafford sought to answer the question "how can something that the Oakland Athletics do affect me?" in order to grasp, in much the same way as "baseball fans believe that they gain from their team's success, that Jesus' death and resurrection are in fact to our credit." Stafford concluded that "trust in vicarious benefits is a fundamental part of our make-up. It is an ineradicable belief of the heart that speaks of something more than we understand. We believe, though we cannot explain, that our heroes' victories are our own."[51]

If most of the muscular Christian usage of sports rhetoric and symbols resembled these two examples, things would be in reasonably good order theologically, and a folk theology of muscular Christianity might never have emerged. That is not the case, however, for at least two reasons. First, athletes and sports-related personnel are assumed to have adequate biblical and theological knowledge, based largely on the legitimation they enjoy as sports heroes. In public settings they talk about what they know best—the world of sport—and use the symbols and rhetoric of that world. Typically, they attempt to add some spiritual principle or theological insight which is often misguided, if not clearly incorrect, because that is why they were invited to speak in the first place.

For example, an elite-sport speaker recently sought to make such a connection for evangelical students at a Christian college. In his talk, he invoked a number of current

221

sports cliches, including the need to be "focused." After describing the importance of focusing in athletic performance, he then shifted into a folk theologizing mode. He spoke more ambiguously of the necessity of focusing on Jesus as a parallel experience of similar importance. In the absence of a sound biblical or theological background, muscular Christian heroes utilize the symbols they know best. They then extrapolate to a theology that is grounded more in SportsWorld rhetoric than orthodox Christian teaching.

This chapel speaker's awkward use of the folk theology of sport also illustrates a second reason for the folk theologizing. What the chapel speaker did was essentially the reverse of what the missionary speaker and author Stafford attempted above. Both of them began with a biblical or theological principle and then appealed to their audiences' familiarity with sports to illustrate and illuminate their points. They were able to do so because they were theologically informed evangelicals whose primary identities were outside the sports subculture. For them, the rhetoric and symbols of sport were only a secondary means to making their theological point.

Another example of the folk theology of muscular Christianity is found in the speaking and writing of former NFL linebacker Dave Simmons, also one of the modern moral crusaders. Simmons has a background in Campus Crusade and AIA, and he reflects positively his experiences in football and ministry. He is the founder of Dad the Family Shepherd, a "ministry that assists the local church to equip their men to be better fathers."[52] In his book *Dad the Family Coach,* Simmons begins with an observation about how the NFL "underwent a revolution in leadership philosophy." Its "blood-n-guts, 'You're an animal'" coaches were replaced by more of a business-administration approach to coaching by "masters of football craft" who "were not afraid to invest their hearts into their teams—they treated the players with dignity."[53]

From this observation, Simmons shifts to the main point of the chapter—that "leadership in the home must be more dimensional than just spelling out the rules and squeezing kids into conformity. A wise family shepherd uses state-of-the-art skills, his mind, and his heart. He is pleased to impart not only his message but his life." This practical, pop-psychology appeal is buttressed with a biblical reference. "The Bible describes good leadership as a careful blend of skills and heart: 'So he shepherded them according to the integrity of his heart, and guided them with his skillful hands' (Ps. 78:72)."[54] In less than two brief paragraphs, Simmons moves from sports symbols to those of pop psychology to a requisite Bible verse, deftly employing the folk theology of muscular Christianity to communicate how fathers should lead their children.

Still other common examples of folk theologizing occur when evangelical muscular Christians interpret the apostle Paul's four primary uses of sporting metaphors. As Oriard has suggested, the church has a long history of using these Pauline texts in efforts to connect "religious and secular ideas, accommodating religious tradition to an increasingly secularized world." Thus, "Paul wrote to the Philippians of 'press[ing] toward the mark, for the prize of the high calling of God in Christ Jesus' (Phil. 3:14); to the Corinthians of running a race 'that ye may obtain [the prize]' (1 Cor. 9:24); to the Ephesians of 'wrestl[ing] not against flesh and blood, but against principalities, against powers, against the rulers of the darkness of the world' (Eph. 6:12); to Timothy of having 'fought a good fight' and 'finished my course,' for which a crown of righteousness awaited him in heaven (2 Tim. 4:7–8)."[55]

Obviously, current muscular Christians have every right to use these texts in their preaching. Perhaps not so obvious, however, is the difference between how past Christians and current muscular Christians approach these texts and their athletic metaphors. Many of today's speakers look at these texts primarily from the perspective of the sports subculture, not primarily as preachers or theologians. But like all preachers, they "see what they want to see" in preparing their sermons. These modern speakers see twentieth-century American sport first; only secondarily do they see the

223

spiritual principles that Paul might have had in mind in the first century. An inadequate background in theology and hermeneutics is compounded by their primary hermeneutical perspective originating in SportsWorld.

One might suggest that these speakers have perpetuated the myth and folk theology of muscular Christianity because no alternative models are available. This is probably not accurate. For example, *homo ludens,* or humans as players, is a longstanding Christian notion. Similarly, Christians of various traditions have constructed a "theology of play." Play has often been celebrated as a "signal of transcendence" and as a shared human expression of being created in the image of God.[56] Evangelical writers and theologians have contributed to this discussion, although their ideas have not been widely read within the muscular Christian movement.[57] Andrew Wingfield-Digby, for example, recently observed from a British-evangelical perspective, "Play is a gift from God, and . . . as God's image-bearers humanity has play woven into its fabric. In Scripture, play is an anticipated social activity of God's people."[58] The more likely explanation for the emergent folk theology, then, is that it is more readily consonant with evangelicals' commitment to evangelism and saving souls by whatever means, with less interest in conceptualizing an *a priori* theological basis for their activity.

Of course, there are exceptions, including Hershiser, Dravecky, and Byrd. Similarly, Max Helton's background in theology and ministry stands him in good stead when he speaks to his NASCAR audience. But their presence only amplifies the larger problem. The unsystematic folk theology has become the dominant rhetorical system. In an ironic way, evangelical muscular Christians' behavior is consistent with historian Hatch's observation that earlier evangelicals had "organized their faith around the issue of communicating the gospel."[59] To put it differently, instead of the "medium being the message" for these modern muscular Christians, their use of sports rhetoric to communicate the gospel is at least as important as the essence of that gospel.

Communicating Evangelical Muscular Christianity: Taking a *Second Look* at *Sports Spectrum*

If a fairly explicit and popularly accepted folk theology has been created by evangelical muscular Christians, then the question remains, By what means have they communicated so broadly? In an era of mass communication, there is probably more than one answer, but one primary means has been a *Sports Illustrated* look-alike, now called *Sports Spectrum*.

In the early 1980s two basketball players who knew of each other from their competitive days in the old American Basketball Association, Julius Erving and Ralph Drollinger, along with representatives of Campus Crusade, discussed the possibility of a new magazine. It would feature prominent athletes and present their Christian commitments in an effort to influence Americans already fascinated with sports. The result was *SportsFocus* magazine, which debuted in February 1985 with an action photo of Erving on the first cover. Drollinger was the publisher, and he explained the magazine's purpose—to look "at sports from a different viewpoint," namely that "the Christian faith has a lot to offer people."[60] That first issue combined the slickness of *Sports Illustrated* with the message of a traditional gospel tract. It emphasized "Features," which were mainly biographical pieces on such well-known heroes as Erving, Willie Gault, and Alberto Salazar.

SportsFocus did not survive beyond its first issue. Instead, it reappeared the following year as *NewFocus*. Erving was out; Drollinger was executive editor, and the new publisher was Martin DeHaan, a radio preacher and head of Grand Rapids–based Radio Bible Class. But *NewFocus* did not survive either. In 1987 *Second Look* appeared—the third manifestation in three years. Over the next two years, six issues were published, and finally in 1989 *Second Look* appeared in regular bimonthly intervals.

A final, substantially revised, fourth version of the magazine appeared suddenly in November 1990 when *Second*

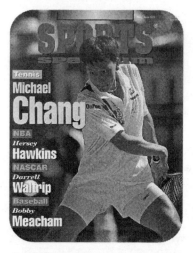

Tennis
Michael
Chang
NBA
Hersey
Hawkins
NASCAR
Darrell
Waltrip
Baseball
Bobby
Meacham

Sports Spectrum has become a popular means of communicating the muscular Christian message by featuring prominent athletes.

Look became *Sports Spectrum*. The biographical "Features" were still a staple, usually with three or four prominent athletes pictured and their Christian relevance interpreted. A new column, "Airing It Out," often included an ample amount of the folk theology of muscular Christianity. It extrapolated a biblical principle to some occurrence in the elite-sport subculture,[61] although with little obvious theological or biblical underpinning. By late 1995 circulation was nearing seventy thousand, and the magazine had begun to turn a profit.[62]

Sports Spectrum magazine begat *Sports Spectrum* radio in early 1991. This format quickly caught on, and at this writing, more than two hundred stations carry it each week. The hour-long broadcast is hosted by Chuck Swirsky, former sports director at WGN, Chicago, but more recently of CJCL in Toronto. Swirsky also supplies "The Swirsky Report" each month to the magazine. The broadcast and the column combine sports trivia with short items on various muscular Christian personalities.[63]

For the nearly four years of *Second Look* between 1987 and 1990, many of the issues emphasized a central theme or topic—from motivation in late 1987 to morality in 1988 and comebacks (featuring Dave Dravecky) in 1990. Unsurprisingly, most of the sixteen topics fit quite well within one or more of the five elements of the myth of modern muscular Christianity. First, the notion of heroic models is a most obvious appeal in both *Second Look* and *Sports Spectrum*. Implicitly, although visibly, much of the magazines' emphasis has been on the biographical accounts of successful athletes who also are practicing muscular Christians. For example, the July-August 1992 issue contained a special section on the approaching Barcelona Olympic Games. Of the many possible ways this subject might have been treated, *Sports Spectrum* focused on the Olympians. It offered stories about six of them who were known to be muscular Christians, including Leroy Burrell, Dave Johnson, Jennifer Azzi, and Paul Wylie.[64]

To the credit of *Second Look*, however, one of the topical issues in 1990 was heroes. Alongside articles on Tim Burke, Kevin Johnson, and Madeline Mims, two more cautionary articles discussed the difficulties in identifying sports heroes. Glenn Davis, then of baseball's Houston Astros, was cited for his opposition to alcohol; he asked the Astros' announcers not to toast him with "This Bud's for you" after each home run he hit.[65] But at best, the message on heroic models was mixed over several years, with a cumulative effect of emphasizing the accomplishments of individual athletes.

Competitive virtue, a second element of the myth, abounds within the pages of *Second Look* and *Sports Spectrum*. One 1988 issue of *Second Look* was given to the topic of morality, and Anthony Munoz of the Cincinnati Bengals was featured for his personal fight against pornography and his refusal in 1986 to be featured in *Playboy* because of the lifestyle it represents.[66] But besides this kind of personal morality, *Second Look* emphasized several topics as virtues arising from competition, including toughness and consistency in two 1989 issues. Golfer Betsy King was cited for her consistency—as well as her trust and patience—as apparent results of her spiritual commitment and her work as a teaching pro.[67]

A third element of the modern myth, therapeutic self-control, was also evident in *Second Look*. Topics such as motivation in 1987, endurance in 1988, and self-image in 1989 are representative of exactly the overlapping rhetoric of athletic training tips, popular psychology, and biblical aphorisms so widespread in the movement. On motivation, former American professional soccer great, Kyle Rote Jr., a frequent SOA speaker and contributor to *Second Look*, declared that "internal" motivation is clearly superior to "external" motivation because "you'll always be able to give your best, regardless of the circumstances." And former Seattle Seahawk and current Congressman Steve Largent explained that he had been motivated to prepare himself "physically, mentally, spiritually, and emotionally to be a great football player." To clinch this theme, Bible teacher John MacArthur cited several "motivational principles" from the pen of the apostle Paul in his "coaching role."[68]

Similarly, on the self-image topic, former pitcher Dravecky was extolled for his ability to "keep his self-image separate from his performance" because "it comes from God. That's the key to keeping a healthy self-esteem in the high-pressure, ego-inflated world of big-league sports."[69]

The final two elements of the muscular Christian myth—pragmatic utility and meritocratic democracy—are less obvious but nevertheless present in *Second Look*. In fact, the whole *raison d'être* for publishing the magazine is its pragmatic utility in helping evangelicals communicate the gospel. The topic of authority was a theme for one 1989 issue, and former football coach Grant Teaff reflected on how a coach can "get the most he can out of his athletes," an explicitly pragmatic statement of a value underlying his profession. Another article explored the fine—and sometimes ambiguous—line between cheating and merely attempting to "gain an edge." One former baseball coach was cited for asserting, "It doesn't come down to right or wrong; it's 'What do I have to do to succeed.'"[70]

Finally, on the element of meritocratic democracy, the best example may have been indirect and nearly contradictory. In an issue on unfairness, the very difficulty of dealing with apparent unfairness in sport was treated uncertainly, given the normative assumption that athletic competition is inherently democratic and therefore should be fair. The best illustration of this was a recounting of pitcher Todd Worrell's experience when he and the St. Louis Cardinals lost the 1985 World Series, in large part because of one bad call by umpire Don Denkinger.[71] Interestingly, although Worrell might have been treated more as a heroic model for his deportment on the field and in the post-series interviews, he was depicted more for representing the democratic values and the difficulty of dealing with injustice in sport.

Second Look and *Sports Spectrum* appear to have become a primary means by which the myth and folk theology of evangelical muscular Christianity are being circulated to an ever-increasing audience. Yet it is important to observe that the magazines have tended not to deal critically with problem areas in sport or to propose any counterperspective about anti-Christian excesses. Two possible exceptions have been laments over money and drugs in sport. When money and materialism are discussed, the emphasis has been on escalating salaries. The perspective is clearly pro-ownership and pro-management, with no attention to the structural greed or manipulation of tax benefits by ownership or how any of this works to the disadvantage of amateur participation.[72]

On the topic of drugs, the case of Steve Howe, the talented but troubled baseball pitcher, is instructive. After Howe had been suspended for repeated cocaine abuse, he was featured in an interview by Kyle Rote Jr. in July-August 1990. Howe then stated, "The Lord allowed me to walk away from the game, having shaken the drug issue. And that is a testimony to what Christ can do. So even if I only throw one pitch, even if I don't get back into the major leagues, the drug cloud is removed."[73] Howe did return to the major leagues, only to have the cloud return when he was arrested for drug abuse and suspended again from baseball. Along with the trials of Darryl Strawberry, Eric Greene, and others, Steve Howe's story is a perplexing one, and arguably one on which there should be some muscular Christian insight. Instead, *Sports Illustrated* probably has been more helpful in providing an understanding of Steve Howe, although puzzling over "this fragile man, this precarious life: Where does it go from here?"[74] Meanwhile *Sports Spectrum* to this point has missed opportunities to offer more realistic and biblically based understandings of modern sport, its mythology, its troubled athletes, and how all this fits together in American life.

While *Sports Spectrum,* in both its magazine and radio formats, has become a significant means of communicating the myth and folk theology of muscular Christianity, its parent organization, Radio Bible Class of Grand Rapids, has assumed an increasingly prominent place in the workings of SOA. In a familiar late twentieth-century evangelical fashion, with no formal structural connection between Radio Bible Class, *Sports Spectrum,* and SOA, the mutual needs of the magazine and SOA were met interpersonally and within the evangelical network in a typically symbiotic style. In a real sense financially, Radio Bible Class rescued the dying dreams of Julius Erving and Ralph Drollinger. This happened in large part because of the background and vision several Radio Bible Class management-level individuals shared from their experiences in intercollegiate athletics at small Christian colleges. Those men already believed the myth. Their organization accepted short-term financial losses until the magazine became profitable, while all the time spreading the gospel and folk theology of muscular Christianity, SOA, and its activities.

As this century nears its conclusion, the institutional structure and the mythical status of modern evangelical muscular Christianity seem well in place. The numbers of individuals and organizations spreading the gospel of muscular Christianity continue to increase. The larger cultural familiarity with the movement's personalities and their message has never been greater, with the popular heroes proclaiming their commitments for all who will listen. Enrollment increases at Christian colleges, and the place of intercollegiate athletics on the scores of campuses affiliated with the NCCAA and the CCCU is as prominent as ever. Evangelical megachurches have similarly caught the vision for using sport in their ministries. Sermons, interviews, and popular literature alike abound with the rhetoric and mythology of sport, with religious and cultural publics primed to hear the latest explanations of the Christian support of sport. Clearly there is little more the movement and its leaders could wish for in planning for the future of evangelical muscular Christianity.

Conclusion

Evangelical muscular Christianity has existed for at least 140 years. During that time, it relocated in America from England, developed indigenous versions reflecting its new cultural and geographical locations, unexpectedly fell apart, then reconstituted among World War II–era Protestant fundamentalists and evolved into the diffuse, multilayered movement now poised to move into the twenty-first century.

What have been most persistent throughout are the twin muscular Christian goals of "making the bad of society good" and "making the good of society better." Even before Thomas Higginson issued his *Atlantic Monthly* series on muscular Christianity devoted to explaining how sport might contribute to improving the lot of good, middle-class Americans, Awful Gardner had become a religious and cultural celebrity—a bad sportsman made good through his revivalist conversion. As Gardner recounted his compelling story, people listened in large part because of his twin connection to sport and revivalist religion.

Thirty years later, everything came together at Northfield. Young collegians spent their summers recreating and listening to challenges from the Moodys, Drummonds, Motts, and Staggs—muscular Christians all. The YMCA and the SVM were in place as the organizational apparatus to propel evangelical muscular Christianity into the twentieth century. Northfield further provided muscular Christians with their rallying watchword of "the evangelization of the world in this generation" as their *raison d'être*. Simultaneously, the evolving culture of sport provided the increasingly popular cultural and mythological basis on which the movement might thrive.

Thirty years later, nearly everything had changed. The key Northfield generation had departed. The YMCA and SVM changed considerably, at least in how they viewed the essential muscular Christian connection between participation in sports and evangelical religion. The twin institutional set-

231

tings of sport and evangelical Christianity developed in directions that had been detectable a generation earlier, but was anyone noticing then? Furthermore, American culture in the Golden Age of the '20s was not the same as that of the Gilded Age of the '90s.

Most important, those very muscular Christians who seemed most likely to provide the second-generation linkage between their forebears from Northfield and the approaching golden age of sport lost their youthful vision in their mature years. In addition, the previously supportive evangelical milieu turned against sport and against the direction American culture took, while focusing inwardly on the intramural battles between modernists and fundamentalists. For muscular Christians to convene something like the Northfield meetings of 1886 or 1887 in the cultural contexts of 1926 or 1927 was unthinkable.

What happened thirty years later was an unexpected rediscovery of the sports appeal by successors of the very fundamentalists who had turned their collective back on sports. Uppermost in their minds, however, were revival and the need to attract youthful listeners. Sport provided exactly the attraction they needed. No one set out to reinvent muscular Christianity, but Gil Dodds, Billy Graham, and Youth for Christ served as inadvertent "brothers of reinvention." Along the way, sport also provided a means by which these marginalized fundamentalists could reenter the cultural conversation, in part by their Christianizing of existing forms of the myth surrounding sport.

Sports Ambassadors, the Fellowship of Christian Athletes, and Athletes in Action then developed the organizational apparatus for institutionalizing evangelical muscular Christianity as the YMCA and SVM had not done seventy-five years earlier. As organizational representatives of what would become Sports Outreach America, these organizations also encouraged ties between sport and the evangelical church and between sport and evangelical colleges. Simultaneously, the churches and colleges adopted wholeheartedly the evangelical version of the muscular Christian myth. Accordingly, sport for them lost much of its intrinsic value but was readily recognized for its cultural power and its ability to attract potential converts—to evangelical religion, its churches, and its college athletic programs.

As the myth of muscular Christianity in its original Tom Brown–like forms gave way to the twin Northfield visions supporting evangelical activity, so the evangelical muscular Christian myth of the late twentieth century has devised a supporting folk theology that provides its adherents with a vocabulary and rhetoric legitimizing their involvement. Most recently, this myth has become a basis for the new muscular Christian moral crusaders entering the contemporary culture wars on the side of orthodoxy, convinced of the privileged position they enjoy as participants in both elite sport and evangelical Christianity.

In terms more sociological than historical, what this story of muscular Christians says is that evangelical religion and sport have developed symbiotic relationships around their shared meanings and shifting boundaries. Evangelical Christianity in America has been driven primarily by its revivalist and conversionist purposes, with theology an important but supporting variable. D. L. Moody wished the YMCA would be more concerned with conversion. It was not until his encounters with C. T. and J. E. K. Studd in England that he imagined how the Northfield meetings might accomplish that

The modern muscular Christian movement is now in its third generation. On the left, during a 1998 tour, is Matt Cook, grandson of Sports Ambassadors' first executive, Bud Schaeffer.

end and perhaps evangelize the world in the process. Billy Sunday wished sport had been more amendable to his personal revivalist agenda, and accordingly he reduced sport literally to the status of metaphor in his sermons. Billy Graham quickly realized the potential sport had for his revivalist crusades, and he seized every opportunity to present sports heroes to help attract converts.

But the boundaries also extended from sport toward evangelical religion for the purposes of their symbiotic enhancement. Sport in the late nineteenth century needed the cultural legitimacy enjoyed by evangelical religion. But the more obvious examples came in the last third of the twentieth century, with the organizational support of sports chaplains and other muscular Christian operatives in the interest of strengthening the public relations and social control functions already latent within sport.

In the process of building these symbiotic relationships, evangelical religion and sport found each other at a variety of conceptual levels—from that of individual muscular Christian heroes to those occupying the role of sports chaplains to the organizational and institutional interconnections enjoyed by sport, religion, and college to the subcultural and cultural levels of shared values and meanings. In all of this, the evangelical church has provided the necessary organizational and subcultural ties. American evangelicalism may not be unique, but it certainly has distinctive characteristics, including its pragmatic ability to endorse aspects of its milieu that helped muscular Christians accomplish their primary goals of conversion and evangelization.

While most of this story has been told from the perspective of evangelical religion, sport has been the necessary second ingredient. Evangelical muscular Christianity was possible in the 1880s because of the rapid acceptance of sport in American life, especially as it encouraged opportunities for the YMCA on college campuses. When sport moved in increasingly secular directions in the early twentieth century, Protestants moved accordingly—but in two disparate directions.

While mainline Protestants continued to endorse sport apart from its value for conversion, fundamentalists (including Billy Sunday in 1893) grew increasingly suspicious of sport and minimized its value. Then, when sport redefined its niche as part of the American way of life in the post–World War II era, evangelical religion was quite happy to reestablish its ties. Similarly, as elite sport once again moves in increasingly secular directions in the late twentieth century, evangelicals have been most willing to follow it and seek to adapt it for their competitive advantages in their churches and colleges.

This institutional symbiosis suggests two further points of convergence. One is more historical—the similarities between the first and second engagements of muscular Christianity. Around the central theme of revival and conversion, nineteenth-century evangelicals adapted an existing myth that sport intrinsically could make the good of society better, once they realized that sport also had great potential for enhancing their revival and conversion goals. In the process, they reduced sport to a merely extrinsic tool in the hands of revivalists and missionaries. Sixty years later, their mid-twentieth-century evangelical counterparts rediscovered the conversion value sport possessed and subsequently adapted it for their purposes, built their own institutional structures, and created a rhetoric to support their activity—thus moving significantly beyond their muscular Christian ancestors.

A second point of convergence between muscular Christianity then and now has been its role in schools of varying types. From Tom Brown to Luther Gulick to Amos Alonzo Stagg to Gil Dodds to the FCA, AIA, and the NCCAA, evangelical muscular Christians have often found high schools and colleges the most conducive milieus for their activity. Along the way, their emphases have shifted from character building to proselytizing, recruiting, and marketing, but the primary target audiences of adolescent and young adult males have been the constant in the story.

Perhaps most surprising is the degree of coherence and similarity among the various forms and manifestations of con-

235

temporary muscular Christianity. Granted, the evangelical subculture has provided a homogeneous foundation for much of the movement's myth and institutionalization of the past forty years, but in a postmodern world given to culturally relative values and organizational forms, evangelical muscular Christianity today looks surprisingly similar to that of its World War II–era origins. Therein may lie both its strength and its weakness.

As the muscular Christian movement has found common cause with the orthodox position in the culture wars, it risks separating from a more moderate constituency that might have found its ethical commitments attractive a decade or two earlier. In the process, muscular Christianity risks establishing a stricter boundary between it and those it seeks to attract as well as repeating the separatism of its fundamentalist predecessors in the early 1900s. As evangelical muscular Christianity looks to the twenty-first century, it enjoys affirmation from within its subculture but also faces the potential for increasing suspicion from without. For many in the movement, however, that potential two-edged sword is rather a confirmation that they are continuing on the right course.

As the century nears its conclusion, the institutional structure and the mythical status of modern evangelical muscular Christianity seem well in place. The numbers of individuals and organizations spreading the gospel of muscular Christianity continue to increase, and the larger cultural familiarity with the movement's men and their message has never been greater. Enrollments increase at Christian colleges, and the place of intercollegiate athletics on the scores of campuses affiliated with the NCCAA and the CCCU is as prominent as ever. What more could the movement and its leaders wish for in planning for the future?

Afterword

Could There Be Another Disengagement?

Evangelicals often have not been known for their ability to learn from the past, and the general orientation they share with their sporting ministries is one of evangelizing and communicating the gospel with the presumed immediate premillennial future in mind. If on the one hand the muscular Christian movement is as widespread and successful as ever, its leaders have every reason to be optimistic about its future. Elsewhere one of us has written that the movement is not likely to disappear. But the question remains whether it can adapt the "organizational structure and the resources to meet the needs of a changing international setting."[1] In other words, rather than asking optimistically, What more could the movement and its leaders wish for? perhaps a more helpful inquiry is, Under what circumstances could there be another disengagement of evangelical religion and sport?

If modern evangelical muscular Christian leaders could go back one hundred years to the post-Northfield days, hypothetically they would find their predecessors—including Moody, McBurney, Gulick, Stagg, Naismith, Studd, and Mott—were as optimistic about the future of religion-in-sport as they, the modern leaders, rightly can be today. But then "everything fell apart" in a rapid and unexpected fashion, so that within two decades things changed greatly. The argument in chapter 3, simply stated, was that the disengagement of religion and sport occurred because of changes at four levels—individuals, organizations, institutions, and culture. One might borrow that model and adapt it to the present muscular Christian reality. Is there any likelihood that another disengagement of religion and sport might occur? Are there any indications that something other than a promising future is in store? Obviously, the answers are speculative, but they point to adaptive strategies the movement may have to pursue as it enters the twenty-first century.

1. Individual Muscular Christian Actors

In the mid-1890s no one could have anticipated the deaths of Moody and McBurney, the philosophical shifts taken by Stagg and Naismith, or the departure of Sunday from their muscular Christian attachments. Individuals matter, and for evangelicals the charismatic, entrepreneurial leaders continued to play significant roles even as the larger movement routinized institutionally. The 1990s are not the 1890s, but in two areas, individuals continue to make a difference.

The first area, and the more apparent, is within the leadership of modern muscular Christianity. What has happened repeatedly is that people move on to other positions or withdraw. One of the first SOA leaders was David Burnham, and since he left about 1989, no single person with comparable ability has taken his place. Similarly, Ralph Drollinger recently departed from SOA for personal reasons. And Eddie Waxer— who is a continuing, behind-the-scenes presence—devotes his efforts to expanding the ISC, with little time available for SOA's concerns. In a strictly functional sense, the work probably is still being done. The question is whether it is done as effectively with the longer-term interests of the evolving movement in view.

A second group of muscular Christians who may yet make a difference is less obvious but perhaps as critical. They are the elite college and professional athletes. One major difference between muscular Christian participants of the 1890s and the 1990s is the proportion of influence and visibility borne by representatives of that elite group. Their numbers were almost totally lacking from the nineteenth-century group, although Billy Sunday is one example. But over the past thirty years or so, more and more elite athletes have identified with the movement. Unfortunately, the activities of some of these high-profile muscular Christian proponents have hindered rather than aided the movement. The problem is larger than Steve Howe and Darryl Strawberry, although perhaps without a discernible pattern. Barry Sanders was identified with A. C. Green's Athletes for Abstinence, only to father a child out of wedlock and then announce a revised ethical understanding. Andre Agassi proclaimed his commitment to Bible study, but "image is everything" is probably his public's perception of him. Horace Grant led the Chicago Bulls' prayer group, only to display his body for nude photographs as his divorce was being finalized.[2] They are not alone.

The dilemma for muscular Christian leaders is probably at once obvious and insolvable. By attaching their credibility and legitimacy to their ability to attract heroic models from secular sport, they have accepted a two-edged sword. Meanwhile, something other than the five-point myth and folk theology of the movement has yet to capture the attention of a majority of the elite participants. So the question is how many "failures" any movement can endure before its credibility and the veracity of its message are at risk.

2. Muscular Christian Organizational Structures

In the 1890s nearly the sole organizational basis of muscular Christianity was the YMCA. As Hopkins and Zald and Denton have demonstrated, the YMCA went through a time of significant transformation, and muscular Christianity was one loser in the process.[3] Organizationally, muscular Christianity looks quite different in the 1990s. The range of groups and their diverse activities bode well for the twenty-first century.

Within the movement, however, two relatively new organizational forms mentioned in chapter 6 fit less well, and their effects on institutionalized muscular Christianity are less predictable. First, with the rise of the megachurch, evangelical Protestantism has undergone a significant change at the local level, especially in middle-class suburban settings. Given their size, abundant resources, and diverse programming, it probably is no surprise megachurches have taken on sports ministry, especially in an appeal to young males. On the surface, the megachurches would seem to have a lot to offer the muscular Christian movement.

Ironically, the opposite may be true, and here the cliché "time will tell" fits. In many megachurches, a philosophy of being "seeker-sensitive" is still evolving. This would appear to make them particularly vulnerable to the secular values-orientation of late twentieth-century sport. This philosophy may not be different from the "market orientation" that has long characterized evangelicals, but the megachurches differ in two other ways. One is in the sheer power of programming that their human and financial resources make possible. The megachurches have the potential to learn from SOA and its affiliates, and then to strike out on their own as independent "vendors" of sports ministry services, while guarding closely the financial resources that might otherwise be available to the movement as a whole. A second difference is qualitative. Generally, seeker-sensitive megachurches accept much of the popular culture's mode of expression, including sport, to attract potential followers. Here some of the tendencies that eventually led to the demise of muscular Christianity in the YMCA seem familiar. But it's too early to know, so time will tell.

A second organizational transition is occurring among the 110 conservative Protestant colleges belonging to the NCCAA. As mentioned earlier, some of the stronger colleges have left the NCCAA for the greener pastures of the NAIA. That leaves the NCCAA with disproportionately smaller, less stable programs that are often located in the smaller, more separatist Bible colleges. The separatism is compounded by an almost totally extrinsic view of sport. The NCCAA extols as a virtue the position that "athletics are a means to an end."[4] The extrinsic commitment reinforced by the latent separatism of the group does not bode well for the future of the movement. There is a risk of the NCCAA's becoming irrelevant within sport and within the larger culture.

What cannot be predicted, however, is the long-term stability of the NAIA. One possible scenario is that the NAIA might collapse. Many of the current NCCAA and CCCU colleges have serious misgivings about joining the NCAA, and only a handful of Christian colleges now belong to that organization. Should the NAIA fail, the NCCAA could become its successor among Christian colleges. In that event, the negative effects for SOA and its member groups would seem less damaging.

3. Muscular Christian Institutional Contexts

With the disengagement of religion and sport nearly a century ago, institutional changes in sport, religion, and college affected the existing relationship between the three. The relationship is quite different at the end of the twentieth century, especially given the realities of symbiosis and elective affinity between evangelicals and sport that led to their reengagement and institutionalization. However, three institutional factors conceivably could affect the future relationship.

First, sport might decide to turn its back on religion and upset the symbiosis. Sport has never benefited as much as the church from their relationship, and the management and leadership of big-time sport are dominated by a "bottom line" corporate mentality more secular in its ethos than even a generation ago. Maybe the "damage control" function of muscular Christianity is less necessary now; maybe chaplains are more of a hindrance than a help. Perhaps pluralistic tendencies within Protestantism will result in a glut of chaplains—all chasing the same muscular Christian constituency. Conceivably, if enough sports managers become convinced that religion is impeding performance on the field,[5] the bottom-line position might be, "Cut off access to the chaplains and availability of space for meetings; it's the on-the-field results that count; fans have short memories about their heroes' (im)morality."

Similarly, there is some evidence that the number of media representatives opposed to the muscular Christian movement is increasing and becoming a stronger force reacting to it. On the one hand, many members of the secular media never have had a good grasp of what the elite athletes are seeking to communicate, in part because the media have difficulty interpreting the symbols (and clichés) of folk theology. While there is some evidence of an increase in the overall coverage of muscular Christian activity,[6] on the other hand articles such as Rick Reilly's in *Sports Illustrated* after the 1991 Super Bowl are not uncommon. In the midst of an essay highly critical of the growing number of players from opposing teams gathering for "prayer circles" after NFL games, Reilly wrote, "Let them exercise it on their own time. . . . Promotional prayer is wholly inappropriate to a sporting event. . . . I hope that the NFL will have the good sense to curtail these huddles—and, if not, that television will have the sense to ignore them."[7]

The other two institutional factors are more historically laden and tied to the post–World War II evangelicalism that gave rise to the present institutional arrangement. Conservative Protestantism then represented a lower-middle-class, white, male-dominated world that emphasized revivalism, evangelism, and an individualistic ethic. No wonder the present SOA groups and the chaplains fit the demographic profile they do. Two more recent realities in sport pose serious challenges to that conservative mode. The first is the place for women in the movement. Here the leaders are caught on the horns of more than one dilemma. On the one hand, the movement is tied to religious and educational realities that reflect a larger worldview generally supportive of culturally and religiously conservative ideas about gender roles. On the other hand, the movement is ostensibly interested in and related to the rapidly increasing numerical and political presence of women in sport. As one example of where the movement is located, the first eight years of *SportsFocus, NewFocus, Second Look,* and *Sports Spectrum* featured only one female athlete on their covers—triathlete Kirsten Hanssen in 1989. Betsy King would be the second in March-April 1993, although she had been a "Features" subject four years earlier. Meanwhile, the May-June 1992 issue included an article titled "Going for the Victory at Home," featuring the wives of four prominent male muscular Christians.[8] Simply stated, with fewer female athletes, and fewer women generally, "at home" in the 1990s, the movement is going to have to address the changing gender balance in sport, particularly with issues of gender equity and the legal and ethical implications of Title IX.

The final institutional reality—also within the evangelical church—is racially and ethnically related. When the reengagement of religion and sport occurred in the 1950s, the evangelical church and elite sport were dominated by whites. One glance at participants in major athletic events today demonstrates how much this has changed. There is little evidence, however, that the current leadership has adapted to—or is thinking of a strategy to address—this major change. On the one hand, this inability to adapt makes some sense, as the movement still reflects its postwar, small-town and suburban, fundamentalist origins. On the other hand, the current leadership may be older and more middle class, but it is no less white. This organizational reality is reinforced by the messages and symbols that originate in the dominant white culture. Potentially fewer connections to the increasingly diverse presence in athletics will be possible if the white sports ministers continue using primarily the cultural and religious symbols they know best.

4. Muscular Christian Subcultures

A final factor that might result in another disengagement of religion and sport is reminiscent of the second disestablishment of religion after World War I. Then the cultural resonance of an earlier Protestant ethos simply went unheeded. In the 1990s the problem is more one of a possible "mutual subcultural delegitimation." Here Douglas' concept of symbolic boundaries is again helpful.[9] What has made the symbiosis of religion and sport so enduring are the overlapping symbols, deriving in part from the religion of the American way of life discussed in chapter 5. But the cultural consensus those overlapping symbols relied upon no longer exists in a time of postmodernism and culture wars. Sport and religion each have "taken their lumps" in American life, despite the persistence of the myths of muscular Christianity. The elite performers being served by the sports ministries are often at odds financially and organizationally with owners and managers of sports teams, whose values are often supported by the same muscular Christian groups. In Douglas' terms, the symbolic boundaries once so overlapping and consonant have shifted. Culturally, sport and religion less frequently speak the same language. The values have changed, and the symbols used to articulate those values are different. The subcultural adhesive is weakening, and the mutual legitimation religion and sport enjoyed is being tested. A recent statement from Robert Lipsyte on "Why Sports Don't Matter Anymore" gets at this idea, at least from within sport. "It's late in the American game and hope for the home team fades. . . . Sports no longer reflect the America of our dreams, and the stars of sport are no longer the idealized versions of ourselves. . . . If that mirror is truly reflecting who and what we are now, we are selfish, shortsighted, morally bankrupt, approaching impotence."[10]

The result is that at the four levels—for the overlapping reasons we discussed—the previously symbiotic relationship between evangelical religion and sport may be less fixed and certain than it appears at first glance. The picture is mixed and complex. The new moral crusaders have brought morality back into muscular Christianity, and a fivefold myth is being expressed broadly in folk religious terms. Yet there are at least hints that among selected individuals, organizations, institutions, and subcultural connections, perhaps the emperor of evangelical muscular Christianity is no longer fully clothed.

The history of any movement unfolds unpredictably, and the immediate picture for evangelical muscular Christianity is certainly surer and brighter than the possible long-term consequences suggested here. Given evangelicalism's expanding organizational acumen and cultural presence, we acknowledge the prospects that favor the staying power of the organization and myth undergirding the modern movement. But the comparison of the contemporary situation to the apparently optimistic and seemingly parallel future for muscular Christianity a century ago—while not exact—includes some signs that things are not quite what they appear. Less dramatic, but more certain, are inevitable changes in both the organization and ethos of the movement, so that its next twenty years are likely to result in more new patterns of leadership and organization than the recent past has seen.

Notes

Introduction

1. Kathryn Teresa Long, *The Revival of 1857–58: Interpreting an American Religious Awakening* (New York: Oxford University, 1998), 39–45. See also J. Edwin Orr, *The Event of the Century: The 1857–1858 Awakening* (Wheaton: International Awakening Press, 1989), 310–11.

2. *New York Tribune*, 31 March 1858, 2. Beyond Long's work, which sketches the influence of the 1857–58 revivals on muscular Christianity, see Timothy L. Smith, *Revivalism and Social Reform* (New York: Abingdon Press, 1957) for a treatment of the revival as a part of the larger context of the reform movements of the nineteenth century.

3. A brief but excellent overview of the traditional interpretation of the American muscular Christian movement is contained in Benjamin Rader, *American Sports: From the Age of Folk Games to the Age of Spectators* (Englewood Cliffs, N.J.: Prentice-Hall, 1983), 146–69. The early historical analysis provided in Guy Lewis, "The Muscular Christianity Movement," *JOHPER* 37 (May 1966): 27–28, reflects such traditional scholarship and the tone of historians during the middle of the twentieth century. Other broad-based studies include Gerald Redmond, "The First *Tom Brown's Schooldays*: Origins and Evolution of 'Muscular Christianity' in Children's Literature," *Quest* 30 (summer 1978): 4–18, and William E. Winn, "*Tom Brown's School Days* and the Development of 'Muscular Christianity,'" *Church History* 29 (1960): 64–73. Most of these social analyses may have been affected by P. C. McIntosh, *Physical Education in England since 1800* (London: A. Bell and Sons, 1968), whose thorough research on English physical education served as a basis for understanding the roots of muscular Christianity in English education. McIntosh's more recent work, *Fair Play: Ethics in Sport and Physical Education* (London: Heinemann, 1979) has been referenced extensively in American works, though the author is British. Earle F. Zeigler, *History of Physical Education and Sport* (Englewood Cliffs, N.J.: Prentice-Hall, 1979), 88ff., represents the group of physical education historians who provide a longer historical view of muscular Christianity. Melvin Adelman, *A Sporting Time: New York City and the Rise of Modern Athletics, 1820–1870* (Champaign, Ill.: University of Illinois Press, 1986) emphasizes this broader context for the development of muscular Christianity in his significant study.

4. Excellent sources for exploring the Kingsley-Hughes literature include Donald E. Hall, ed., *Muscular Christianity: Embodying the Victorian Age* (Cambridge: Cambridge University Press, 1994); Brenda Colloms, *Charles Kingsley: The Lion of Eversley* (London: Duckworth Co., 1975); John Raymond de Symons Honey, *Tom Brown's Universe: The Development of the English Public School in the Nineteenth Century* (New York: Quadrangle, New York Times Book Co., 1977); George J. Worth, *Thomas Hughes* (Boston: Twayne, 1984); Norman Vance, *The Sinews of the Spirit: The Ideal of Christian Manliness in Victorian Literature and Religious Thought* (Cambridge: Cambridge University Press, 1985); Robert B. Heilman, "Muscular Christianity," *Notes and Queries* 185, no. 2 (July 17, 1943), 44–45; Henry R. Harrington, "Charles Kingsley's Fallen Athlete," *Victorian Studies* 21, no. 1 (1977): 73–86.

5. Hughes's use of the Tom Brown myth captured the imagination of the youth of the English-speaking world. Soon the term Tom Brown took on a meaning that included but went beyond Hughes's concepts of morality and manliness. Various religious and nonreligious groups gradually used the concept to advance an agenda related to healthful living, fitness, and many other forms of personal and social development.

6. The literature on muscular Christianity is diverse and extensive. In the scholarship of nineteenth-century sport, the term was often tied to British and Victorian concepts of manliness, fair play, and character development—all through vigorous striving in sports. Traditional histories have emphasized that understanding. More recent studies of muscular Christianity are becoming more diverse. Two examples by J. A. Mangan inform this view. "Christ and the Imperial Game Fields: Evangelical Athletes of the Empire," *BJSH* 1, no. 2: 184–201, provides an excellent British perspective. His studies of British public schools, especially *Athleticism in the Victorian and Edwardian Public School: The Emergence and Consolidation of an Educational Ideology* (Cambridge: Cambridge University Press, 1981), provide a helpful background for understanding the worldwide reach of muscular Christian ideals. Mangan especially deserves credit for reenergizing this area of scholarship.

7. See Mark Girouard, *The Return to Camelot: Chivalry and the English Gentleman* (New Haven: Yale University Press, 1981), especially chap. 9 on muscular chivalry.

8. Thomas Hughes, *Tom Brown at Oxford* (London: Macmillan, 1861), 83.

9. Redmond, "The First *Tom Brown's Schooldays*," 7, paraphrasing Peter McIntosh in part.

10. McIntosh, *Fair Play*, 27.

11. Michael Oriard, *Sporting with the Gods: The Rhetoric of Play and Game in American Culture* (Cambridge: Cambridge University Press, 1991), 11; Andrew W. Miracle Jr. and C. Roger Rees, *Lessons of the Locker Room* (Amherst, N.Y.: Prometheus Books, 1994), 40, citing Christopher Armstrong in part. S. W. Pope, *Patriotic Games: Sporting Traditions in the American Imagination, 1876–1926* (New York: Oxford University, 1997) provides an interesting, alternative view of how sports managers used holidays and other patriotic venues to shape an American identity through sport.

12. Charles Kingsley, *Health and Education*, cited in McIntosh, *Fair Play*, 28.

13. Given environmental and social conditions of the nineteenth century, health and fitness concerns emerged alongside and sometimes related to the

muscular Christian movement. Since many of these newer immigrants were Catholic, there developed a subcultural muscular Christianity related to Catholicism and not to Protestantism. That story deserves its own telling.

14. Literature representing these broad concerns include Linda J. Boorish, "The Robust Woman and the Muscular Christian: Catherine Beecher, Thomas Higginson, and Their Vision of American Society, Health and Physical Activities," *IJHS* 4 (September 1987): 139–54, and Bruce Haley, *The Healthy Body and Victorian Culture* (Cambridge: Harvard University Press, 1978). Perhaps the most influential American scholar of nineteenth-century fitness and sport framed by Victorian culture is Roberta J. Park. Her numerous articles illuminate a century of intellectual history with fitness as the theme. Companion pieces to Park are Donald J. Mrozek, *Sport and American Mentality, 1880–1910* (Knoxville: University of Tennessee Press, 1983), and Harvey Green, *Fit for America: American Health, Fitness, Sport and American Society* (New York: Pantheon Books, 1986).

15. One helpful source making these distinctions among the different approaches to sport made by various religious traditions is Robert J. Higgs, "Muscular Christianity, Holy Play, and Spiritual Exercises: Confusion about Christ and Sports and Religion," *Arete* 1, no. 1 (fall 1983): 59–85. An example of a distinctive Roman Catholic perspective is Michael Novak, *The Joy of Sports* (New York: Basic, 1976).

16. Three representative writers from other academic areas who have attempted to understand the post–World War II evangelical Protestant approach to sport and sports evangelism are Shirl J. Hoffman, ed., *Sport and Religion* (Champaign, Ill.: Human Kinetics, 1992), especially the four section introductions and the reprint on pages 111–25 of his own "Evangelicalism and the Revitalization of Religious Ritual in Sport," *Arete* 2, no. 2 (spring 1985): 63–87; Brian W. W. Aitken, "The Emergence of Born-Again Sport," *Studies in Religion* 18, no. 4 (fall 1989): 391–405; and Christopher L. Stevenson, "The Christian-Athlete: An Interactionist-Developmental Analysis," *Sociology of Sport Journal* 8, no. 4 (December 1991): 362–79.

Chapter 1: The Rise of Evangelicals and the Development of Sport in America

1. Robert E. Speer, *A Memorial of a True Life: A Biography of . . . Hugh McAllister Beaver* (New York: Fleming H. Revell, 1898), 18 and 21, quoting an 1892 edition of Henry Clay Trumbull's, *The Knightly Soldier: A Biography of Major Henry Ward Camp.* Camp was reared in a church pastored by Horace Bushnell, one of the leading churchmen of the period.

2. Ibid., 22.

3. *North Carolina Presbyterian*, 2 January 1867, 2. We appreciate Robin Baker calling this article to our attention.

4. Ibid.

5. Ibid.

6. "A Christian Club," *New York Times*, 18 July 1869, 5.

7. Harvey Green, *Fit for America: American Health, Fitness, Sport and American Society* (New York: Pantheon Books, 1986), 183, 192, 343.

8. While many scholars agree that muscular Christianity played a role in the development of modern sport, their views diverge as to the centrality of that role and its long-range effect. Some, such as Guy Lewis (*JOHPER*, 1966, 27), consign the term to a description of social reform affecting only a small segment of the population. Nevertheless, they ascribe to muscular Christianity a key role in developing modern American sport. Others, such as Melvin Adelman (*A Sporting Time*, 279), minimize the role of muscular Christians in modern sport and suggest that moral and character development through sport existed long before the term was coined. One could posit, of course, that essence precedes existence and that the term is not as significant as the movement or people it represented. Nevertheless, even among scholars who identify a unique role for muscular Christianity, few have examined the work of muscular Christians over time or analyzed the role of a particular religious subgroup such as evangelical Protestants as significant contributors to the movement. As one recent indication of this lacuna in scholarship, the otherwise satisfactory twenty-five-page bibliography on American sport history by Robert Lewis devotes about three sentences to religion. "The Puritans had not opposed games as such but questioned the frivolous dissipation of time and talent. . . . Throughout the nineteenth century religious revivals kept alive the evangelical distinction between the worldly and the gathered saints dedicated to God's work. Moralists insisted that recreations be 'rational': improving in character, consistent with reason and righteousness." Robert K. Lewis, "American Sport History: A Bibliographic Guide," *American Studies International* 29, no. 1 (April 1991): 44.

9. C. Howard Hopkins, *History of the Y.M.C.A. in North America* (New York: Association Press, 1951), 382ff.

10. William H. Freeman, *Physical Education and Sport in a Changing Society*, 4th ed. (New York: Macmillan Co., 1992), 129; Bruce L. Bennett, "Physical Education and Religion" (unpublished notes, 15 January 1962), 4. An edited summary of this paper appeared in the *Physical Educator* 19 (October 1962): 85–86.

11. Editorial, "The Necessity of Recreation," *Spirit of the Times* 26 (27 December 1856): 546, as quoted in Deobold Van Dalen and Bruce Bennett, *A World History of Physical Education* (Englewood Cliffs, N.J.: Prentice-Hall, 1971), 412.

12. Most research on the rise of muscular Christianity in the United States has focused on the writings of eastern intellectuals and their arguments for sports and recreation. However, writings of Perry Miller and more recent researchers describe not only similarities but also distinctions between transcendentalists and early revivalists in working out the Puritan ideal of the covenanted community. The transcendentalists especially carried a burden of optimism that the nation's destiny was to establish a perfect society in America. Better health and fitness were manifestations of that society.

13. Thomas Wentworth Higginson, "Saints and Their Bodies," *Atlantic Monthly* 1 (1858): 582–95. John Lucas, "Thomas Wentworth Higginson: Early Apostle of Health and Fitness," *JOHPER* (February 1971): 30–33, provides a balanced, though brief, view of Higginson and his work. Given the breadth of Higginson's life and career (1823–1911), it is unfortunate that discussions of his contributions are often limited to connections with early muscular Christianity. As president of Williams College and as a leader in the early professionalization of physical education, Higginson's impact on athletics was not narrow.

14. Ernest Lee Tuveson, *Redeemer Nation: The Idea of America's Millennial Role* (Chicago: University of Chicago Press, 1968) is a classical interpretation of the importance of the reinforcing religious and civil visions of America's place in the world, especially in the Civil War era.

15. Perry Miller, *The Life of the Mind in America: From the Revolution to the Civil War* (New York: Harcourt, Brace and World, 1955), 56ff. Also, see Timothy L. Smith, *Revivalism and Social Reform* (New York: Abingdon Press, 1957), for an analysis of the social work of the revivalists. From the larger perspective of an overarching concept of play and sport, Richard A. Swanson, "American Protestantism and Play: 1865–1915" (Ph.D. diss., Ohio State University, 1967) is helpful.

16. James E. Kirby, "Matthew Simpson and the Mission of America," *Church History* 36, no. 3 (September 1967): 301.

17. See Stanley N. Gundry, *Love Them In: The Proclamation Theology of D. L. Moody* (Chicago: Moody, 1976), 175. Postmillennialism provided a rationale for the conversion of mankind and the amelioration and cure of the ills of the world. It was a philosophy of history, and a generally optimistic one at that. Through the efforts of Christians, the kingdom would be brought to reality before Christ returned. Society itself would be reorganized in accordance with the laws of God. The postmillennial philosophy of history was the cornerstone in the foundation of most, if not all, of the social-reform movements promoted by American evangelicals in the mid-nineteenth century, and the view continued after the Civil War, though it began to lose ground. The prayer revival of 1857–58 served to quicken these hopes that had long lived in American Protestantism.

18. Because American Protestantism was oriented to postmillennialism at midcentury, emerging social institutions such as the YMCA had postmillennial orientations. Nevertheless, that view was not acted upon with equal understanding by all participants. For an overview of the decline of postmillennialism, see James H. Moorhead, "The Erosion of Postmillennialism in American Religious Thought, 1865–1925," *Church History* 53, no. 1 (March 1984): 61–77.

19. The history of millennial influence is difficult to sort through, given the intricacies of evangelical theology. Helpful are Stanley J. Grenz, *The Millennial Maze* (Downers Grove, Ill.: InterVarsity Press, 1992); Ernest R. Sandeen, *The Roots of Fundamentalism: British and American Millenarianism, 1800–1930* (Chicago: University of Chicago Press, 1970); and Timothy P. Weber, *Living in the Shadow of the Second Coming: American Premillennialism, 1875–1925* (Grand Rapids: Zondervan, 1983). For an excellent overview of the premillennial position and its fit into American evangelicalism, see George M. Marsden, *Fundamentalism and American Culture: The Shaping of Twentieth-Century Evangelicalism, 1870–1925* (New York: Oxford University, 1980).

20. Ronald L. Numbers and Jonathan M. Butler, *The Disappointed: Millerism and Millenarianism in the Nineteenth Century* (Bloomington, Ind.: Indiana University Press, 1987) provides a helpful background on the Millerite predecessors of evangelical premillennialists; Ruth Alden Doan, "Millerism and Evangelical Culture," in Numbers and Butler, *The Disappointed*, 118–38, is especially valuable on the connections between groups.

21. John R. Betts, *America's Sporting Heritage, 1850–1950* (Lexington: Addison-Wesley, 1974), 156ff. Betts concluded, "No one can deny the significance of sportsmen, athletes, journalists, and pioneers in many organizations, and no

one can disregard the multitude of forces transforming the social scene. The technological revolution is not the sole determining factor in the rise of sport, but to ignore its influence would result only in a more or less superficial understanding of the history of the prominent social institutions of modern America."

22. James W. Fraser, *Pedagogue for God's Kingdom* (New York: University Press of America, 1985), 183. Timothy Smith, "Protestant Schooling and American Nationality, 1800–1850," *The Journal of American History* 53 (1966–67): 679–94, and David Tyack, "The Kingdom of God and the Common School," *Harvard Educational Review* 36 (fall 1966): 447–69, include analyses of the positive roles of evangelicals in the development of public schools.

23. Fraser, *Pedagogue,* 184.

24. Lyman Beecher wrote, "Let the Catholics mingle with us as Americans and come with their children under the full action of our common schools and Republican institutions and the various powers of assimilation, we are prepared cheerfully to abide the consequences" (Fraser, *Pedagogue,* 184).

25. Calvin Stowe, Beecher's son-in-law and one of the leaders of the movement for public schools, put it, "These are facts which show plainly, that notwithstanding the diversity of sects, there is common ground on which the seriously pious of all sects substantially agree" (Fraser, *Pedagogue,* 183).

26. *The American Educational Reader: Fifth Grade* (New York: Ivison, Blakeman, Taylor and Co., 1873), 34–35.

27. Van Dalen and Bennett, *A World History of Physical Education,* 408. Commitment to character development through athletics, however, emerged prominently only when students pressured faculty to include such activities. Van Dalen and Bennett conclude that, "Original emphasis on athletic movements came from institutions of higher learning, mostly attended by students living away from home. Athletics was an original contribution by the student body. Beginning as free, spontaneous sports and games, athletics became organized by students apart from the school proper, largely in opposition to it. Later it followed faculty advisory control and official adoption by educational authorities." Student action had propelled athletics into the American educational system. Now muscular Christians would sanctify it for all of society.

28. Smith, *Revivalism,* 63ff., regards the 1850s revivals as an important transition time in American religion and one that set the course for evangelicalism for the next century.

29. The authors are indebted to John D. Hannah of Dallas Theological Seminary for several key interpretations of Charles Finney's contributions to the American revival movement.

30. Luther Gulick, Secretary of the League, SPC Archives, GV 563 Y6A4. See also Ethel J. Dorgan, *Luther Halsey Gulick, 1865–1918* (New York: Teachers College, 1934), 54. Hopkins, *History,* 378–85, provides an informative discussion of morality work of the YMCA. The emphasis of the White Cross Society on sexual purity in the 1880s is one example of the attempt to combine personal and social efforts for improvement.

31. Clyde Binfield, *George Williams and the Y.M.C.A.* (London: Heinemann, 1973), 20–21. See also Kenneth Scott Latourette, *World Service: A History of the Foreign Work and World Service of the Young Men's Christian Association of the United States and Canada* (New York: Association Press, 1957), 21ff., and *Fifty Years' Work amongst Young Men in All Lands: A Review of the Work of the Young Men's Christian Association* (London: Botolph, 1894).

32. Francis Gulick Jewett, *Luther Halsey Gulick: Missionary in Hawaii, Micronesia, Japan, and China* (Boston: Congregational Sunday School and Publishing Society, 1896), 15.

33. Clifford E. Clark Jr., *Henry Ward Beecher: Spokesman for a Middle-Class America* (Urbana, Ill.: University of Illinois Press, 1978), 132–34. See also Kathryn Teresa Long, *The Revival of 1857–58: Interpreting an American Religious Awakening* (New York: Oxford University, 1998) for an interpretation of how the revival of 1858 broke new ground through the use of lay leadership, its urban orientation, and its emphasis on business culture. Also, cf. William C. Beecher and Samuel Scoville, *A Biography of Henry Ward Beecher* (New York: Charles L. Webster and Co., 1888), 375. Beecher took a keen interest in the revival. He postponed his other activities and devoted full-time to playing off the revival. He held daily prayer meetings and met individually with those in doubt. But his approach reflected changes in society and within the church and revealed how much he had modified his faith. Beecher no longer threatened his congregation with eternal damnation. The love of God, rather than the fear of retribution, became the chief reason for conversion. "If this remedy fails, I know of no other," he stated. "If love will not save you, fear will be of no avail," he wrote (Clark, *Henry Ward Beecher*, 134).

The difference between Beecher's attitude and that of Charles Finney was obvious when Beecher declared that "I very soon saw that in conducting a revival my business was to bring to bear upon men the influence of the gospel . . . and then to let every one repent, become converted and come into the church according to his temperament. If when he has got in, he says, 'I love God and hate sin,' that is enough to begin with" (ibid., citing William Beecher quoting Henry Ward Beecher, "Lecture Room Talk," 13 November 1860). Beecher understood conversion as the gradual development of character rather than as the instantaneous experience of divine grace.

34. Furman Bishop, *The College Game* (Indianapolis: Bobbs-Merrill, 1974), 22.

35. Michael Oriard, *Sporting with the Gods: The Rhetoric of Play and Game in American Culture* (Cambridge: Cambridge University Press, 1991), 177.

36. J. H. Sawyer, "Henry Ward Beecher and Catherine E. Beecher and Their Influence on the Physical Work of the Young Men's Christian Association," 6, in Gulick's Theses at the Springfield College Archives, Special Collection, hereafter referred to as SCA-SC.

37. William G. McLoughlin, *The Meaning of Henry Ward Beecher: An Essay on the Shifting Values of Mid-Victorian America, 1840–1870* (New York: Alfred A. Knopf, 1970), 151, quoting Beecher.

38. Henry Ward Beecher, *Eyes and Ears* (Boston: Ticknor and Fields, 1863), 205–6.

39. Henry Ward Beecher, *A Treasure of Illustration* (New York: Fleming H. Revell, 1904), 50.

40. "Amusements," *New Englander* (1867): 411.

41. Ibid., 421–22.

42. McLoughlin, *Meaning*, 258.

43. Ibid., 68.

44. Hopkins, *History*, 187, offers a short analysis of this "almost forgotten story." However, Smith, *Revivalism*, 76, feels that Hopkins insufficiently stressed

the YMCA's "intimate bond with the churches." This void may have helped isolate "sport" history from "religious" history.

45. Immediately after Moody's death, William R. Moody, *The Life of Dwight L. Moody* (New York: Fleming H. Revell, 1900), 55–62, reflected Moody's early work and clearly identified him with muscular Christianity.

46. Gene A. Getz, *MBI: The Story of Moody Bible Institute* (Chicago: Moody Press, 1969), 26.

47. Marsden, *Fundamentalism,* 33.

48. Binfield, *Williams,* 222, connects Finney with Moody and the extended YMCA movement in Britain and on the continent.

49. Margaret Lamberts Bendroth, *Fundamentalism and Gender, 1875 to the Present* (New Haven: Yale University, 1993), 20

50. Smith, *Revivalism,* 63.

51. Long, *Revival of 1857–58,* emphasizes the role of secular and religious press in extending the revival and in popularizing converts such as Gardner.

52. Kathryn T. Long, "The Power of Interpretation: The Revival of 1857–58 and the Historiography of Revivalism in America," *Religion and American Culture* 4, no. 1 (winter 1994): 77–105.

53. Martin Marty, *Righteous Empire* (New York: Dial, 1970), 180.

54. Ruth Rouse, *The World's Student Christian Federation: A History of the First Thirty Years* (London: SCM Press, 1948), 27; Hopkins, *History,* 278–79; Charles Ober, *Luther Wishard: Projector of World Movements* (New York: Association Press, 1927).

55. L. L. Doggett, *Life of Robert R. McBurney* (Cleveland: F. M. Barton, 1902), 204–5.

56. Ibid., 193.

57. Ibid., 194. McLoughlin's excellent analysis of the Finney, Beecher, Moody, and Sunday connection emphasizes the differing ideas of progress among them. Moody, struggling to convert the poorest elements of Chicago's South Side, was convinced that the world had been getting steadily worse since Adam's fall. Beecher categorically disagreed. After talking to Moody, he told a friend: "I thought I saw the secret of his working and plans. He is a believer in the second advent of Christ, and in our times. He thinks it is no use to attempt to work for this world." Moody searched the Bible for God's views and concluded, "I don't find any place where God says the world is to grow better and better. . . . I find that the earth is to grow worse and worse. . . . I look upon this world as a wrecked vessel: God has given me a lifeboat and said to me, 'Moody, save all you can'" (McLoughlin, *Meaning,* 121).

58. James B. Reynolds, *Two Centuries of Christian Activity at Yale* (New York: G. P. Putnam's Sons, 1901), 107.

59. Doggett, *McBurney,* 194.

60. Ibid., 87, 95.

61. Ibid., 100.

62. Ibid., 192ff.

63. J. C. Pollock, *Moody: A Biographical Portrait of the Pacesetter in Modern Mass Evangelism* (New York: Macmillan Co., 1963), 121ff.–227ff. Doggett, *McBurney,* 5ff. Emmett Dedmon, *Great Enterprises: 100 Years of the YMCA of Metropolitan Chicago* (New York: Rand McNally, 1957), 76ff.

64. See Gundry, *Love,* 175–93, for a description of Moody's development of a premillennial position, and Sandeen, *Roots,* for the Niagara conference in

1875 and the prophecy conference in 1878, which established a firm premillennial position in evangelical circles.

65. Doggett, *McBurney*, 205.

66. Pollock, *Moody*, 198.

67. J. Edmund Welch, "Edward Hitchcock, M.D., Founder of Physical Education in the College Curriculum" (Ed.D. diss., George Peabody, 1962), 22.

68. Alanson Fish, "Life, Work, and Influence of Dio Lewis," Gulick Theses, SCA-SC, a Gulick student's work written in 1898.

69. Mary Eastman, *The Biography of Dio Lewis* (New York: Fowler and Wells, 1891), 30.

70. Gulick, "Sargent," n.d., SCA-SC.

71. Binfield, *Williams*, 5, 20.

72. Binfield's work explores extensively the connections of the YMCA to the ongoing revivals. Binfield links the YMCA leadership with the Keswicks (Binfield, *Williams*, 222ff.). As described below, even McBurney, who was regarded as liberal by some, acknowledged throughout his career that changing lives was the critical element of the YMCA work.

73. L. L. Doggett, *Studies in Association Work* (New York: Association Press, 1905), 19.

74. Hopkins, *History*, 380.

75. Ibid.

76. Ibid., 379.

77. Ibid., 378.

78. Mayer N. Zald and Patricia Denton, "From Evangelism to General Service: The Transformation of the YMCA," *Administrative Science Quarterly* 8, no. 2 (September 1963): 215ff.

79. Hopkins, *History*, 379. Drummond moved in and out of various segments of society. A personal friendship with Moody, developed from his student days, carried through his career until Moody's death in 1899. In his tour of American colleges in 1886 when he was at Yale, Drummond was so busy with social encounters that he had to "escape" to a cemetery to respond to his mail. Later that same day he wrote, "I had a delightful day at Hartford last Friday after writing you—called on Mark Twain, Mrs. Harriet Beecher Stowe, and the widow of Horace Bushnell." George Adam Smith, *The Life of Henry Drummond* (New York: McClure, Phillips and Co., 1901), 380.

80. Hopkins, *History*, 372.

81. Marty, *Righteous*, 177–82. This two-party model continues to be helpful, despite recent challenges; cf. Douglas Jacobsen and William Vance Trollinger Jr., "Historiography of American Protestantism: The Two-Party Paradigm and Beyond," *Fides et Historia* 25, no. 3 (fall 1993): 4–15. Marty's first "public party" held on to existing postmillennial commitments theologically, but they "gradually lost faith in revivalism and worked instead with [secular] techniques and processes which strove for some transformation of the world" (Marty, *Righteous*, 179). In addition, their thinking was influenced by philosophical trends that discounted the supernatural and emphasized unchangeable laws that determine the course of events. They "began gradually to abandon the dramatically supernatural aspects of the postmillennial view of history" (Marsden, *Fundamentalism*, 50).

Meanwhile Marty's second "private party" responded more pessimistically to "the shattering effects of the [Civil] war, the trauma of strikes and financial panics in the 1870s and 1880s, [and] the formation of an urban world with its apparently intractable problems" (Marty, *Righteous,* 180). While their post-millennial, public, fellow Protestants optimistically maintained faith in the possibility of "the redemption and sanctification of our whole social system" (Grenz, *Millennial,* 158), the private, premillennial Protestants sought to combine an existing supernatural worldview with a more literal interpretation of the Bible and less favorable views toward secular progress. "During the 1860's, premillennialism of this sort was rapidly rising in popularity" (Marsden, *Fundamentalism,* 51).

82. Weber, *Living,* 26.

83. Ibid., 28.

84. Besides supernaturalism, biblical literalism, and pessimistic views of modern society, the premillennialists generally endorsed a new version of Finney's perfectionism that came to be known as "Keswick holiness." "By 1870, holiness teachings of one sort or another seemed to be everywhere in American revivalist Protestantism" (Marsden, *Fundamentalism,* 75), and the Keswick vocabulary emphasized several distinctly manly themes such as "power" and "victory" which "undoubtedly increased the movement's masculine appeal" (Bendroth, *Fundamentalism,* 22). The possibility of "victorious living" over sinful temptations plus the "power for service" as Christian workers became staples in the private, Keswick-influenced, premillennial party of evangelical Protestants who were about to become the dominant force in the engagement of muscular Christianity.

85. "Intercollegiate Football," *New Englander and Yale Review* 45 (December 1886): 1047.

86. Hopkins, *History,* 383.

87. Ibid., 183.

88. Ibid., 189.

89. Laurence L. Doggett, *History of the Young Men's Christian Association* (New York: Association Press, 1922), 102; Allen Guttmann, *A Whole New Ball Game* (Chapel Hill: University of North Carolina, 1988), uses the immigration and socialization theme as background for the development of basketball in the YMCA.

90. Hopkins, *History,* 203.

91. Ibid., 189–202. The following succinct description of the YMCA was presented in Latourette, *World Service,* 22: "The Young Men's Christian Association was born of warm evangelism. It was for young men. It was closely related to urban business. It was for members of the 'white-collar' class. It had at heart not only the spiritual welfare but also other aspects of the well-being of young men. It was lay. It was Protestant, but transcended denominational boundaries. It had the continuing financial support and guidance of older men who had attained wealth and prominence through the 'free enterprise' tradition of the nineteenth century."

92. Norman Grubb, *C. T. Studd* (Ft. Washington, Pa.: Christian Liberty Press, 1982), 17ff. Much of the following Studd material is taken from Grubb's commentary. Grubb was C. T. Studd's son-in-law.

93. Richard C. Morse, *My Life with Young Men: Fifty Years in the Young Men's Christian Association* (New York: Association Press, 1918), 344. Grubb, *Studd,* 31ff.

94. Grubb, *Studd,* 33.

95. Ibid., 55.

96. Ibid., 110.

97. Cf. David Howard, *Student Power in World Evangelism* (Downers Grove, Ill.: InterVarsity Press, 1970).

98. Pollock, *Moody*, 252. Allan Gibson Steel (1858–1914) was perhaps the greatest cricket player of the nineteenth century.

99. Grubb, *Studd*, 29–30.

Chapter 2: The Engagement of Religion and Sport

1. Charles K. Ober, *Luther D. Wishard: Projector of World Movements* (New York: Association Press, 1927), 117–18. See also Richard C. Morse, *My Life with Young Men: Fifty Years in the Young Men's Christian Association* (New York: Association Press, 1918), 351.

2. Ober, *Wishard*, 116.

3. *Collegiate Bulletin of the Young Men's Christian Association* 8, no. 6 (March 1886): 1.

4. Ibid.

5. Luther Gulick's call for young men to join the association the following year in "a movement toward Christian character in sport" fit this pattern. Gulick argued, "Our associations are not merely groups of men working for self improvement. They are groups of men working for the extension of Christ's Kingdom among young men. The Athletic League is based upon the idea that Christ's Kingdom should include the athletic world, that the influence of athletics upon character must be on the side of honesty and Christian courtesy, and not upon the side of dishonesty and brutality. The League undertakes, just so far as possible, to bring about a change in this athletic spirit. . . . The former domination of athletics by men having other standards than those of the association has been alluded to. Our physical directors, on the other hand, constitute a body of Christian men who, we hope, in the course of time, by virtue of higher and stronger motives and character, will change this situation for the better. Associated effort is far more effective than individual effort. The League offers the channel of affiliation through which these men may co-operate for the higher ends" (Luther Gulick, Secretary of the League, SPC Archives GV 563 Y6 A4).

6. Ernest R. Sandeen, *The Roots of Fundamentalism: British and American Millenarianism, 1800–1930* (Chicago: University of Chicago Press, 1970), 180. Much of Speer's writing reflects the Keswick influence, especially *Christ and Life* (New York: Fleming H. Revell, 1901).

7. C. Howard Hopkins, *History of the Y.M.C.A. in North America* (New York: Association Press, 1951), 385.

8. Ober, *Wishard*, 122. C. Howard Hopkins, *John R. Mott, 1865–1955* (Grand Rapids: Eerdmans, 1979) provides a balanced view of Mott and the youth missionary movement.

9. See *Report of the First International Convention of the Student Volunteer Movement for Foreign Missions, 1891* (Boston: T. O. Metcalf, 1891) and quadrennial reports thereafter through 1936 for the work of SVM. Studd and Mott are illustrative of a group of dedicated muscular Christians who helped carry the message of world evangelism with youthful ardor. Others included Charles Ober, who served as student director of Northfield from 1885 to 1890 after

joining Luther Wishard in 1884 as associate for the international committee. Robert P. Wilder, whose family was linked to the Haystack Meeting of 1806, which had energized a missionary outburst early in the nineteenth century, organized college students for missionary activity.

10. Ibid., 34.

11. Ibid.

12. Ober, *Wishard,* 116. Drummond followed the same pattern after his visit to the United States the following year (1887). According to Ober quoting Wishard, "Drummond fully met—yes, highly surpassed—our expectations in the impressions he made on the students, but greatly to our disappointment, we found him utterly disinclined to carry anything home in the way of organized methods. This is another example of the differences between the American and British approaches to muscular Christianity" (Ruth Rouse, *The World's Student Christian Federation: A History of the First Thirty Years* [London: SCM Press, 1948], 36).

13. *Collegiate Bulletin* 8, no. 6 (March 1886): 1.

14. Ibid., 258.

15. Kenneth Scott Latourette, *World Service: A History of the Foreign Work and World Service of the Young Men's Christian Association of the United States and Canada* (New York: Association Press, 1957), 37.

16. T. J. Shanks, *College of Colleges: Led by D. L. Moody* (Chicago: Fleming H. Revell, 1887), 24ff. Reports for the next year were also edited by Shanks and were titled *College Students at Northfield, or A College of Colleges, No. 2.* A third volume edited by Fred L. Norton was again titled *A College of Colleges Led by D. L. Moody.* From this point each will be cited as *College* with the year following in parentheses.

17. J. C. Pollock, *Moody: A Biographical Portrait of the Pacesetter in Modern Mass Evangelism* (New York: Macmillan, 1963), 258.

18. Ibid., 257.

19. Ibid.

20. James B. Reynolds, et al., *Two Centuries of Christian Activity at Yale* (New York: G. P. Putnam's Sons, 1901), 250.

21. *Intercollegian* 12, no. 1 (October 1889): 6.

22. Harper is an interesting member of this group. A child prodigy in foreign languages, he had gained national recognition while still in his twenties. While teaching at Denison College in Ohio, Harper was converted and baptized, then spent the next decade speaking on the Chautauqua circuit and at Bible conferences as well as pursuing his teaching career. He went to Yale in 1886 and established national credentials before moving to the University of Chicago as its first president in 1892. See Theodore Morrison, *Chautauqua: A Center for Education, Religion, and the Arts in America* (Chicago: University of Chicago Press, 1974), 73ff. for further discussion of the early career of Harper.

23. Timothy P. Weber, *Living in the Shadow of the Second Coming,* enlarged edition (Grand Rapids: Zondervan, 1983), 74.

24. Dana L. Robert, "The Legacy of Arthur Tappan Pierson," *International Bulletin of Missionary Research* 8, no. 3 (July 1984): 120.

25. John R. Mott, "The Student Missionary Uprising," *The Missionary Review of the World* (November 1889): 824.

26. Arthur T. Pierson, "The Signal Cry of the New Crusade," *The Missionary Review of the World* (July 1891): 537–40; cf. Dana L. Robert, "The Origin of the Student Volunteer Watchword: 'The Evangelization of the World in this Generation,'" *International Bulletin of Missionary Research* 10, no. 4 (October 1986): 146–47. In November that year, Pierson addressed the prophecy conference in Chicago on the topic "Our Lord's Second Coming, a Motive to World-wide Evangelism." His inclusivist denominational posture combined with a hard-edged premillennialism he had adopted in the late 1870s, and his "urgency and enthusiasm for the missionary enterprise were directly related to his millennial hopes."

27. Dana L. Robert, "The 'Crisis of Missions': Premillennial Mission Theory and the Origins of Independent Evangelical Missions," in *Earthen Vessels: American Evangelicals and Foreign Missions, 1880–1980*, eds. Joel A. Carpenter and Wilbert R. Shenk (Grand Rapids: William B. Eerdmans, 1990), 36.

28. Tissington Tatlow, *The Story of the Student Christian Movement of Great Britain and Ireland* (London: Student Christian Movement Press, 1933), 12.

29. *College* (1887), 235–36. It is interesting that the British speakers and observers made the most explicit connections between manliness and Christianity. Americans, in practice, would imply such a connection but not dictate it.

30. *College* (1887), 26.

31. Ibid.

32. Ibid., 263.

33. *Intercollegian* 10, no. 4: 29.

34. *Intercollegian* 12, no. 1: 6–7.

35. See Mott, "Student Missionary Uprising," 825, for an explicit invocation of the Cambridge Band and a decision "to adopt a similar plan." Probably Mott personally never endorsed premillennialism as a basis of world evangelization.

36. Dwight L. Moody, "Our Lord's Return," *New Sermons, Addresses, and Prayers* (New York: Henry S. Goodspeed, 1877), 535.

37. Weber, *Living*, 53.

38. Ralph Henry Gabriel, *Religion and Learning at Yale* (New Haven: Yale University, 1958), 210. Some muscular Christians began to be labeled pejoratively as "the Dwight Hall Heelers."

39. SCA-SC, "Minutes," 29 September 1894.

40. *College* (1887), 263.

41. John Mott, *The Present World Situation* (New York: Student Volunteers for Foreign Mission, 1915), 3.

42. National Council of Congregational Churches, Thirteenth Triennial Session, 19.

43. Robert J. Cole, ed., *Students in the Present Mission Crisis* (New York, 1910), 31. The Minutes of the SVM meetings are thorough and cover a half-century of quadrennial meetings. Also William H. Beahm, "Factors in the Development of the Student Volunteer Movement for Foreign Missions" (Ph.D. diss., University of Chicago, 1941) is helpful.

44. Cole, *Present Mission Crisis*, 173.

45. "Religion in Yale University," *New Englander and Yale Review* 45 (December 1886): 1047.

46. *Young Men's Era*, 10 December 1891, 779.

47. Rouse, *World's Christian*, 29.

48. Walter Pilkington, *Hamilton College: 1812–1962* (New York: Hamilton College, 1962), 202.

49. Albion W. Small, college president and head of the sociology department at the University of Chicago, as quoted in Richard J. Storr, *Harper's University: The Beginnings* (Chicago: University of Chicago Press, 1966), 179.

50. See Ethel Dorgan, *Luther Halsey Gulick, 1865–1918* (New York: Columbia University Press, 1934), and Frances Gulick Jewett, *Luther Halsey Gulick: Missionary* (Boston: Congregational Sunday School and Publishing Society, 1896).

51. SCA-SC, Box 1896, "Special Training for Gymnasium Instructors."

52. SCA-SC, "Athletic League."

53. SCA-SC, Box 1896. See Gulick's address to the 29th YMCA convention in 1891.

54. The early Gulick was similar in viewpoint to the early Harper. Their philosophies of and approaches to evangelism appear to have been much more clearly and openly stated during the 1880s than a decade later.

55. SCA-SC, Box 1896.

56. SCA-SC, Von DeSteiner.

57. Dorgan, *Gulick*, 27.

58. SCA-SC, article titled "Fundamental Basis of the Young Men's Christian Association," n.d. His lecture on the legitimate place of athletics in the YMCA, given at the 1894 Massachusetts State Convention, argued against those in the association who opposed athletics because it would lead to specialization and contribute to the evil that athletics was meant to overcome. Gulick's solution was the development of the pentathlon and handicapped point systems, which would produce all-around athletes or level the playing field.

59. L. L. Doggett, *Life of Robert R. McBurney* (Cleveland: F. M. Barton, 1902), 203ff. See Benjamin Rader, *American Sport Heritage* (New York: Prentice-Hall, 1983), 149ff., for an explanation of how muscular Christianity furnished the rationale for "controlling young men" and lessening the perceived negative influences of the city, early maturity, economic greed, and sexual impurity (usually masturbation). Rader indicates that there was a Rousseauian naivete of "paradise lost" by the closing of the frontier and the emergence of the modern city. Sports, many of the boy-workers came to believe, could serve as an effective surrogate for the lost rural experience.

60. Luther Gulick, "The Legitimate Phase of Athletics in the YMCA," SCA-SC, BV1145 G8.

61. Luther Gulick, Secretary of the League, SCA-SC, GV 563 Y6 A4.

62. Ibid.

63. Luther H. Gulick, "The Doctrine of 'Hands Off' in Play," *Proceedings of the Third Annual Playground Congress* (New York: Playground Association of America, 1909), 3.

64. Donald J. Mrozek, *Sport and American Mentality, 1880–1910* (Knoxville: University of Tennessee Press, 1983), 226–35, esp. 227. See also Allen Guttmann, *From Ritual to Record: The Nature of Modern Sports* (New York: Columbia University Press, 1978).

65. John A. Lucas and Ronald A. Smith, *Saga of American Sport* (Philadelphia: Lea and Febiger, 1978), 216ff.

66. Ellis Lucia, *Mr. Football: Amos Alonzo Stagg* (South Brunswick: A. S. Barnes, 1970), 42, 189ff.

67. University of Chicago Archives, Harper Papers, box XIV, folder 38, hereafter cited as UCA, Harper. Considerable mythology accompanied Stagg, which he to some degree expanded and exploited. For example, he was fond of relating the story of how Harper had "upped" the financial incentive for Stagg to come to Chicago because Stagg "kept silent and thought" when Harper was making the offer (Amos Alonzo Stagg and Wesley Winans Stout, *Touchdown* [New York: Longmans, 1927], 143). As evident in Stagg's correspondance, Stagg actually sought advice from Harper about which job he should take, since he had offers from Pennsylvania, Yale, and Johns Hopkins to coach. Stagg's arguments evidently raised his salary. He stated that he "felt he was not doing right by myself in agreeing to come to Chicago for so small a salary" (Letter, UCA, Harper, box XIV, folder 38).

68. Ibid., 105ff.

69. Ibid.

70. Ibid., 130. See Hopkins, *Mott,* 49ff., for a discussion of Harper and Stagg's influence on Mott. Alexander Weyand, *The Saga of American Football* (New York: Macmillan, 1955), 34ff., explores Stagg's role in the development of football at the conclusion of his career.

71. Reynolds, et al., eds., *Two Centuries,* 264ff. Gabriel, *Religion and Learning,* 202. Stagg and Stout, *Touchdown,* 110.

72. Ibid., 42, 100–101. For insight into Harper's views see James P. Ward, *The Bible and the University: The Messianic Vision of William Rainey Harper* (Chicago: University of Chicago Press, 1987). One of Stagg's colleagues stated clearly that "the secretaryship is one branch of ministry. . . . I am giving my life to the ministry. My pulpit is sometimes on the athletic field. . . ." (see *College* [1889], 84).

73. Storr, *Harper's,* 179; SCA-SC, "Autobiography."

74. Lucia, *Mr. Football,* 189. Stagg indicated that sport was a manifestation of faith, calling for clean living, honest thinking, and level dealing.

75. Gilbert Patten's Merriwell served as the prototype for the American amateur athlete during the first half of the twentieth century much as Tom Brown had served those of the last half of the nineteenth century.

76. *Young Men's Era,* 10 December 1891, 778.

Chapter 3: The Disengagement of Evangelical Muscular Christians from Sport

1. *American Physical Education Review* (May 1914): 12–13.

2. Bernice Larsen Webb has completed the most thorough study of Naismith in *The Basketball Man: James Naismith* (Lawrence, Kans.: University Press of Kansas, 1973). Yet her research and much of the reference information about Naismith's invention of basketball are rooted in material from the 1930s. A document that Naismith dictated the decade before his death was edited and enhanced by several individuals before it was published in 1941 by the YMCA as *Basketball: Its Origins and Development* (New York: Association Press, 1941). Later it was again edited, by Robert Cheney, and republished as *Basketball's Origins: Creative Problem Solving in the Gilded Age* (Cambridge, N.Y.: Bear Publications, 1976). The original version was reissued in 1996 by the University of Nebraska Press in its Bison Books series. Recent interpretations

still follow the framework established by these Naismith reflections, e.g,. see Allen Guttmann, *A Whole New Ball Game: An Interpretation of American Sports* (Chapel Hill: University of North Carolina Press, 1988), 70–75. Most interviews of family and friends occurred after the 1960s. The time lapse between an event and the memory of that event has created a unique oral tradition. Some of the most critical pieces of information were passed down from Naismith forty years after an event occurred. The core of this section is derived from these sources as well as interviews conducted by one of the authors with those who knew him personally: Thomas Ryther, Bertha Weiler, and Henry Shenk.

3. Cheney, *Basketball's Origins*, ii.

4. The relationship between Phog Allen and James Naismith deserves further research. An interesting interplay between the two reflects conflict over coaching versus not coaching, American sporting traditions versus British traditions, and disciple and mentor roles in their relationship. Naismith was never able to articulate his views in the way his mentor, Luther Gulick, did. And in fact Gulick's position on supervision was almost opposite Naismith's. Speaking before the third annual Playground Congress in 1909, Gulick endorsed the idea of strong leadership (Luther Gulick, "Doctrine of 'Hands Off' in Play," 3, 10 SCA-SC) at SCA. "Within the last few years there has arisen a pernicious doctrine with reference to children—the doctrine of 'hands off.' It is based on the idea that children grow up wholesomely if only they are let alone. . . ." Gulick argued the reverse, that game activity needed adult supervision and guidance. "Through these play leaders there is from generation to generation a transfer of character, as in the case of the young man mentioned, who transformed the young manhood of a country community by his contact with the boys in playing baseball."

5. Burton St. John, *North American Students and World Advance* (New York: Student Volunteer Movement for Foreign Missions, 1920), 76.

6. Ibid., 90.

7. Milton T. Stauffer, ed., *Christian Students and World Problems* (New York: Student Volunteer Movement for Foreign Missions, 1924), 87.

8. Ibid., 64.

9. Clifford W. Putney, "Going Upscale: The YMCA and Post War America," *Journal of Sport History* 20, no. 2 (1993): 162; cf. Putney, "Muscular Christianity: The Strenuous Mood in American Protestantism, 1880–1920" (Ph.D. diss., Brandeis University, 1994).

10. Ibid.

11. Laurence R. Veysey, *The Emergence of the American University* (Chicago: University of Chicago Press, 1956), 2, 4, 9.

12. George M. Marsden, *The Soul of the American University: From Protestant Establishment to Established Unbelief* (New York: Oxford, 1994), 237–38.

13. Veysey, *Emergence*, 265–66.

14. Marsden, *Soul*, 279, 283, quoting the Carnegie Foundation for the Advancement of Teaching, *Second Annual Report of the President and Treasurer* (1907), 53–54, in Richard Hofstadter and Walter P. Metzger, *The Development of Academic Freedom in the United States* (New York: Columbia University Press, 1955), 362.

15. Marsden, *Soul*, 268, citing Harold Bolce, "Rallying Round the Cross," *Cosmopolitan* 47 (September 1909): 492; Marsden, *Soul*, 309.

16. Robert Taft, *Across the Years on Mount Oread, 1866 . . . 1941* (Lawrence, Kans.: University of Kansas, 1941), 95.

17. William McLoughlin describes Billy Sunday's preaching as "an amalgamation of the views of Finney, Moody, and Beecher." William G. McLoughlin, *Billy Sunday Was His Real Name* (Chicago: University of Chicago Press, 1955), 121. He adds, "Finney's preaching marked the climax of the first phase of this recurrent revival; Moody's campaigns marked the climax of the second phase; and Sunday . . . was to climax the final, culminating phase," 38. Also, Lee Thomas, *Billy I* (Van Nuys, Calif.: Son-Rise Books, 1974), 34, describes Sunday as "America's first superstar athlete to accept Jesus Christ as his Lord and Savior." However, Thomas portrays Sunday's move from sports performance to evangelist as complex and presents Sunday as much more hesitant to leave baseball than do other scholars (Thomas, *Billy I*, 66ff.).

18. McLoughlin, *Billy*, 142. His attitude toward fighting sin demonstrates his theatrically pugnacious frame of reference: "I'm against sin. I'll kick it as long as I've got a foot, and I'll fight it as long as I've got a fist. I'll butt it as long as I've got a head. I'll bite it as long as I've got a tooth. And when I'm old and fistless and footless and toothless, I'll gum it till I go home to Glory and it goes home to perdition!" D. Bruce Lockerbie, *Billy Sunday* (Waco: Word, 1965), 63. McGloughlin explores how this fighting theme was played out in his meetings, 84ff.

19. Thomas, *Billy I*, 63ff.

20. Elijah P. Brown, *The Real Billy Sunday: The Life and Work of Rev. William Ashley Sunday, D.D., the Baseball Evangelist* (New York: Fleming H. Revell Company, 1914), 27ff.

21. Billy Sunday, "Why I Left Professional Baseball," *Young Men's Era* 19, no. 30 (27 July 1893): 1.

22. Andrew Miracle and Roger Rees, *Lessons of the Locker Room: The Myth of School Sports* (Amherst, N.Y.: Prometheus Books, 1994), 43.

23. Perhaps reflecting Billy Sunday's personal analysis, William Ellis, *Billy Sunday: The Man and His Message* (Philadelphia: Winston Co., 1914), 48, indicates that Sunday refused an invitation to become a physical director for the YMCA because "His religious zeal from the first outshone his physical prowess."

24. Thomas, *Billy I*, 67ff; Lockerbie, *Billy*, 4ff.

25. Sunday obviously used his reputation as a former professional baseball player, a perspective presented by his colleague Homer Rodeheaver, *Twenty Years with Billy Sunday* (Winona Lake, Ind.: The Rodeheaver Hall-Mack Co., 1936), 88ff., and Brown, who used *The Baseball Evangelist* as a subtitle for his work *The Real Billy Sunday*.

26. McLoughlin, *Billy*, 138.

27. David Moberg, *The Great Reversal* (Philadelphia: Lippincott, 1977).

28. Norman Grubb, *C. T. Studd* (Ft. Washington, Pa.: Christian Liberty Press, 1982), 33.

29. Douglas Frank, *Less Than Conquerors: How Evangelicals Entered the Twentieth Century* (Grand Rapids: William B. Eerdmans, 1986).

30. Finis Farr, *Black Champion: The Life and Times of Jack Johnson* (1964; reprint, Greenwich, Conn.: Fawcett Publications, 1969), 69, 108 (page citations are to the reprint edition).

31. C. Allyn Russell, *Voices of American Fundamentalism: Seven Biographical Studies* (Philadelphia: Westminster, 1976), 61, 203.

32. "That Boxing Match," *Moody Bible Institute Monthly* 22, no. 1 (September 1921): 548; "Clergymen and Base Ball," *Moody Bible Institute Monthly* 22, no. 12 (August 1922): 1155; "Protection of the Sabbath As a Civil Institution," *Moody Bible Institute Monthly* 21, no. 6 (February 1921): 264; "Stopping Sunday Base-ball," *Moody Bible Institute Monthly* 23, no. 2 (October 1922): 64.

33. C. Howard Hopkins, *History of the Y.M.C.A. in North America* (New York: Association Press, 1951), 511.

34. Ibid., 645.

35. Ibid., 521.

36. "Finds Student Y in Perilous Position," *Christian Century* 44 (23 June 1927): 787–88.

37. The classical study by Mayer Zald and Patricia Denton, "From Evangelism to General Service: The Transformation of the YMCA," *Administrative Science Quarterly* 8, no. 2 (September 1963): 214–34, explores this institutional change.

38. Robert T. Handy, "The American Religious Depression, 1925–1935," *Church History* 29, no. 1 (1960).

39. Robert T. Handy, *A Christian America*, 2d ed. (New York: Oxford University, 1984), 177–81.

40. Gulick, "Doctrine," 3. Roosevelt appears to have endorsed the concept of "natural physical" education while at the same time implementing institutional control through organizations such as the NCAA when he called for greater oversight and institutional control during the 1905–6 football crisis.

41. "Football As Our Greatest Popular Spectacle," *Literary Digest* 75, no. 9 (2 December 1922).

42. John R. Tunis, "Changing Trends in Sport," *Harper's Magazine* 170, no. 1 (December 1934): 86.

43. Tony Ladd, "Sexual Discrimination in Youth Sport: The Case of Margaret Gisolo," in Reet Howell, *Her Story in Sport: A Historical Anthology of Women in Sports* (West Point, N.Y.: Leisure Press, 1982), 579–89.

44. Tony Ladd, "Reform in Educational Sport: Lessons from History" (paper presented to the American Culture Association, Toronto, March 1990).

45. Howard Savage, *American College Athletics* (New York: Carnegie Foundation, 1929).

Chapter 4: Toward the Reengagement of Evangelicalism and Sport

1. Several helpful biographies of Billy Graham provide details of his life and career in revivalism. These include John Pollock, *Billy Graham: The Authorized Biography* (New York: McGraw-Hill, 1966); Marshall Frady, *Billy Graham: Parable of American Righteousness* (Boston: Little, Brown, 1979); David Lockard, *The Unheard Billy Graham* (Waco: Word, 1971); William G. McLoughlin, *Billy Graham, Revivalist in a Secular Age* (New York: Ronald, 1960). Probably the best work on Graham is William Martin, *A Prophet with Honor: The Billy Graham Story* (New York: William Morrow, 1991), including pp. 100–101 for background on the Charlotte revival of 1947. Graham's recent autobiography, *Just As I Am: The Autobiography of Billy Graham* (San Francisco: HarperCollins, 1997), provides another perspective.

2. Frady, *Billy Graham*, 174.

3. "Mr. Dodds Goes to Town," *Time* 39, no. 10 (9 March 1942): 52, is a likely first mention of Dodds.

4. John R. Tunis, "The Great Sports Myth," *Harper's Monthly* 156, no. 934 (March 1928): 430.

5. Warren I. Susman, *Culture As History: The Transformation of American Society in the Twentieth Century* (New York: Pantheon, 1984), 158, 168; chap. 9, "The Culture of the Thirties," originally appeared as "The Thirties," in *The Developing of an American Culture,* 2d ed., eds. Stanley Coben and Lorman Ratner (New York: St. Martin's Press, 1983).

6. Susman, *Culture,* 154, 180–81, includes the allusion to Niebuhr.

7. Robert T. Handy, *A Christian America,* 2d ed. (New York: Oxford University, 1984), 177.

8. Robert S. Lynd and Helen Merrell Lynd, *Middletown: A Study in Modern American Culture* (New York: Harcourt, Brace and World, 1929), 406; Lynd and Lynd, *Middletown in Transition* (New York: Harcourt, Brace and Co., 1937), 311.

9. "Why No revival?" *Christian Century* 52, no. 38 (18 September 1935): 1168.

10. William Pierson Merrill, "Is Religion Dying?" *Scribner's Magazine* 94, no. 5 (November 1933): 292.

11. Robert T. Handy, "The American Religious Depression, 1925–35," *Church History* 29, no. 1 (1960): 3–16; Winthrop S. Hudson, *The Great Tradition of the American Churches* (New York: Harper and Bros., 1953), 196.

12. Richard D. Mandell, *Sport: A Cultural History* (New York: Columbia University Press, 1984), 219, 221.

13. Robert L. Duffus, "The Age of Play," *The Independent* 113, no. 3890 (20 December 1924): 539–40, 556; George Trevor, "King Football Answers the Depression," *The Literary Digest* 116, no. 12 (16 September 1933): 24, 33; "Pro Football versus Collegiate," *The Literary Digest* 122, no. 18 (31 October 1936); "More Light on Night Baseball," *The Literary Digest* 106, no. 13: 20; cf. J. F. Steiner, "Recreation and Leisure Time Activities," in *Recent Social Trends in the United States* (New York: McGraw-Hill, 1933), esp. 925–35.

14. William C. White, "Bye, Bye, Blue Laws," *Scribner's Magazine* 94, no. 2 (August 1933): 108.

15. William J. Baker, *Sports in the Western World,* rev. ed. (Urbana, Ill.: University of Illinois Press, 1988), 244; "Pari-mutuel Tonic Puts New Life in Race Season," *The Literary Digest* 116, no. 5 (29 July 1933): 27; cf. "Race-bets: $500,000,000 a Year Thrills," *The Literary Digest* 122, no. 26 (26 December 1936): 34–35.

16. Jesse Frederick Steiner, *Americans at Play: Recent Trends in Recreation and Leisure Time Activities* (New York: McGraw-Hill, 1933), v, 155, 180.

17. Martin Marty, *Righteous Empire* (New York: Dial, 1970), 177–82; Ernest R. Sandeen, *The Roots of Fundamentalism* (Chicago: University of Chicago Press, 1970), esp. 243–50; George M. Marsden, *Fundamentalism and American Culture: The Shaping of Twentieth-Century Evangelicalism, 1870–1925* (New York: Oxford University, 1980).

18. George M. Marsden, *Understanding Fundamentalism and Evangelicalism* (Grand Rapids: William B. Eerdmans, 1991), 60.

19. Merrill, "Is Religion Dying?" 290; "Billy Sunday, the Last of His Line," *Christian Century* 52, no. 47 (20 November 1935): 1476.

20. Marsden, *Understanding*, 61, 66.

21. "The Third Force in Christendom," *Life* (9 June 1958): 113; Henry P. Van Dusen, "The Third Force's Lessons for Others," *Life* (9 June 1958): 122–23; William G. McLoughlin, "Is There a Third Force in Christendom?" *Daedelus* 96 (1967): 59.

22. Marsden, "The Paradox of Revivalist Fundamentalism," chap. 4 in *Fundamentalism*, 43–48; Marsden, *Understanding*, 66, 68.

23. Joel A. Carpenter, *Revive Us Again: The Reawakening of American Fundamentalism* (New York: Oxford University, 1997), 131; cf. "A Directory of Evangelical Radio Broadcasts," *Sunday School Times* 74 (23 January 1932): 44–45.

24. Quentin J. Schultze, "Evangelical Radio and the Rise of the Electronic Church, 1921–1948," *Journal of Broadcasting and Electronic Media* 32, no. 3 (summer 1988): 293, 295, 302.

25. Joel A. Carpenter, "From Fundamentalism to the New Evangelical Coalition," in *Evangelicalism and Modern America*, ed. George M. Marsden (Grand Rapids: William B. Eerdmans, 1984), 3–16; Frank S. Mead, "Apostle to Youth," *Christian Herald* 68, no. 9 (September 1945): 15–17, 51; George Sweeting, *The Jack Wyrtzen Story* (Grand Rapids: Zondervan, 1960).

26. Robert Wuthnow, *The Restructuring of American Religion* (Princeton, N.J.: Princeton University, 1988), 42; McLoughlin, "Is There a Third Force?" 67; Carpenter, "From Fundamentalism," 15, citing Geoffrey Perrett, *Days of Sadness, Years of Triumph* (New York: Penguin, 1973), 347–50, in part; Mel Larson, *Youth for Christ: Twentieth Century Wonder* (Grand Rapids: Zondervan, 1947), 26–29, citing Hoover in *The American* (March 1946), in part.

27. Mark Senter III, "The Youth for Christ Movement As an Educational Agency and Its Impact upon Protestant Churches: 1931–1979" (Ph.D. diss., Loyola University of Chicago, 1989), 128–29.

28. Ibid., 139; Bob Bahr, *Man with a Vision: The Story of Percy Crawford* (Chicago: Moody Press, c. 1961); Joel A. Carpenter, "Revive Us Again: Alienation, Hope, and the Resurgence of Fundamentalism, 1930–1950," in *Transforming Faith: The Sacred and Secular in Modern American History*, eds. M. L. Bradbury and James B. Gilbert (New York: Greenwood, 1989), 114.

29. Sweeting, *Jack Wyrtzen*, 24–26, 48; Bahr, *Man*, 52–54; Mead, "Apostle to Youth," 15–16.

30. Sweeting, *Jack Wyrtzen*, 49–50, 60; Larson, *Youth for Christ*, 42–46.

31. Clarence Woodbury, "Bobby Soxers Sing Hallelujah," *American Magazine* 14, no. 3 (March 1946): 123; Forrest Forbes, *God Hath Chosen: The Story of Jack Wyrtzen and the Word of Life Hour* (Grand Rapids: Zondervan, 1948), 59–65.

32. Sweeting, *Jack Wyrtzen*, 74, citing *New York World Telegram* in part; Woodbury, "Bobby Soxers," 124.

33. Bruce Shelley, "The Rise of Evangelical Youth Movements," *Fides et Historia* 18, no. 1 (January 1986): 48–50; Torrey Johnson and Robert Cook, *Reaching Youth for Christ* (Chicago: Moody, 1944), 9–14; Carpenter, "Revive Us," 114–15.

34. Joel A. Carpenter, "Youth for Christ and the New Evangelicals' Place in the Life of the Nation," *Religion and the Life of the Nation*, ed. Rowland T. Sherrill (Urbana, Ill.: University of Illinois Press, 1990), 134.

35. Shelley, "Rise of Evangelical," 49; Mel Larson, *Young Man on Fire: The Story of Torrey Johnson and Youth for Christ* (Chicago: Youth Publications,

1945), 79–93; Taylor provides a version of Johnson's enlisting his support in Herbert J. Taylor, *God Has a Plan for You* (Old Tappan, N.J.: Fleming H. Revell, 1968), 64–65.

36. "Minutes, YFC Leaders' Conference, 1945," Youth for Christ collection, Billy Graham Center archives, Wheaton; James Hefley, *God Goes to High School* (Waco: Word, 1970), 23–24.

37. "Wanted: A Miracle of Good Weather and the 'Youth for Christ' Rally Got It," *Newsweek* 25, no. 24 (11 June 1945): 84.

38. Martin, *Prophet*, 95, 631; "Hearst Papers Now Boost Youth for Christ Movement," *United Evangelical Action* 6, no. 10 (2 July 1945): 1; "William Randolph Hearst's Editorial Endorsement of 'Youth for Christ,'" *United Evangelical Action* 6, no. 11 (16 July 1945): 13.

39. Harold E. Fey, "What about 'Youth for Christ'?" *Christian Century* 62, no. 25 (20 June 1945): 729, 731; cf. "Has Youth for Christ Gone Fascist?" *Christian Century* 52, no. 46 (14 November 1945): 1243–44.

40. Leslie Conrad Jr., "Non-Denominational Youth Movements," *International Journal of Religious Education* 32, no. 10 (June 1956): 16, 38.

41. "Lauds 'Youth for Christ,'" *New York Times*, 27 October 1945, 44; "Anti-Semitism Is Denied," *New York Times*, 16 December 1945, 31; "Youth for Christ," *Time* (4 February 1946): 46–47; Larson, *Young Man*, 91; Willard M. Aldrich, "Young People Are a Crop," *Moody Monthly* 45 (November 1944): 138, 140.

42. Larson, *Young Man*, 89; Larson, *Youth for Christ*, 56, 82–89; Martin, *Prophet*, 90–91; "Minutes, YFC."

43. Mel Larson, *Twentieth Century Crusade: The Story of Youth for Christ* (Grand Rapids: Zondervan, 1953), 17–20; Martin, *Prophet*, 92–105.

44. Arthur Daley, "Somehow They Always Run Faster," *New York Times Magazine* (29 February 1948): 14, 44–45.

45. Mel Larson, *Gil Dodds: The Flying Parson* (Chicago: Evangelical Beacon, 1945), 17–26.

46. Ibid., 27–29.

47. Daley, "Somehow," 45.

48. Larson, *Gil Dodds* (1945), 34–37.

49. Ibid., 37–41.

50. "Mr. Dodds," 52; Larson, *Gil Dodds* (1945), 44–46.

51. "He's Faster Than the Devil," *American Magazine* 134, no. 5 (November 1942): 87.

52. Larson, *Gil Dodds* (1945), 50–54.

53. "No. 1 Amateur," *Newsweek* 23, no. 2 (10 January 1944): 75–76.

54. "Pious Miler," *Time* 45, no. 5 (29 January 1945): 55–56; Larson, *Gil Dodds* (1945), 59–63; Larson, *Young Man*, 89.

55. Mel Larson, *Gil Dodds: The Flying Parson*, 2d ed. (Grand Rapids: Zondervan, 1948), 71; Larson, *Gil Dodds* (1945), 38.

56. Gene Farmer, "Best Indoor Mile," *Life* 24, no. 7 (16 February 1948): 95–96; "No. 1," 76.

57. Cf. Larson, *Gil Dodds* (1945); Larson, *Gil Dodds* (1948), 13–16; Larson, *Youth for Christ*, 43; Sweeting, *Jack Wyrtzen*, 69–70.

58. Larson, *Gil Dodds* (1948), 8, 69–70.

59. "Pious Miler," 55; "Wanted: a Miracle," 84.

60. "Minutes"; Martin, *Prophet*, 91–94; Larson, *Gil Dodds* (1948), 73–76.

61. Larson, *Gil Dodds* (1948), 8, 69–70.

62. Frady, *Billy Graham*, 160; Larson, *Youth for Christ*, 109.

63. Larson, *Gil Dodds* (1948), 77.

64. "Preacher's Comeback," *Time* 49, no. 5 (3 February 1947): 54, 56; "Track: the Lord's Miler," *Newsweek* 29, no. 5 (3 February 1947): 65–66; "King of the Mile," *Life* 22, no. 7 (17 February 1947): 85–86.

65. Larson, *Gil Dodds* (1948), 76–85; "Track: Gil Dodds Again," *Newsweek* 31, no. 6 (9 February 1948): 69–70.

66. "Dodds to Run in Trials," *New York Times*, 8 July 1948, 28; "Leg Injury Forces Miler Out of Trial," *New York Times*, 9 July 1948, 14.

67. Arthur Daley, "Sports of the Times: In Pursuit of Olympic Glory," *New York Times*, 9 July 1948, 14; Joseph M. Sheehan, "Whitfield Gained the Spotlight in Final Olympic Track Tryouts," *New York Times*, 12 July 1948, 16; "Yankee Stadium Scene of 1,100 Conversions," *United Evangelical Action* 7, no. 13 (15 August 1948): 15; "Gil Dodds—The Hard Luck Kid," in *Sport Annual* (New York: Bartholomew House, 1949).

68. Larson, *Twentieth Century*, 26–28; "American Leaders Are Prominent in YFC Meet," *United Evangelical Action* 7, no. 10 (July 1948): 15, 18; "11,800 Hear Scandinavian YFC Team in Four Days," (16 August 1949), unidentified source, courtesy of Erma Dodds Whitaker.

69. "Pierce, Dodds to Korea," *United Evangelical Action* 9, no. 5 (15 April 1950): 8; Bob Pierce and Gil Dodds, "God Reached Korea before Bullets," *Youth for Christ Magazine* (August 1950): 8–9; 46–47; "Americans Going to YFC World Congress," *United Evangelical Action* 9, no. 12 (1 August 1950): 9.

70. "Bibles and Basketball Aid in Formosa Mission," *United Evangelical Action* 11, no. 3 (15 March 1952): 43.

71. Dick Hillis, *Born to Climb* (Waco: Word, 1967), 20; "Bibles and Basketball," 43.

72. "Formosa Gospel Crusade: China Christian Cable" (2 July 1952), Overseas Crusades collection, Billy Graham Center Archives, Wheaton.

73. "Formosa Gospel Crusade: China Christian Cable" (27 August 1952), Overseas Crusades collection, Billy Graham Center archives, Wheaton.

74. Marsden, *Understanding*, esp. 62–72; Carpenter, "From Fundamentalism," esp. 9–16.

75. Larson, *Youth for Christ*, 86–87. Exactly why Wyrtzen never affiliated is unclear, but he quickly moved to establish his own entities apart from YFC that also reflected a more separatist agenda.

76. Initially, YFC leaders probably did not actively seek—nor necessarily know how to seek—the approval of government and media elites. They did court the favor of successful businessmen, however, which indirectly may have opened up these other cultural targets.

77. Martin, *Prophet*; cf. Ron Frank, "Graham's Youth for Christ Years: What Was Their Significance" (paper, Wheaton College Graduate School, May 1986). Frank emphasizes Graham's shift at Charlotte to an adult audience, perhaps for the first time.

78. Frady, *Billy Graham*, 174.

79. Why Youth for Christ apparently had less success with sport in Europe than in Asia is not clear. One possibility is that no individual took on the role of promoting sports in Europe as Dick Hillis did in Asia; the readiness of the Asian

crowds for the YFC methods of sports evangelism was another difference from Europe.

Chapter 5: Institutionalizing Muscular Christianity since the 1950s

1. Carol Flake, *Redemptorama: Culture, Politics, and the New Evangelicalism* (New York: Doubleday Anchor, 1984), 95–96.

2. Bill Glass, *Get in the Game!* (Waco: Word, 1965), 12–13.

3. Ibid., 13, 18.

4. Ibid., 23, 32.

5. Ibid., 32–39.

6. Ibid., 39–40.

7. Ibid., 3–4, 42.

8. Ibid., 47–49; Bill Glass, *Free at Last* (Waco: Word, 1976), 23–24.

9. Bud Schaeffer, letter to supporters, c. July 1955, Overseas Crusades collection, Billy Graham Center archives, Wheaton, Ill.

10. Helen N. Dodd, letter to Dr. Dick Hillis, 26 June 1975, Overseas Crusades collection; Jack King, letter to Helen Dodd, 2 July 1975, Sports Ambassadors collection; "First Annual Sports Ambassadors Evaluation Conference" (c. 1977), Sports Ambassadors collection, Billy Graham Center archives, Wheaton, Ill.

11. Joseph Dunn, *Sharing the Victory* (New York: Quick Fox, 1980), 6–7.

12. Ibid., 14, 17, 20–25.

13. Ibid., 33, 36.

14. Ibid., 37.

15. Ibid., 37–39.

16. "Hero Worship Harnessed," *Sports Illustrated* 4, no. 6 (6 February 1956):46, citing Palmer Hoyt in part; Dunn, *Sharing*, 39–40.

17. Dunn, *Sharing*, 42–46; "A Muscular Boost for Christian Doctrine," *Life* 41, no. 12 (17 September 1956): 67–68; "Christians in Sport," *Newsweek* 48, no. 10 (3 September 1956): 58.

18. "Forty Years of Influence—Fellowship of Christian Athletes Annual Report" (Kansas City, Mo.: Fellowship of Christian Athletes, 1994); Dunn, *Sharing*, 110–11; statistical update courtesy of Ron Frank.

19. Dunn, *Sharing*, 130–32.

20. Richard Quebedeaux, *I Found It! The Story of Bill Bright and Campus Crusade* (New York: Harper and Row, 1979), 4–12; Bill Bright, *Come, Help Change the World* (Old Tappan, N.J.: Fleming H. Revell, 1970), 35–38.

21. Quebedeaux, *I Found*, 17–18; Bright, *Come, Help*, 39–41.

22. Quebedeaux, *I Found*, 142–43.

23. Ibid., 144.

24. Ibid., esp. 80–91.

25. Flake, *Redemptorama*, 100.

26. Quebedeaux, *I Found*, 17, 143.

27. "Serving Christ through Baseball" (Warsaw, Ind.: Unlimited Potential, Inc., c. 1990); Tom Roy, interview with James A. Mathisen, Dallas, 26 April 1990.

28. Jim Grassi, "The Ultimate Fishing Challenge" (Brainerd, Minn.: Infisherman Inc., 1989); "Race Track Chaplaincy of America" (Race Track Chaplaincy of America, Illinois Division, n.d.); Bill McDonald, "These Bikers Ride Religiously," *Chicago Tribune*, 17 February 1991, section 17, 10.

29. Peter Golenbock, *Dynasty: The New York Yankees, 1949–1964* (1975; reprint, New York: Berkley Books, 1985), 289, 386–401, 424–26, 474 (page numbers refer to reprint edition).

30. Ibid., 395–96, 399.

31. Watson Spoelstra, "What's the Score?" *Youth for Christ* (October 1960), 23.

32. Tim Stafford, "In the Catacombs of Candlestick," *Christianity Today* 37, no. 5 (26 April 1993): 23.

33. Glass, *Get In,* 19; Glass also connects himself to Richardson in *Get In,* 45.

34. Ibid., 47, 111, 125–26.

35. L. Fisher, *God's Voice to the Pro* (Boca Raton, Fla.: Sports World Chaplaincy, 1969), esp. 63–64; Zola Levitt, *Somebody Called "Doc"* (Carol Stream, Ill.: Creation House, 1972), 26–33.

36. "Training for Life's Ultimate Victory" (Issaquah, Wash.: Pro Athletes Outreach, c. 1990).

37. Max Helton, interviews with James A. Mathisen, Dallas, 28 April 1991, and Cambridge Junction, Mich., 20 June 1992.

38. W. Lloyd Warner, *The Family of God: A Symbolic Study of Christian Life in America* (1959; reprint, New Haven: Yale University, 1961), 216–59 (page numbers refer to reprint edition); cf. Warner, *American Life: Dream and Reality* (Chicago: University of Chicago Press, 1953), 1–26.

39. Dwight D. Eisenhower, "Text of Eisenhower Speech," *New York Times,* 23 December 1952, 16; the speech was delivered to the Freedoms Foundation, 22 December 1952.

40. Will Herberg, *Protestant—Catholic—Jew,* rev. ed. (Garden City, N.Y.: Doubleday Anchor, 1960), 95.

41. Martin E. Marty, *The New Shape of American Religion* (New York: Harper and Bros., 1959), 67–68.

42. William J. Baker, *Sports in the Western World,* rev. ed. (Urbana, Ill.: University of Illinois, 1988), 304.

43. Richard Espy, *The Politics of the Olympic Games* (Berkeley: University of California, 1981), 38, citing David B. Kanin, "The Role of Sport in the International System" (paper presented at the Annual Convention of the International Studies Association, Toronto, 25–29 February 1976).

44. Frederick W. Cozens and Florence Scovil Stumpf, *Sports in American Life* (Chicago: University of Chicago Press, 1953), 248.

45. For a descriptive treatment of American sport as a folk religion, see James A. Mathisen, "From Civil Religion to Folk Religion: The Case of American Sport," in *Sport and Religion,* ed. Shirl J. Hoffman (Champaign, Ill.: Human Kinetics, 1992), 17–33.

46. Robert Lipsyte, *SportsWorld: An American Dreamland* (New York: Quadrangle/New York Times, 1975), x, xiv–xv.

47. Allen Guttmann, *The Olympics: A History of the Modern Games* (Urbana, Ill.: University of Illinois, 1992), esp. chap. 9, "A Time of Troubles."

48. Neil Amdur, "Mrs. King Defeats Riggs, 6-4, 6-3, 6-3, amid Circus Atmosphere," *New York Times,* 21 September 1973, 1, 31; Grace Lichtenstein, "Mrs. King Calls Victory 'Culmination' of a Career," *New York Times,* 21 September 1973, 31; Richard D. Mandell, *Sport: A Cultural History* (New York: Columbia University, 1984), 235.

49. "Are Sports Good for the Soul?" *Newsweek* 77, no. 2 (11 January 1971): 51–52.

50. Jesse Frederick Steiner, *Americans at Play: Recent Trends in Recreation and Leisure Time Activities* (New York: McGraw-Hill, 1933), 179–80.

51. Russell W. Ramsey, *God's Joyful Runner* (South Plainfield, N.J.: Bridge Publishing, 1987), vii, 57, 64–68; Mel Larson, *Gil Dodds: The Flying Parson* (Chicago: Evangelical Beacon, 1945), 33, 50.

52. Ed T. Darling, "Amusements: 20 Questions, 20 Answers," *Youth for Christ* 12, no. 5 (August 1954): 5; Donn Moomaw, "Seminary for Me," *Youth for Christ* 12, no. 6 (September 1954): 9; cf. Mel Larson, *Ten Famous Christian Athletes* (Wheaton: Miracle Books, 1958): 24, 58.

53. Glass, *Get In*, 51–52, 119–21; cf. Marvin Olasky, "Land without a Sabbath," *World* (22 May 1993): 24–25.

54. Michael Oriard, *Sporting with the Gods: The Rhetoric of Play and Game in American Culture* (Cambridge: Cambridge University Press, 1991), 253.

55. Robert Wuthnow, *The Restructuring of American Religion: Society and Faith since World War II* (Princeton: Princeton University, 1988), 107, 109.

56. Stafford, "In the Catacombs," 22–25; Pat Richie, "Ministering to Professional Athletes" (audiotape of presentation to Sports Outreach America, Dallas, 27 April 1990).

57. Richie, "Ministering."

58. Helton, interviews with Mathisen; "Motor Racing Outreach: 1994, Year in Review" (Harrisburg, N.C.: Motor Racing Outreach, 1995).

59. Pete Nowell, "Minister's Flock in the Fast Lane," *Chicago Tribune*, 10 February 1995, section 2, 8.

60. Cris Stevens, interview with James A. Mathisen, Dallas, 26 April 1990, "News from the Town Fellowship . . ." (Knoxville: Alternative Ministries, 1990).

61. On King's leadership role, see Karen Rudolph Drollinger, "Back in the Swing of Things," *Sports Spectrum* 7, no. 3 (March-April 1993): 6–9.

62. Henry Soles, interview with James A. Mathisen, Wheaton, Ill., 14 June 1991.

63. "PBF—Serving the Pro Basketball Family," (Waterford, Calif.: Pro Basketball Fellowship, c. 1992).

64. This point is developed further in chap. 7; cf. David Leon Moore, "Ballplayers Putting Faith in Christ," *USA Today*, 26 July 1991, 1C.

65. Written records of the early motivations of these organizers are incomplete; cf. Eddie Waxer, interviews with James A. Mathisen, Dallas, 27 April 1990, and Atlanta, 29 April 1995.

66. The tenuous relationship between AIA and the FCA, for example, has continued for nearly three decades. In the 1990s the FCA's relatively stronger financial support has relieved some of the tension, although FCA Executive Director Wendell Deyo "confessed" publicly his lack of trust in AIA at the Sports Outreach American meeting in Atlanta in April 1995. The two groups recently have undertaken some joint ventures, perhaps for the first time.

67. "Wheaton's All-American Burnham Scores in Classes and Pulpit, Too," *Youth for Christ* 11, no. 8 (November 1954): 8–9; Larson, *Ten Famous Athletes*, 27–35.

68. Waxer, interviews with Mathisen; Quebedeaux, *I Found*, 145–46.

69. Andrew Wingfield-Digby, "Sport," in *New Dictionary of Christian Ethics and Pastoral Theology*, eds. David J. Atkinson and David H. Fields (Leicester, England: Inter-Varsity Press, 1995), 809–10.

70. "International Sports Coalition" (Boca Raton, Fla.: International Sports Coalition, c. 1988); Waxer, interview with Mathisen, 27 April 1990.

71. "International Sports Coalition: Annual Reports, 1992, 1993, 1994" (Marietta, Ga.: International Sports Coalition, 1995); Waxer, interview with Mathisen, 29 April 1995.

72. Ralph Drollinger, "Five Trends in Sports Ministry for the '90s" (plenary presentation, Sports Outreach America, Dallas, 28 April 1991); cf. "Sports Outreach America: 1995 Annual Conference," Atlanta, 27–29 April 1995.

Chapter 6: Interinstitutional Muscular Christianity: Church, College, and Sport in Modern America

1. Advertisement for Liberty University, Lynchburg, Va., which appeared in various evangelical publications, including *Campus Life* and *Christianity Today*, 1994–95.

2. Douglas Lederman, "Liberty U. Seeks Success in Football to Spread Fundamentalist Message," *Chronicle of Higher Education*, 15 March 1989, A29, 32; Barry Jacobs, "Liberty Builds from the Ground Up," *New York Times*, 21 March 1989, 49, 51; Leigh Montville, "Thou Shalt Not Lose," *Sports Illustrated* 71, no. 20 (13 November 1989): 82–86, 90, 92, 94.

3. Lederman, "Liberty U.," 29, 32.

4. Jacobs, "Liberty," 51.

5. Robert H. Boyle, "Oral Roberts: Small but Oh, My," *Sports Illustrated* 33, no. 21 (30 November 1970): 64–65.

6. Andrew M. Greeley, *The Denominational Society* (Glenview, Ill.: Scott, Foresman and Co., 1972), 1, 254.

7. Much of this vast literature can be traced back to H. Richard Niebuhr, *The Social Sources of Denominationalism* (New York: World, 1929). A more recent representative statement is Wade Clark Roof and William McKinney, "Denominational America and the New Religious Pluralism," *Annals of the American Academy of Political and Social Science* 480 (1985): 24–38.

8. Robert Wuthnow, *The Restructuring of American Religion: Society and Faith since World War II* (Princeton, N.J.: Princeton University, 1988), esp. chaps. 5–6.

9. A complete discussion of what evangelicalism includes is beyond the scope of this study. George Marsden is helpful on the history of evangelicalism, especially his "Introduction: The Evangelical Denomination," in *Evangelicalism and Modern America*, ed. George Marsden (Grand Rapids: William B. Eerdmans, 1984), vii–xvi. Both Wuthnow, *Restructuring*, 173–85, and James Davison Hunter, *American Evangelicalism* (New Brunswick, N.J.: Rutgers University Press, 1983) and *Evangelicalism: The Coming Generation* (Chicago: University of Chicago Press, 1987), esp. chap. 1, are insightful sociologically.

10. The importance of dissenting views in American religion is stated effectively in Edwin Scott Gaustad, *Dissent in American Religion* (Chicago: University of Chicago Press, 1973).

11. The market-driven aspect of American religion, including the role played historically by resourceful entrepreneurs, is documented by Roger Finke and Rodney Stark, *The Churching of America, 1776–1990: Winners and Losers in Our Religious Economy* (New Brunswick, N.J.: Rutgers University Press, 1992).

12. Mayer Zald and Patricia Denton, "From Evangelism to General Service Organization: The Transformation of the YMCA," *Administrative Science Quarterly* 8 (September 1963): 213–34.

13. James DeForest Murch, *Cooperation without Compromise: A History of the National Association of Evangelicals* (Grand Rapids: William B. Eerdmans, 1956); Bruce L. Shelley, *Evangelicalism in America* (Grand Rapids: William B. Eerdmans, 1967).

14. George Marsden, *Reforming Fundamentalism* (Grand Rapids: William B. Eerdmans, 1989); Hunter, *Evangelicalism*.

15. Mary Douglas, *Purity and Danger* (Baltimore: Penguin, 1966); Wuthnow, *Restructuring*, 9–10.

16. Bill Glass, *Get in the Game!* (Waco: Word, 1965); that this boundary continues to be debated, despite changes of the 1950s–'60s, cf. Marvin Olasky, "Land without a Sabbath," *World* (22 May 1993): 24–25.

17. Ernest R. Sandeen, *The Roots of Fundamentalism: British and American Millenarianism, 1800–1930* (Chicago: University of Chicago Press, 1970).

18. Probably the Wheaton-Taylor connection was the earliest and strongest, as the story is told here. Many of the early Youth for Christ leaders, including Billy Graham and Gil Dodds, had Wheaton ties. The first Venture for Victory teams were coached by Don Odle from Taylor and supported by Taylor students and alumni. Dodds attended Gordon before moving to Chicago, and it provided an East Coast connection to Wheaton and Taylor.

19. These terms are used here to convey relationships at a level of seriousness and abstraction probably somewhere between their precise meanings in theoretical sociology and their everyday usage. Taken together, they depict a conservative and stable interpretation of the relationships usually found between church, college, and sport.

20. "Are Sports Good for the Soul?" *Newsweek* 77, no. 2 (11 January 1971): 51.

21. Although journalists and biographers have examined Graham from nearly every conceivable angle, his relationship to sport and to elite athletes remains a gap in the literature on him. William Martin, *A Prophet with Honor: The Billy Graham Story* (New York: William Morrow, 1991) is probably the best single work on Graham, but information on his interest in sports is sparse. In his recent autobiography, Graham does not provide much insight into his interest in sports, other than including one photograph of himself batting in a pickup baseball game; he also refers to athletes Michael Chang, Gary Player, Bernard Langer, and coach Tom Landry as "role models in our society" and "friends of mine over the years [who] have been involved in our Crusades" (Billy Graham, *Just As I Am: The Autobiography of Billy Graham* [San Francisco: HarperCollins, 1997], 296, 687).

22. "Are Sports Good?" 51.

23. Kuhn is often perceived as an enigmatic figure, but he usually acted in ways consonant with the wishes of baseball's powerful owners and administrators. His sympathies for Baseball Chapel have been reported widely. For exam-

ple, Tim Stafford wrote that "Watson Spoelstra took the idea and, using his contacts with baseball commissioner Bowie Kuhn, formed Baseball Chapel" ("In the Catacombs of Candlestick," *Christianity Today* 37, no. 5 [26 April 1993]: 23).

24. Curry Kirkpatrick, "Born to Serve," *Sports Illustrated* 70, no. 9 (3 March 1989): 73.

25. Hershiser places this incident in context in Orel Hershiser with Jerry B. Jenkins, *Out of the Blue* (Brentwood, Tenn.: Wolgemuth and Hyatt, 1989). Dravecky's story appears in Dave Dravecky with Tim Stafford, *Comeback* (Grand Rapids: Zondervan, 1990), and he continues as one of modern muscular Christianity's more articulate spokespersons.

26. J. C. Pollock, *The Cambridge Seven* (London: Inter-Varsity Fellowship, 1955). For a less positive interpretation of these British muscular Christians, cf. Patrick Scott, "Cricket and the Religious World in the Victorian Period," *Church Quarterly* 2, no. 3 (October 1970): 134–44.

27. Andrew W. Miracle Jr. and C. Roger Rees, *Lessons of the Locker Room: The Myth of School Sports* (Amherst, N.Y.: Prometheus Books, 1994), 42.

28. Dean M. Kelley, *Why Conservative Churches Are Growing* (New York: Harper and Row, 1972).

29. While the "official" NCCAA history attributes its origins to Wilhelmi and the Canton group, it is also true that Ron Hines, not Wilhelmi, spearheaded the 1968 tournament. Cf. "History and Philosophy of the NCCAA," in *National Christian College Athletic Association—Official Division I Handbook,* revised (Marion, Ind.: NCCAA, 1994), and "NCCAA Founder Authors Book," *NCCAA News Update* 5, no. 4 (July 1994): 4. Given one of the authors' attendance at and recollections of the 1968 tournament in Detroit, the relatively important role Hines played there probably is not given its due now in the NCCAA official recounting of the record.

30. Steve Morley, telephone interview with James A. Mathisen, 4 April 1995.

31. "History and Philosophy," and "Directory," in *National Christian.*

32. "Purpose," in *National Christian.*

33. Lederman, "Liberty U.," A32.

34. Barry May, "Report to the NCCAA National Convention from the Executive Director" (Marion, Ind.: NCCAA, 1995).

35. Barry May and Kelly Wood, interviews with James A. Mathisen, Marion, Ind., 18 March 1995.

36. Ron Bishop, "What Charles Barkley, Barney, and Christian Coaches Have in Common" (plenary presentation, Annual Meeting of the National Christian College Athletic Association, Marion, Ind., 17 March 1995).

37. "History," in *National Christian,* 3.

38. "Preparing Tomorrow's Christian Leaders through Athletics" (Marion, Ind.: NCCAA, c. 1995).

39. Nancy T. Ammerman, "North American Protestant Fundamentalism," in *Fundamentalisms Observed,* eds. Martin E. Marty and R. Scott Appleby (Chicago: University of Chicago Press, 1991), 32.

40. Ibid., 21.

41. "Bible Schools That Are True to the Faith," *Sunday School Times* 72, no. 5 (1 February 1930): 63.

42. Ammerman, "North American," 33.

43. C. Robert Pace, *Education and Evangelism: A Profile of Protestant Colleges* (New York: McGraw-Hill, 1972), 2.

44. Ibid., 205.

45. William C. Ringenberg, *The Christian College: A History of Protestant Higher Education in America* (Grand Rapids: William B. Eerdmans, 1984), 204.

46. Ibid., 205.

47. "Christian College Coalition . . . Integrating Scholarship, Faith and Service" (Washington, D.C.: Christian College Coalition, 1994).

48. Cf. the two lists of member institutions in 1994–95—for the CCC in "Christian College Coalition" and for the NCCAA in "1994–95 Membership Directory" (Marion, Ind.: NCCAA, 1994), 17.

49. Ken Sidey, "Football Scores with Enrollment and Evangelism," *Christianity Today* 34, no. 12 (10 September 1990): 65.

50. "Play with the Pros in College," advertisement for Trinity College, Deerfield, Ill., which appeared in various evangelical publications, including *Campus Life* and *Christianity Today*, 1990–91.

51. "A Winning Tradition," advertisement for Grand Rapids Baptist College, Grand Rapids, Mich., which appeared in various evangelical publications, including *Campus Life*, 1990–91.

52. "Think BIG about Your Future at APU," advertisement for Azusa Pacific University, Azusa, Calif., which appeared in various evangelical publications, including *Campus Life*, 1994–95.

53. "Geneva . . . A Winning Tradition, a Christian Perspective," advertisement for Geneva College, Beaver Falls, Pa., which appeared in various evangelical publications, including *Campus Life*, 1991–92.

54. "Northwestern College of Iowa—The 'A' Team," advertisement for Northwestern College, Orange City, Iowa, which appeared in various evangelical publications, including *Campus Life*, 1991–92.

55. "Sports at Atlantic Union College," advertisement for Atlantic Union College, South Lancaster, Mass., which appeared in *Campus Life* magazine, 1990–91.

56. Mark Troyer, interview with James A. Mathisen, Atlanta, 29 April 1995; cf. "Proposal," Asbury College Athletic Department to Asbury College Administration, 21 March 1995.

57. "President Opposes Intercollegiate Sports for Asbury College," *Asbury Collegian*, 22 November 1947, 1.

58. Ibid.

59. Robb Joynt, "ICS and the Other Christian Schools," *Asbury Collegian*, 27 November 1968, 6; "Two points of view," *Asbury Collegian*, 27 November 1968, 6; Skip Elliott, "A Sports Editor's Analysis," *Asbury Collegian*, 27 November 1968, 6, 12. We appreciate Mark Elliott making these articles available to us.

60. Elliot, "Sports Editor's Analysis," 6, 12.

61. J. Paul Ray, "Comments on Intercollegiate Basketball," 17–18 February 1976, Asbury College archives; Greg Mesimore, letter to Dennis Kinlaw, 20 September 1976, Asbury College archives.

62. "Proposal," Asbury College Athletic Committee to Asbury College Administration, 20 May 1987, Asbury College archives.

63. "Proposal," Asbury College Athletic Department; Troyer, interview with Mathisen.

64. As of this writing, no systematic analysis of the growth, essential characteristics, and distinctive philosophy of the megachurch movement exists.

275

What does exist are journalistic and other first-person accounts, often about individual churches and their apparent success.

65. Between 1991 and 1995, this "presence" increased significantly. At the 1995 SOA meeting in Atlanta, "church recreators" led a panel discussion in which they announced their plans for an organizational meeting of ministers of sports and recreation. On the short term, it is unclear what effect this new organization might have upon SOA.

66. David Gibson, interview with James A. Mathisen, Atlanta, 28 April 1995.

67. Eugene DePorter, interview with James A. Mathisen, Atlanta, 28 April 1995.

68. Len VandenBos, interview with James A. Mathisen, Wheaton, Ill., 12 June 1995.

69. Jim Riley, telephone interview with James A. Mathisen, 16 May 1995.

70. 8th Annual Centurion Classic, Marquette Manor Baptist Church, Downers Grove, Ill., 3–8 April 1995; Rich Sevilla, interview with James A. Mathisen, Bolingbrook, Ill., 9 June 1995.

Chapter 7: Interpreting the Ethos of Modern Evangelical Muscular Christianity: Religion and Sport in New Patterns of Cultural Reinforcement

1. Richard Hoffer and Shelley Smith, "Putting His House in Order," *Sports Illustrated* 82, no. 2 (16 January 1995): 32.

2. Arthur J. Daley, "Dartmouth 3, Cornell 0, Official Score As Ithacans Refuse Victory," *New York Times,* 19 November 1940, 31.

3. "Cornell Wants 'No Long Count,' President Tells Students," *New York Times,* 20 November 1940, 29.

4. Daley, "Dartmouth 3," 31.

5. William F. Reed, "College Report: A Loser in Victory," *Sports Illustrated* 73, no. 16 (15 October 1990): 96.

6. "Sportsmanship and Violence," *More Than a Game* A&E Cable Network television program, narr. Frank Gifford, 1991.

7. Edward Gilbreath, "Manhood's Great Awakening," *Christianity Today* 38, no. 2 (6 February 1995): 22.

8. "Winning the Races," *Christianity Today* 39, no. 2 (6 February 1995): 23, citing Bill McCartney, *Seven Promises of a Promise Keeper.*

9. Gilbreath, "Manhood's," 22.

10. Ibid., 26.

11. James Davison Hunter, *Culture Wars: The Struggle to Define America* (New York: Basic Books, 1991), esp. 43–51.

12. The idea of a "creed" of American sport was developed a generation ago by Harry Edwards, *Sociology of Sport* (Homewood, Ill.: Dorsey, 1973), 103–30. Edwards suggested two "creedal strands" in American sport consisting of seven "major tenets" that bear some similarity to the "myths" of muscular Christianity discussed here.

13. "New Morality Called Lie by Bill Glass," *The Indianapolis Star,* 26 October 1970, 1; "Decadent World Running out of Time, Glass Tells Crowd," *Findlay (Ohio) Republican Courier,* 30 August 1971, D2.

14. "People: Evangelist Raps Jets' Namath," unidentified source, Bill Glass collection no. 455, Billy Graham Center archives, Wheaton, Ill.; Charles McCarthy, "Bill Glass Calls for 'Radical Dedication,'" *Fresno Bee,* 27 September

1971; Dan Hruby, "Namath under Fire," *San Jose Mercury-News*, 13 August 1972, 93; Richard Levin, "From Football to the Pulpit," *Los Angeles Herald-Examiner*, 6 September 1973, C2.

15. John Underwood, letter to Bill Glass, 25 March 1971, Bill Glass collection no. 455, Billy Graham Center archives, Wheaton, Ill.; Bill Glass, letter to Wilbur F. Eastman Jr., Prentice-Hall, 30 March 1971, Bill Glass collection no. 455, Billy Graham Center archives, Wheaton, Ill.

16. Levin, "From Football," C2.

17. Bill Glass, *Free at Last* (Waco: Word, 1976), 30.

18. "Basic Counselor Training for Total Prison Weekends" (Cedar Hill, Tex.: Bill Glass Foundation, n.d.).

19. Robert Wuthnow, *The Restructuring of American Religion: Society and Faith since World War II* (Princeton, N.J.: Princeton University, 1988), 207, 209.

20. Ibid., 211.

21. Jimmy Greenfield, "'No One's Perfect': Gambling Detracted from Jordan's Image," *Chicago Tribune*, 14 January 1999, section 4, 10; cf. Mark Starr, "Gambling Man," *Newsweek* 121, no. 24 (14 June 1993): 72–74; Jerry Kirshenbaum, "High Stakes," *Sports Illustrated* 78, no. 23 (14 June 1993): 13; Richard Demak, "The Investigation: Did the NBA Really Probe Michael Jordan's Activities?" *Sports Illustrated* 76, no. 14 (13 April 1992): 11.

22. Wuthnow, *Restructuring*, esp. 201–14.

23. Christopher L. Stevenson, "The Christian-Athlete: An Interactionist-Developmental Analysis," *Sociology of Sport Journal* 8, no. 4 (December 1991): 362–79.

24. Hunter, *Culture Wars*, chap. 4.

25. Gilbreath, "Manhood's," 26.

26. A. C. Green with J. C. Webster, *Victory* (Orlando, Fla.: Creation House, 1994), 87.

27. Ibid., 230–31.

28. Ibid., 212–13.

29. Ibid., 131.

30. Ibid.

31. Gilbreath, "Manhood's," 26.

32. The philosophical discussion regarding the role of physical activity is addressed in numerous general sources in the physical education literature. Examples are Daryl Siedentop, *Introduction to Physical Education, Fitness, and Sports*, 2d ed. (Mountain View, Calif: Mayfield Publishing Co., 1994), and Delbert Oberteuffer, et al., *Physical Education: A Textbook for Professional Students*, 4th ed. (New York: Harper and Row, 1970).

33. Michael Oriard, *Sporting with the Gods: The Rhetoric of Play and Game in American Culture* (Cambridge: Cambridge University Press, 1991), 10–11.

34. Ibid., 12.

35. Based on the authors' participant observations over several years, references to Liddell and Studd occur occasionally but without any self-conscious effort to construct a "seamless web" in the form of a myth of muscular Christianity to which the current SOA-affiliated participants attach themselves. "Intellectuals" in the movement, such as Ralph Drollinger and Bill Sutherland, however, are quite familiar with these earlier figures; cf. Russell W. Ramsey, *God's Joyful Runner* (South Plainfield, N.J.: Bridge, 1987), on Liddell.

36. Nathan O. Hatch, "Evangelicalism As a Democratic Movement," in *Evangelicalism and Modern America,* ed. George Marsden (Grand Rapids: William B. Eerdmans, 1984), 78.

37. "History and Philosophy of the NCCAA," *National Christian College Athletic Association—Official Division I Handbook,* revised (Marion, Ind.: NCCAA, 1994), 3.

38. Eddie Waxer, interview with James A. Mathisen, Dallas, 27 April 1990.

39. Hatch, "Evangelicalism," 72–73.

40. Gary Warner, *Competition* (Elgin, Ill.: David C. Cook, 1979), 191, citing pastor and former athlete Nelson Price.

41. David Leon Moore, "Ballplayers Putting Faith in Christ," *USA Today,* 26 July 1991, 1C.

42. Warner, *Competition,* 204–5.

43. Dennis Byrd with Michael D'Orso, *Rise Up and Walk* (New York: HarperCollins, 1993). Byrd's dramatic story subsequently became a made-for-television movie.

44. Donald J. Mrozek, *Sport and American Mentality, 1880–1910* (Knoxville: University of Tennessee, 1983), 227.

45. Robert N. Bellah, Richard Madsen, William M. Sullivan, Ann Swidler, and Steven M. Tipton, *Habits of the Heart: Individualism and Commitment in American Life* (Berkeley: University of California, 1985), 60.

46. Wes Neal, *Total Release Performance* (Branson, Mo.: Institute for Athletic Perfection, 1975), 23.

47. Wes Neal, "Garbage In, Garbage Out," *Second Look* 2, no. 2 (1988): 15.

48. Carol Flake, *Redemptorama: Culture, Politics, and the New Evangelicalism* (New York: Viking Penguin, 1984), 93.

49. David Hesselgrave, "His Coming and Our Going" (sermon preached at First Baptist Church, Geneva, Ill., 20 October 1990).

50. Tim Stafford, "Baseball and the Atonement," *Christianity Today* 32, no. 6 (8 April 1988): 22.

51. Ibid., 23–24.

52. Dave Simmons, *Dad the Family Coach* (Wheaton: Victor Books, 1991), back cover.

53. Ibid., 149.

54. Ibid., 149–50.

55. Oriard, *Sporting,* 153.

56. Johan Huizinga, *Homo Ludens: A Study of the Play-Element in Culture* (Boston: Beacon Press, 1950) is a classic on this subject. Peter L. Berger in *A Rumor of Angels* (Garden City, N.Y.: Doubleday, 1969), 57–60, argues that play is one of several "signals" of God's transcendence that humans express.

57. Robert K. Johnston, *The Christian at Play* (Grand Rapids: William B. Eerdmans, 1983) is a helpful contribution. Other evangelically oriented works include Arthur F. Holmes, *Contours of a World View* (Grand Rapids: William B. Eerdmans, 1983), especially chap. 15 on "Play," and Leland Ryken, "Play," in *New Dictionary of Christian Ethics and Pastoral Theology,* eds. David J. Atkinson and David H. Field (Leicester, England: Inter-Varsity Press, 1995), 664–65.

58. A. Wingfield-Digby, "Sport," in Atkinson and Field, *New,* 809.

59. Hatch, "Evangelicalism," 78.

60. Ralph Drollinger, "Dear Reader," *SportsFocus,* special issue (February 1985): 8.

61. Dave Branon, "Airing It Out—Getting and Giving," *Sports Spectrum* 4, no. 6 (November-December 1990): 31.

62. Tom Felton, interview with James A. Mathisen, Atlanta, 29 April 1995.

63. The combination of "Stats Central" and "The Swirsky Report," with questions answered by Chuck Swirsky, began in *Sports Spectrum* 5, no. 2 (March-April 1991), although "Stats Central" began in the previous issue, with the announcement of the forthcoming Swirsky column.

64. Ken Walker, John Carvalho, Greg Johnson, Karen Drollinger, and Dave Branon, "From Pelota to Peace: the Olympics," *Sports Spectrum* 6, no. 4 (July-August 1992): 12–22.

65. Sara L. Anderson, "Who's on First?" *Second Look* 4, no. 2 (March-April 1990): 15.

66. Sara L. Anderson, "The Smut Stops Here," *Second Look* 2, no. 2 (1988): 12–14.

67. Rick Wattman, "Her Majesty the King," *Second Look* 3, no. 6 (November-December 1989): 16–18.

68. Kyle Rote Jr., "A Second Look at Motivation," *Second Look* 1, no. 4 (1987): 2; Karen Rudolph Drollinger, "Going Long," *Second Look* 1, no. 4 (1987): 7; John MacArthur Jr., "Striving for the Ultimate Reward," *Second Look* 1, no. 4 (1987): 19–21.

69. Dave Egner, "The View from the Top," *Second Look* 4, no. 5 (September-October 1990): 22.

70. Grant Teaff, "Excellence Hanging in the Balance," *Second Look* 3, no. 3 (May-June 1989): 11; Paul Hoeman, "Shame and Fortune," *Second Look* 3, no. 3 (May-June 1989): 17.

71. Bill Horlacher, "Rookie to the Rescue," *Second Look* 1, no. 1 (1987): 14–16.

72. Articles decrying the greed and materialism in sport are nearly annual occurrences. Examples include Dave Branon, "The Billion-Dollar Question," *Sports Spectrum* 6, no. 2 (March-April 1992): 31; Mike Sandrolini, "In the Money," *Sports Spectrum* 5, no. 4 (July-August 1991): 26–28; Dave Branon, "Getting and Giving," *Sports Spectrum* 4, no. 6 (November-December 1990): 31; and Sara L. Anderson, "Sports Salaries: Do the Dollars Make Sense?" *Second Look* 2, no. 1 (1988): 16–19.

73. Kyle Rote Jr., "That Was Then, This Is Now," *Second Look* 4, no. 4 (July-August 1990): 18.

74. Richard Hoffer, "A Career of Living Dangerously," *Sports Illustrated* 76, no. 4 (3 February 1992): 38–41.

Afterword: Could There Be Another Disengagement?

1. James A. Mathisen, "Toward an Understanding of 'Muscular Christianity': Religion, Sport, and Culture in the Modern World," in *Christianity and Leisure: Issues in a Pluralistic Society,* eds. Paul Heintzman, Glen A. Van Andel, and Thomas L. Visker (Dordt, Iowa: Dordt College, 1994), 204.

2. Perhaps the real problem is that some of these elite athletes have been promoted by the muscular Christian groups, with little real sense of the depth or endurance of their commitments to Christian principles. After Barry Sanders

was featured by *Sports Spectrum* in November-December 1992, the magazine took unusual measures in its January 1995 issue. It published a letter from one Sanders fan who said Sanders' behavior "tore me up." It also included a statement from the Washington Redskins' Darrell Green that Sanders "may not have been as grounded in the gospel." Cf. "Praying for Barry," *Sports Spectrum* 9, no. 1 (January 1995): 4; Allen Palmeri, "The Brothers Green," *Sports Spectrum* 9, no. 1 (January 1995): 29. Andre Agassi's muscular Christianity, while he has never been the subject of a *Sports Spectrum* article, was dismissed by John Feinstein, *Hard Courts* (New York: Villard, 1991), 23, 365, as "a publicity tool" and another of his "fads," such as being into weight training. In addition, Horace Grant was the subject of two *Sports Spectrum* articles, both written by the Chicago Bulls' cochaplain: Scott Bradley, "Coming of Age," *Sports Spectrum* 5, no. 6 (November-December 1991): 6–9; and "My Life with Da Bulls," *Sports Spectrum* 7, no. 9 (November 1993): 22–25.

3. C. Howard Hopkins, *History of the Y.M.C.A. in North America* (New York: Association Press, 1951); Mayer N. Zald and Patricia Denton, "From Evangelism to General Service: The Transformation of the YMCA," *Administrative Science Quarterly* 2 (September 1963): 215ff.

4. "History and Philosophy of the NCCAA," *National Christian College Athletic Association—Official Division I Handbook* (Marion, Ind.: NCCAA, 1994), 3.

5. This implication recurs that once athletes become muscular Christians, they will lose "their competitive edge." For whatever reasons, it has occurred most often among baseball players; cf. of Bob Knepper in Jill Lieber, "Some Say No Leica," *Sports Illustrated* 68, no. 25 (20 June 1988): 48–51; of Darryl Strawberry in David Lee Moore, "Ballplayers Putting Faith in Christ," *USA Today*, 26 July 1991, 1C; and of the entire Seattle Mariners team, alleged to have "put an all-Christian team on the field" while losing frequently, Bob Sherwin, "Playing for a Higher Authority," *Seattle Times*, 27 July 1986, D8. We appreciate Mike Hamilton calling this last article to our attention.

6. Granted, the secular coverage of Gil Dodds in the 1940s—especially by his friend Arthur Daley—was quite adequate, and the next surge came with the positive treatment of the FCA in its early days in the mid-1950s, as noted in chap. 5. *The New Yorker* noticed the New York Jets chapel gathering as early as 1973; cf. "The Talk of the Town—Service," *The New Yorker* 49, no. 39 (19 November 1973): 46–47. Perhaps the first attempt at an in-depth interpretation of the modern muscular Christian movement came from Frank Deford in a three-part series in *Sports Illustrated* in 1976, beginning with "Religion in Sport," *Sports Illustrated* 44, no. 16 (19 April 1976): 88–102. Carol Flake's chap. 4, "The Spirit of Winning: Sports and the Total Man," then provided a witty overview of key elements in the movement in *Redemptorama: Culture, Politics, and the New Evangelicalism* (Garden City, N.Y.: Doubleday, 1984). In the last ten to fifteen years, however, these spotty treatments have become more numerous and systematic. 1991, for example, was a banner year, with major stories on muscular Christians in the *New York Times*, ABC's *20/20* and *Nightline*, *USA Today*, and *Sports Illustrated*. In September 1991 the *Pittsburgh Press* featured a weeklong, six-part series subsequently syndicated in other daily newspapers. More recently, *USA Today's Baseball Weekly* featured "The Gospel vs. the Game" on its cover and included five pages of coverage; cf. Tim Wendel, "Religion in the Clubhouse: Divine or Divisive?" *Baseball Weekly*, 8–14 June 1994, 36–38, 40; and ESPN carried an hour-

long program on religion in sport, "A Time to Play, a Time to Pray," on 19 May 1995. The coverage of professional football players such as Reggie White and Randall Cunningham has been quite extensive—mixed for White and more positive for Cunningham; on White, cf. William C. Rhoden, "The Spirit That Moves the Packers, *New York Times,* 11 January 1997; Timothy W. Smith, "White Wants His Pulpit between Hash Marks," *New York Times,* 23 January 1997; on Cunningham, cf. Austin Murphy, "Second Coming," *Sports Illustrated* 89, no. 23 (7 December 1998): 36–41; Don Banks, "Quarterback Faith-Keeper," *Minneapolis Star Tribune,* 25 December 1998: C1, C6.

7. Rick Reilly, "Save Your Prayers, Please," *Sports Illustrated* 74, no. 4 (4 February 1991): 86. Some of the critical stories have been "self-inflicted," as the treatment Bob Knepper elicited with his remarks critical of women in sport, especially of aspiring umpire Pam Postema in 1988; cf. Lieber, "Some Say," 48, that "in God's society woman was created in a role of submission to the husband. It's not that woman is inferior, but I don't believe women should be in a leadership role"; cf. "Few Laugh at Knepper 'Joke,'" *The Milwaukee Journal,* 16 June 1988, 12C. Or John Feinstein could not find in himself the possibility of giving Andre Agassi the benefit of a doubt, inasmuch as "his favorite word [is *f*——]," then Agassi must be "invok[ing] being born-again as a publicity tool" (*Hard Courts,* 23, 366, 397). But Feinstein is similarly critical at some length of Michael Chang's muscular Christianity (*Hard Courts,* 22–23, 219–23). More often, the articles have centered on the disruptive influence some muscular Christians were, as the case of Gary Gaetti. Cf. Dave Cunningham, "Gaetti's New Relationship with God Fails to Convert Detractors," *Chicago Tribune,* 26 May 1991, sec. 3, 12; and Hank Hersch, "The Gospel and Gaetti," *Sports Illustrated* 71, no. 8 (21 August 1989): 42–44, 46. Also representative is the skeptical tone of David Davis, "Jesus Saves," *LA Weekly,* 10–16 June 1994, 37, and ESPN's "A Time to Play" that asserted both the disruptive element of Christians in the locker room and that their praying occurs only "for show," and a harsh critique before the 1998 Super Bowl that called the "God Squadders'" activities both "anti-Christian" and "ridiculous;" cf. William Nack, "Does God Care Who Wins the Super Bowl?" *Sports Illustrated* 88, no. 3 (26 January 1998): 46–48. Even the academically oriented *Chronicle of Higher Education* got involved, citing concerns about separation of church and state legalities on public university campuses; cf. Debra E. Blum, "Devout Athletes," *Chronicle of Higher Education,* 9 February 1996, A35–36.

8. Karen Drollinger, "Going for the Victory at Home," *Sports Spectrum* 6, no. 3 (May-June 1992), 26–29.

9. Mary Douglas, *Purity and Danger* (Baltimore: Penguin, 1966).

10. Robert Lipsyte, "Why Sports Don't Matter Anymore," New York Times Magazine, 2 April 1995, 57; apparently Lipsyte wrote in large part in response to the more moderate position taken by Wilfred Sheed, "Why Sports Matter," The Wilson Quarterly 19, no. 1 (winter 1995): 11–25.

Index

113790

289